2013

A TRIBUTE TO SIR
ALEX FERGUSON

BY HARRY HARRIS
FOREWORD BY SIR BOBBY CHARLTON

EMPIRE
PUBLICATIONS

First published in 2013

EMPIRE PUBLICATIONS
1 Newton Street, Manchester M1 1HW
© Harry Harris 2013

ISBN 9781909360167

Printed in Great Britain.

CONTENTS

CREDITS

I WOULD LIKE TO thank Sir Bobby Charlton for his valuable contributions as he is part of the fabric of Manchester United and synonymous with the Sir Matt Busby era, as well as a current director, a global ambassador for the club and so an incredible link to the Sir Alex Ferguson era.

I have known Sir Bobby for many, many years. He is now 75, but I have played football with Sir Bobby, and even against him, when he was well into his 60s. I used to play for the England Press Team and Bobby was a regular, along with Sir Trevor Brooking and others such as Ron Atkinson. During the European Championships, one of the boot manufacturers organised a mirror tournament for the media and on the morning of the big match between England and Russia, the England press team had a squad of 20, while the Russians, who at that time had a tiny media corps, had some of their journalists still travelling back from another game, so only seven turned up for the kick off.

Coach Mike Hart, chief football writer for the *Evening Standard* at the time, delegated the usual England subs, myself included, to switch to the Russian team. I played left back for Russia and tried at least once to tackle Sir Bobby. When the rest of the Russian media turned up, I played for England in the second half, scoring against Russia. I sat in the dressing rooms afterwards amazed that I had played with and against Sir Bobby – it really doesn't get much better for a football reporter Living The Dream!

I would also like to thank David Sadler, of the AFMUP (Association of Former Manchester United Players), for putting me in touch with some of the real legends of Manchester

United. Paul Parker, an old friend, also helped to direct me to some of the players he knows.

My thanks also to the Professional Footballers Association, to Gordon Taylor and Martin Buchan, and to Chris Joslin the PFA's commercial executive in London for helping me to find the right players to interview. A massive thank you to all the United legends past and present who have contributed.

To old friend and former journalist colleague David Meek, I extend my gratitude for his invaluable assistance. David was, for years, The Voice of Old Trafford as football correspondent for the *Manchester Evening News* and despite retirement many years ago, ghost wrote Sir Alex's programme notes right up to his retirement. My thanks, too, to Richard Bevan, chief executive of the LMA.

Thanks also to everyone at Empire Publications, particularly Ashley Shaw, Delennyk Richardson and John Ireland, for taking on such a book project and Anthony Verrill for his assistance.

FOREWORD

"I've known for about three or four years that he would be stepping down and he's changed his mind a couple of times. He's such a fantastic manager. He could go on forever, that's the way he is."

SIR BOBBY CHARLTON

I AM IN PARADISE. I have been involved with Manchester United virtually all of my life pretty much and it's been a fantastic ride – I have loved every minute of it, mostly as a player, and now as a director. I am 75, but I am looking forward to even more good times with Manchester United, I am confident about that. I will keep going for as long as I can. Whatever happens, Manchester United are one of the biggest clubs in world terms and that is fantastic.

While nothing can replace being a player, watching Manchester United every game is like being in paradise. What a fantastic club this is and football in England is the best without a doubt; fast, furious, entertaining and skilful. It is a shame that we have struggled a little bit internationally, but Manchester United are the premier club in England, if not the world, and it is just brilliant, exciting.

As for Sir Alex's retirement. Well I've known for about three or four years that he would be stepping down and he's changed his mind a couple of times. He's such a fantastic manager. He could go on forever, that's the way he is. But maybe with a bit of ill health, on top of not seeing the family, he's thought this is the time to do it. He deserves a break. He's got the hip operation and there's just so much pressure on the position. It's very tough. He just loves the game, and people appreciate that.

David Moyes is a great appointment. Perhaps people will be saying, 'thank God that United are not going to be a threat any more'. But that's a major mistake that they are making. Nothing will change from the philosophy, from Alex Ferguson's philosophy and Matt Busby's philosophy. There will be a great future at United, and the football at Old Trafford will remain the same. It has always been a philosophy to attack; never be boring, never be dull. Sir Alex has always stressed that, and the club has never been better than it is now.

I was just a youngster when United won the title in 1955-56 and won my first League winner's medal the following season playing with Duncan Edwards. Then there was the George Best, Denis Law era, a magical period and with Matt Busby's philosophy to be the best that we can be, he wasn't interested in second best. He wanted to win the League, as that was the only way to qualify for the European Cup, and he wanted to be the best team in Europe, if not the world.

To win 20 League titles is something special, and I am delighted to have contributed to a book that looks at all 20 titles and in particular the contriubution of all the players and managers associated with this fantastic football club.

Sir Bobby Charlton

MAY 2013

FOREWORD

SIR BOBBY CHARLTON

Born: 11 October 1937, Ashington, Northumberland

HONOURS

INTERNATIONAL:
World Cup Winner – 1966
106 caps, record 49 goals
CLUB HONOURS:
Football League First Division winner:
1956–57, 1964–65, 1966–67
FA Cup winner – 1962-63
European Cup winner – 1967–68
Charity Shield winner – 1956, 1957, 1965, 1967
European Player of the Year – 1966
(runner-up – 1967, 1968)
FWA Footballer of the Year – 1966
PFA Merit Award (1974)
BBC Sports Personality of the Year Lifetime Achievement Award
– 2008
UEFA President's Award – 2009

INTRODUCTION

"He is the greatest coach of all time, especially because of all the difficulties he overcame at the start of his career with Manchester and for remaining for so many years on the same bench. It's really incredible. I normally think that after four or five years at the most a coach should move, so to think that he stayed on the same bench for 26 years is incredible. That takes psychological, technical and humane capacity. I had a special relationship with him."

FABIO CAPELLO

20|13 IS A TRIBUTE to one of British football's most successful and glittering managerial careers. Sir Alex Ferguson went out on a high with his 13th Premier League trophy, a record that will never be equalled. 20 Championships in total for Manchester United, 13 for Sir Alex, 38 trophies at Old Trafford including two Champions League trophies, 49 trophies in all with St. Mirren, Aberdeen and United, all of which mark him out as the most successful managerial career in British football. All ending with this final triumph in the year 2013 – perfect symmetry.

This book is a tribute to the enormous success Sir Alex has brought to the club, and his determination to overhaul Liverpool's record of domestic championships. While the Champions League meant so much to Sir Alex, and he would accept that he has under achieved in bringing only two Champions League trophies to the club, he is immensely proud of the fact that the Premier League haul of 13 titles puts Manchester United firmly at the pinnacle of

INTRODUCTION

English football as undisputed champion of champions.

Sir Alex retired after more than 26 years in charge of the club describing his epic reign as an 'honour and a privilege'. He becomes a director and ambassador after he formally retired after United's match with West Bromwich Albion on May 18 – his 1,500th in charge.

No one can surpass his haul of 13 Premier League title, but if he leaves with one major regret it is that he could not match Bob Paisley's record of three European Cups with Liverpool. Having secured Champions League wins in 1999 and 2008, Sir Alex was unable to overhaul that particular record but somehow kept his impossible pledge to end Liverpool's dominance in domestically by transforming the total League Championships won from 18-7 in Liverpool's favour to 20-18 in United's.

As he left the dug out for the last time, a piece of history left with him. Sir Alex was the last of the old fashioned British managers who ruled the club from top to bottom. He arrived at the training ground by 7.15am everyday over those 26 years to oversee his undisputed territory as The Manager in charge of every inch of anything to do with the playing side of Manchester United. The day he announced his resignation sent shock waves throughout the footballing world, prompting statements from the Prime Minister, and politicians eager to push him forward for a peerage.

Prime Minister David Cameron joked that Sir Alex will have to provide a consultancy service to the club he follows, Aston Villa, as they battled relegation. In a speech opening debate in the Commons following the Queen's address, the PM suggested that even Conservative MPs would be recognising the achievements of Sir Alex - a staunch Labour supporter. He said: "It is the day to perhaps sing the praises of Sir Alex Ferguson, a remarkable man in British football who has had an extraordinary, successful career. I am sure that all members, even on the blue team, will want to pay tribute to this member of the red team. Perhaps he could now provide some consultancy services for Aston Villa."

Labour leader Ed Miliband told MPs that Sir Alex was

"the most successful football manager the world has ever seen... phenomenally talented at his job." Adding, "I won't let this day pass without paying tribute to the most successful football manager this world has ever seen – a great supporter of the reds, you might call him. Sir Alex Ferguson, phenomenally talented at his job, winner of 13 championships – (he) can teach us all about hard work and dedication."

Outgoing Manchester United Chief Executive David Gill described his time working with Sir Alex as the 'greatest experience' of his working life and that the club had been planning for his imminent retirement, "I've had the tremendous pleasure of working very closely with Alex for 16 unforgettable years – through the treble, the double, countless trophy wins and numerous signings. We knew that his retirement would come one day and we both have been planning for it by ensuring the quality of the squad and club structures are in first-class condition. Alex's vision, energy and ability have built teams – both on and off the pitch – that his successor can count on as among the best and most loyal in world sport.'

Joel Glazer, joint chairman of the Manchester United board with brother Avie, highlighted the 2008 Champions League final penalty shootout success over Chelsea, "Alex has proven time and time again what a fantastic manager he is but he's also a wonderful person. His determination to succeed and dedication to the club have been truly remarkable. I will always cherish the wonderful memories he has given us, like that magical night in Moscow."

Sir Alex was famed for his infamous 'hairdryer treatment'. Notably in February 2003 when he kick a boot in the changing room which hit David Beckham on the forehead. Beckhams' visible wound created a public fallout and the then England captain left the club months later. Yet, Beckham was full of praise for Sir Alex illustrating the respect for his former boss, as he reacted, "I've just seen the news on Sir Alex. As I have said many times before the boss wasn't just the greatest and best manager I ever played under he was also a father figure to me

INTRODUCTION

from the moment I arrived at the club at the age of 11 until the day I left. Without him I would never have achieved what I have done in my career. He understood how important it was to play for your country and he knew how much it meant to me. After 1998 [when he was sent off in the World Cup] without the manager I would have found it virtually impossible to cope with the attention I was getting on and off the field and for this I will always be grateful to him for his support and protection. I am truly honoured to have been guided by the greatest manager in football and to have had the career that I had under him. Thank you boss and enjoy the rest!"

On Twitter, Rio Ferdinand commented, 'The bosses work ethic, his desire to win + to make us better players were unrivalled. Thanks boss.' Meanwhile FA chairman David Bernstein recognised Sir Alex's "remarkable" contribution to the game. He said: "Sir Alex Ferguson's achievements are truly remarkable – he is genuinely one of the greatest managers of all time and certainly of the modern era. His contribution to English football has been outstanding in every regard and, in the FA's 150th year, it is something that should be celebrated. On behalf of the FA I'd like to wish him a happy and healthy retirement."

First-team coach Rene Meulensteen was told of Ferguson's plans on Wednesday morning and felt the news was not entirely unexpected. "(I found out) this morning when I came to the club. He called us into his office and he said what decision he took. It's always been on the cards – there's speculation every season. I think the manager kept his cards close to his chest. I think he felt the time was right now and he made a decision. He's obviously a man who thinks very, very well so I'm sure he's taken a lot of thought into making this decision. I wish him well. He's been fantastic for this club and I hope all the fans give whoever's going to come in the same support that he gets."

Former United defender Steve Bruce believes any successor to Ferguson will struggle to get close to emulating his record. The Hull manager said, "He's going to be some act to follow. It's impossible to copy somebody like him. He will treat the groundsman just as well as he will treat his star centre-forward. He's got a fantastic humility about him, for all that he's achieved."

The repercussions for United were felt much further afield than the United dressing room for present and past players, far greater than the club might even have imagined. The Board knew there would be a seismic shift in opinion about where the club would go without their talisman manager, but they couldn't have imagined the global intensity of media interest.

After giving emotional speeches to his players and staff at their Carrington training ground, the fall out really began… The decision seem to be strangely timed with rumours flying about in Manchester that a player had leaked information on the club's golf day and at least one betting company announcing on the Monday that a number of large bets had been placed on David Moyes to succeed Sir Alex before the end of the season.

The previous weekend, in his programme notes for a match against Chelsea, Sir Alex had insisted, "I certainly don't have any plans at the moment to walk away from what I believe will be something special and worth being around to see. It's always difficult in football to be absolutely sure of the future because the game has a habit of tripping you up, but I don't live in a fantasy world and believe we have every reason to feel confident about the future of Manchester United. My view stems not from the euphoria of winning back the title we lost last season, but on the way we did it and the make-up of our playing personnel."

In the light of subsequent events, Ferguson's notes seem very curious indeed. As in a statement announcing the end of his managerial career he said: "The decision to retire is one that I have thought a great deal about and one that I have not taken lightly. It is the right time."

David Meek helped write Sir Alex's autobiography and ghost-writes his Old Trafford programme notes. The 82-year-old journalist is trusted by Sir Alex and been writing his programme notes for 26 years. Meek, a journalist I have know for many years, is conservative in his news gathering during his time as covering the fortunes of Manchester United with the

INTRODUCTION

Manchester Evening News, his sources impeccable inside Old Trafford. Meek added to the intrigue when he wondered what really went on behind the scenes after he penned the programme notes in which Sir Alex insisted he wanted to continue managing. Was he 'nudged' towards the exit? "I can't honestly say I'm aware of anything." Meek replied, "We never hear anything from the Glazers but they're in charge. There is the scenario that he was blissfully intending to carry on for another season, true to his programme notes, but then there was a top summit meeting and the suggestion was made (that he retired). I don't think it had to be made forcefully. If he felt the owners no longer had 100 per cent confidence in him, I don't think he'd hesitate [to go]." When pushed if he thought that was realistic, he replied: "Well yeah... I'd love to know. That's the next chapter to the story. Did he go or was he pushed? I knew something was afoot when I rang him [on Tuesday] at his home and I said 'shall I come in tomorrow morning?' He said 'no, I shall be too busy.' That's all he said."

Sir Alex reprimanded Meek for his comments on the Keys and Gray radio show. There was no updated column from Sir Alex in the programme for his final game at Old Trafford days later, instead his resignation quotes were reprinted as he wanted to save his thoughts until his address to the fans after his Farewell Game. The interview he gave Meek for his final home match programme was not used, and Meek changed his 'story' on of Sir Alex's departure, saying on Radio 5 Live's Sportsweek that the manager's Chelsea programme notes had been a 'smokescreen'. Meek said, "He sold us all a dummy. I didn't doubt for a moment he was kidding me."

Well, was he or wasn't he? Only Sir Alex really knows. His son Darren, manager of Peterborough, made it clear that the United boss hadn't quit over ill health and would have coped with the hip operation, but didn't address the issue of stress. Having always cited his health as the primary factor in any decision to retire, the club confirmation only days before the announcement that Sir Alex, who had a heart pacemaker fitted in 2004, would undergo hip surgery in August which inevitably inspired acres of media coverage speculating about his future whether he would bring in David Moyes as his assistant for a year or whether he would finally retire.

It was also reported that two Premier League managers, who remained anonymous, suggested Sir Alex would have quit a year earlier had United not lost the Premier League title race to City. That though, was not confirmed by United but neither was it denied that he confided in wife Cath that he had to shelve plans to retire within hours of City's shock title triumph. Sir Alex comments that followed the final home game with Swansea did stand up the view he had no intent on going out unless it was as a winner.

Was it the stress or something connected to the mysterious nose bleed the year before as David Whelan had told me a year earlier? Former England manager Fabio Capello thought so. Capello, the then manager of the Russian national side, spoke to Sir Alex about it, "I called him and he told me that he decided this way because of excess stress. A few months ago he told me that he was going to stay on. The news of his retirement really surprised me. I called him and he told me that he decided this way because of excess stress. He told me that now he'll go and travel a bit, have fun and see the world with his wife. He was the greatest coach of all time, especially because of all the difficulties he overcame at the start of his career with Manchester and for remaining for so many years on the same bench. It's really incredible. I normally think that after four-five years at the most a coach should move, so to think that he stayed on the same bench for 26 years is incredible. That takes psychological, technical and humane capacity. I had a special relationship with him."

The 'noisy neighbours' absorbed the implications on the eve of their FA Cup final against Wigan at Wembley, hoping it would mean a permanent shift of power across Manchester. Roberto Mancini said: "It was a great honour to beat him at Old Trafford and I wish him good luck for his future. I don't think there'll be another manager like him. To win every trophy for 27 years is an incredible situation." Mancini won the battle of Manchester a year earlier to win the Premier League that included the historic 6-1 win at Old Trafford in 2011. That mattered little, nor did winning the league, as his failure in the Champions League has put his position as manager tinkering on the brink, the speculation that the decision to axe him had already been taken even ahead of the Cup Final.

Even so, despite concentrating on the Cup Final and concerning himself with his won future at the time, Mancini remarked, "In Europe, there are other good managers. I don't know if you can say Sir Alex is the best ever but he is the best in the last 27 years. A top club, a big club like United, you can change the manager. Sir Alex built this team but it is a big club with a big history and I don't think it will change something."

James Milner believed that Sir Alex's departure will have no bearing on City's determination to reclaim the League title, "I don't think that affects us really. We concentrate on our business over here and it's obviously big news but all we are concentrating on us the FA Cup final. It's not going to be any more open than it would have been if he was there next year. He's been an amazing manager for them over the years, his record is ridiculous, unreal, but we are concerned on our side. We are bitterly disappointed how the League went this year, the main thing is that we win a piece of silverware at the weekend, do that and take the momentum of winning a trophy into next season and have a good league campaign.'

Former City captain Paul Lake felt this could prove a 'pivotal moment' in their battle for supremacy. "I would suggest everyone will see it as a chance to establish themselves. We are planning for next season at the same time as what we're doing now. Yes, Sir Alex is going to pass that mantle over to somebody. They will have a fantastic squad of players enriched with success and that mindset – these guys are going to feel 10 foot tall whoever comes in. But we've also experienced that and now know what it takes. We've got that experience under our belts. It could be a very pivotal moment in the power struggle in Manchester but nothing is taken for granted. We've got to bring in different players and there are those that are going to be offloaded. We are building now to regain that title so it could be pivotal but whoever takes that role will still have the guidance and that person to steer them that is one of the greatest managers ever. The challenge is ours but it could be a great moment for us to really turn the screw.'

Lake added, "I've got the utmost respect for Sir Alex Ferguson. I had my testimonial back in 1997. We had no-one to play a game and one of my committee members was talking to Sir Alex and he said 'why haven't you asked me?' He said 'well, you're United' to which Sir Alex said well, ask me the question'. He did and he responded 'of course I will play for Paul and I will make sure David Beckham is there, Paul Scholes is there, the Nevilles are there'. That is the measure of the man. He is an incredible man as well as an amazing manager. As a City fan, though, obviously there was a little kind of feeling that, wow, this is a real opportunity for us. It is an exciting moment and I've seen on Twitter, Facebook and all the social media that it is party time for City fans. There again, there is somebody with a lot of experience that is going to come in with Sir Alex's guidance but I've got to say there was a big part of me that had a huge smile for most of the day. We know his reign has finally come to an end and whoever takes it on has got a huge responsibility - imagine our expectations times 10 or times 100. That person has to fill those shoes, fill that gap and carry on as Sir Alex left off so it is a great moment for us and I personally am really excited by the prospect."

One of Ferguson's biggest rivals in the past 20 years, Arsene Wenger, called the United manager's reign "immaculate". They 'enjoyed' many duels over the years, most notably challenging head-to-head for the Premier League title in the late 1990s and early 2000s. Wenger recognised Sir Alex left huge boots to fill. Wenger said, "It is difficult to imagine English football without him, but it's now a reality and a fact."

Wenger, who will become the longest-serving manager in the country after taking charge at the Gunners in 1996, commented, "I would just like to pay tribute to an unbelievable achievement and a fantastic career. Basically the achievement is immaculate, when you look at the whole structure and consistency of the achievement. It is, of course, something exceptional. It is difficult to imagine English football without him, but it's now a reality and a fact. Of course the next manager has to fill in and show he has the dimension to do that. It is a big task for the guy who comes in."

David Moyes was another long-serving boss, but Wenger anticipated a tough task for the former Everton boss, "What you can say still is that Manchester United are commercially and financially one of the strongest two or three clubs in the world, and that is still a good basis to start when you come in because you know the players are there, the team is there, and the potential is there. They have developed very well and they are in a very, very strong position to deal with the problem they face. But of course it's a great void to fill for Manchester United, because the charisma and personality disappears suddenly in a club which has been dominated by it for such a long time. It's not an easy task to replace a person like that."

David Moyes declined to talk directly about Manchester United when first asked by the media, but he was never evasive, akin to the way Sir Alex handled the press. Asked whether he had considered turning down United's approach, Moyes said: "I have to be honest and say no. I wasn't planning on leaving. My contract was running out but we were planning for pre-season. All we've ever done is keep planning. I've got everything ready for next season and the chairman and everyone knows the route we need to take next season. This is a club competing to be in Europe."

Everton have only finished outside the top half of the table in two of Moyes' 10 full seasons in charge and are sixth in the table with two games of the current campaign remaining. He was proud of the progress the club had made over the past decade. "I'm disappointed to be leaving such a great club. The club has been such a great part of my life," he added.

Moyes' appointment was seen by Stoke boss Tony Pullis as a positive step for young British managers, "David Moyes has come from bottom to the top, and for him to have this chance is brilliant. It's great for all young, aspiring managers, because it shows that young British managers are given a chance at the very top." Moyes has yet to win a major trophy but United captain Nemanja Vidic expected the new boss can continue the club's success. "I'm looking forward to working with David and I believe I will have the same success I had with Sir Alex. David and Sir Alex share some similarities – they are very passionate, they are both winners and you can see the way they approach the games and how they run things."

Harry Redknapp, the relegated QPR boss, first praised him, "Sir Alex has had a massive influence on so many managers. He's achieved so much. Davey is a great boy, a top manager. It's good that a British coach has got the top job." Then, Redknapp spoke out about his undue influence on officials. "A lot of officials would be in awe of him and afraid to upset him. There was such an aura about him because he is a winner. I never had any doubts about that. If there was a bit of time to be added they would make sure they got it right because they did not want to upset him. When Man Utd were losing, they had an average of four minutes and 37 seconds added time, compared with three minutes and 18 seconds when they were winning. Especially young referees, and even one or two of the older ones, were a little bit afraid to upset him."

When Liverpool manager, Rafa Benitez, shared that view. He said: "We know what happens every time we go to Old Trafford and the United staff. They are always going man to man with the referees, especially at half-time when they walk close to the referees and they are talking and talking."

As for the decision to quit, Redknapp added, "I think we all knew it would come suddenly. I thought he would go on for a couple of years yet. He has won the Premier League and maybe feels it is a good time to go out and enjoy his life. Maybe he wants a bit more time to do stuff away from football. He has put great

INTRODUCTION

teams together. He has known the right time to let people go and never been afraid to make the big decisions. Whether it was Roy Keane, David Beckham or Jaap Stam, all the great players have come and gone. He knows the game inside out."

Moyes has not won a major trophy, but Redknapp believed he was the right choice, "It is great for British coaches that Manchester United have picked someone who has come up through the lower divisions. It is good they have given the opportunity to David Moyes, I think he will be fantastic. It is a tough job. Moyes built a great team at Everton and I'm sure he will do a great job at Manchester United."

Big Sam thought Moyes "the perfect candidate" anticipating an emotional atmosphere when he took the Hammers to Goodison Park for Moyes' final home game in charge. "I hope their crowd show their appreciation for him. You can't do anything but applaud him for what he's done in 11 years at Everton. He'll face the challenge head on. It's one of the biggest jobs in club football."

Meanwhile Sir Bobby Charlton was convinced the club made the right choice, "He's maybe been a little bit in awe of everything that happens here – you can't help it when the club has become so big. The mere fact he thinks he can improve it is just fantastic."

Of course there was a precedent at Old Trafford. In 1969 Sir Matt Busby retired but stayed on as general manager, with new boss Wilf McGuinness, promoted from First Team Coach, replaced a little over a year later. However Sir Bobby believed the club had learnt from that mistake. "Alex will help David Moyes. He won't intrude, but he will help him. Like Alex, David has a work ethic and maybe there's something the Scots know that we don't. He's going to be quite happy. He's a well-meaning lad. He's very, very professional and I think he will be a big success at our club."

Michael Carrick was "very excited" to be working with Moyes, "I'm very much looking forward to moving onto a new chapter with the club and personally in my career working under

David. I think he has done an unbelievable job at Everton over a long period of time to keep them up there challenging for Europe. He hasn't had the money of the top four or five clubs to spend but he has always put a team out there that is challenging and I've only heard good things about him from players that have played under him. I'm sure he is going to come here and have a successful time. He's not going to have to change a great deal overnight because things have gone so well of late, but he's his own man and he's going to do his own things and we are all fully behind him as players."

Carrick revealed how he and his team-mates were speechless when Ferguson told them of his decision, "our initial thoughts were we were really disappointed and quite gutted when the manager told us as a team. It was quite sad in the dressing room – that was the initial shock to it but, as time passes, you deal with it and move on. He's arguably the best manager of all time so for him to be sitting in the same changing room telling us that it's his time to retire and giving us the reason, it was quite an emotional time and we were well aware of the importance of it. It was silent.

"What can you say after that? Everyone was digesting the news. It was well documented for a day or two in the media that was there was something coming, we weren't quite sure what. So when the boss pulled us together and told us, that was it. It was hard to take but we fully understand and appreciate everything he has done, not just for this football club but everything he has done for the world of football in the last 30–35 years."

The United players wanted to give their retiring manager a suitable send-off from Old Trafford against Swansea, who had nothing to play for having already qualified for the Europa League having won the Capital One Cup. A full house of 76,000 had the privilege of the last chance to savour the most successful manager in British football history in charge at Old Trafford, and also to say farewell to a footballing legend as Paul Scholes announced his retirement for the second time just ahead of Sir Alex's big farewell. The outstanding England midfield star ended his career at the end of the 2010–11 season, but missed the game so much the 38-year-old opting to resume his career in January 2012, so he signed a one-year deal and it was expected this would be his final, farewell season. His final game at Old Trafford couldn't have been much bigger, Sir Alex's emotional retirement, United presented with the Premier League trophy. Scholes contribution to Sir Alex's 13th title was limited to a handful of appearances as he suffered a knee injury in January.

The reclusive Scholes commented, "Playing football is all I have ever wanted to do, and to have had such a long and successful career at Manchester United, under the greatest manager of all time, has been an honour." Sir Alex paid his own tribute, which made a change from everyone paying their tributes to him! He said: "Paul is a truly unbelievable player. He has always been fully committed to this club and it has been a real privilege to work with him for so many years. Paul will play at Old Trafford on Sunday against Swansea and will collect an unbelievable but well-deserved 11th Premier League medal." Rio tweeted, "One of the best I played alongside also the most naturally gifted player too."

Scholes was one of a vintage batch who graduated through the club's youth system in 1992, alongside Beckham and Gary Neville, and made his debut in 1994. He is only the third United player to surpass 700 appearances, following Sir Bobby Charlton and Ryan Giggs. One of France's greatest ever legends Zinedine Zidane described Scholes as being "in a class of his own" while World Cup-winning Italian boss Marcelo Lippi said he was "one of the most important players for United under Sir Alex".

THE GREATEST

SIR ALEXANDER CHAPMAN FERGUSON has finally left the Old Trafford dug out never to return but he will never be forgotten. How could he be with a stand bearing his name and a statue on the concourse outside, and a banner depicting his triumphs adorning the East Stand that is unlikely to be equalled by any football manager at any single football club in the future.

Cristiano Ronaldo, who played under Ferguson for six years from 2003, tweeted "thanks for everything, Boss" accompanied by a picture of the two together. Roy Hodgson, the England manager, viewed the announcement as "a sad day for English football". Adding, "It marks the end of an era in football management. No one will be able to match his achievements, his dedication, his support for colleagues in need and his team building know-how."

Sepp Blatter, FIFA president tweeted, "His achievements in the game place him without doubt as one of the 'greats'. It was an honour to present Sir Alex with an award at the 2011 Ballon D'Or. Will his longevity at the top ever be repeated?" Michel Platini, Uefa president hailed Sir Alex as a "visionary" who "has made a massive contribution to football across Europe".

Sir Alex now joins another knight of the realm Sir Bobby Charlton, who made more than 600 appearances for United between 1956 and 1973, on the United board. Sir Bobby said, "I am a director at United but I hardly need to worry about a thing because we are winning all the time and it is all down to Sir Alex Ferguson. He would get up in the middle of the night and travel 300 miles if he thought there was someone he could sign. He loves the game. He is such a fantastic manager. Everything he has done has been fantastic."

So farewell Sir Alex. At the age of 71, it was time to go. He'd done it all, got the t-shirt and given us so many great teams and wonderfully gifted players, he left as the undisputed Greatest Of All Time.

We will miss you. Well, Manchester United fans will. United's rivals might be glad to see the back of the laird of Old Trafford but even they must recognise his genius. The neutrals will most definitely miss him. The game will never be quite the same again.

We will miss his bright red nose, chewing gum in his dug out seat looking miserable as sin, the fury at any refereeing decision he doesn't like, Fergie time ie. looking at his watch incessantly as if demanding more over time from his time piece, complaining bitterly that insufficient time was handed down by the officials (only if his team needed it for a comeback, of course), his ruthless manipulation of the transfer market, his love of expensive red wine, inviting managers back to his office after games for a tipple (even those who he had fallen out with down the years such as Kevin Keegan and Kenny Dalglish), banning the press from his media conferences when he took a dislike to something they'd written or said about him and of course that wonderful smile and jig of delight when his team scored yet another late, late winner.

United fans would dread the Fergie tombola, the almost random selection of players that seemed to get more erratic as the years went on but they would revel in his one-eyed dedication to the cause, the Lord Protector who would risk upsetting anybody and everything to get his way.

This unique drive was the real secret of his success at Old Trafford. Sir Alex won 38 trophies during his 26-year reign at Old Trafford. Can there be a more fitting tribute than that fact alone? There could be no better epitaph. Nothing gave him more pleasure than lifting the next big prize and forcing United's trophy room to fund yet another extension.

And what of The Hairdryer? During a marathon round of

interviews following his departure I was asked to explain the origin of the phrase, as, for a change, the interviews following the announcements were as likely to be on news programmes as sports shows. I think it was Brian McClair that first coined the phrase in reference to the feeling of being blasted by the manager for some mistake or other and the rush of hot air that made one's hair stand one end.

In "The Ferguson Effect" a book I penned in 1999 featuring stories from 40 personalities in football and the media who had come across Sir Alex, virtually all of them admitted that they had endured The Hairdryer Treatment at one stage of their lives. Myself included! The players won't miss it, that's for sure!

Above the parochial concerns of the United fans. the man will be remembered for the positive aspects he brought to Old Trafford and to football in the widest sense. Sir Alex delivered United's 20th league title, his 13th Premier League title, before announcing his retirement. A fine way to bow out.

It all began on the now demolished Manor Ground in Oxford on 8 November 1986 and came to a close at United's final game of the season at The Hawthorns and West Bromwich Albion on Sunday, 19 May 2013, whereas he would have preferred the curtain to close at Wembley in the Champions League Final.

It seems a life time ago when Sir Alex took over from Ron Atkinson in 1986, and of course it is, there have been few longer managerial reigns in football and certainly none as successful. If it wasn't for Sir Alex, David Moyes and Arsene Wenger, the average reign of a Premier League boss, currently one year and three months, would be considerably shorter.

But if you want history, tradition and silverware, then look no further than Sir Alex at Old Trafford; two Champions League crowns, the UEFA Cup Winners' Cup, 13 Premier League League titles, five FA Cups, four League Cups, an Inter-Continental Club cup and a World Club Cup. World champions twice or "once more than England" as the United fans are fond of singing.

When the overnight speculation reached a crescendo that Sir Alex was about to retire and in the hours before the big announcement the next morning, I was inundated with media calls to talk about the issue, and of course, my article a year ago, an interview with the Wigan chairman and owner Dave Whelan was much quoted. The Wigan chairman had given me an interview for my ESPN column making it perfectly plain that he was sure that 2012-13 would be Sir Alex's final season in charge of Manchester United and of course it proved to be spot on.

When the big decision was announced, it was done so via Twitter, a medium that Sir Alex had been highly dubious about, indeed he would rather his players didn't use it, as it was always open to abuse; he warned his players about the excesses of the medium. How ironic, indicative of the changing age of football. that United tweeted: "Sir Alex Ferguson retires. #thankyousiralex". A club statement read: "The most successful manager in English football history will bow out after the West Bromwich Albion game on 19 May and join the football club board."

Sir Alex immediately commented, "The decision to retire is one that I have thought a great deal about and one that I have not taken lightly. It is the right time. It was important to me to leave an organisation in the strongest possible shape and I believe I have done so. The quality of this league winning squad, and the balance of ages within it, bodes well for continued success at the highest level whilst the structure of the youth set-up will ensure that the long-term future of the club remains a bright one. Our training facilities are amongst the finest in global sport and our home Old Trafford is rightfully regarded as one of the leading venues in the world. Going forward, I am delighted to take on the roles of both director and ambassador for the club. With these activities, along with my many other interests, I am looking forward to the future. I must pay tribute to my family, their love and support has been essential. My wife Cathy has been the key figure throughout my career."

The announcement was made while US markets were closed, and the club and shareholders waited eagerly to discover what, if any, impact, it would have on the share price. When trading began shares fell by 4.5% at the height of their decline. Hardly a surprise as the club has warned institutions and individual investors in its prospectus ahead of its stock market flotation that its business was dependent on its ability to attract and retain players, and naturally that largely depended on the success rating of the team, which in turn was dependent on the quality of their manager. "Any successor to our current manager may not be as successful as our current manager," the prospectus stressed.

The US based ownership remains unpopular with the United fan base, and it has been a tricky juggling act for Sir Alex to keep the fans happy enough to diminish the protests against the highly leveraged takeover; the best way of quelling disquiet was the steady stream of trophies despite restrictions on the transfer budget inevitably a consequence of the interest repayments on the loads.

The club still runs smoothly enough despite a debt of £370m and finances that remain tightly controlled by the Glazer family. The Americans bought the club for £790m in 2005 in a controversial deal that loaded the club with debt. One of Ferguson's greatest achievements has been to maintain, and indeed accelerate, United's trophy haul despite annual interest payments of up to £70 million, restricted activity in the transfer market and the forced sale of stars such as Cristiano Ronaldo.

'Gold Trafford' is a phenomenal money making machine with global commercial enterprises, and the Glazers have expanded the commercialisation and revenue streams to a degree that has off-set some of these interest repayments. In addition the Glazers have refinanced the loans dispensing with the more expensive and potentially damaging PIK loans. Nevertheless any managerial successor would be entering a club where the priority was not neccessarily acquiring the best players but the most cost effective.

THE GREATEST

Despite constant speculation about Middle East or Chinese takeovers amounting to close to £2 billion, the Glazers have never been inclined to sell their prize sporting asset and, instead, opted for a flotation on the New York stock exchange, having abandoned a similar plan in England, and the Wall Street initiative saw the Glazers sell 16.7 million shares, equal to a 10% stake in the club. Since the flotation in August 2012, Manchester United shares have risen 34%.

The timing or Sir Alex's retirement created all sorts of conspiracy theories. Was it because Jose Mourniho was touted for the Chelsea job and the United board wanted him... was it because David Moyes contract was coming to an end at Everton... was it because of ill health and talk of missing the new season because of a summer hip operation. Was he pushed? The last theory was born out of the manager's persistent denials of any thoughts of retirement. But he might well have learned from his original plan to retire in 2001 before he backtracked explaining it had been a terrible mistake. By announcing his retirement then, in advance, it had an adverse effect on a season in which they surrendered the title to Arsenal.

Yet, just weeks before his retirement, in March, as he prepared to face Real Madrid in the Champions League, he wrote in his programme notes: "This is what it is all about – a packed Old Trafford, the floodlights on, the pitch glistening and two of the greatest and most romantic clubs in the game about to do battle. People ask me why I don't retire after so many years in the game, but how could anyone with an ounce of passion for football in their soul voluntarily walk away from the opportunity to be involved in this kind of occasion?" He has repeated similar sentiments a few times since that statement, insisting he was good for a few more years. He certainly put people off the scent if his intention all along was to quit.

After that gut-wrenching defeat Sir Alex's loyal assistant Mike Phelan pointed out that his Boss was "too distraught" convinced Turkish referee Cuneyt Cakir's decision to send off Nani for a high foot had robbed them of victory. Sir Alex would have liked to have departed with a third Champions League trophy and to win it at Wembley where Sir Matt Busby's United triumphed against Benfica in 1968, as he had a rich sense of United's history and traditions. Perhaps he felt the third European Cup would take more time than he had at his disposal, and that it was no longer a challenge to which he could aspire. Fergie Time was a back handed recognition of his desire to squeeze every last second from a match if there was a glimmer of hope of rescuing a game but Father Time had caught up with the man at last in his pursuit of that elusive third Champions League.

Undoubtedly the highest high point of his entire, illustrious United career was the night in Barcelona's Nou Camp in May 1999 when stoppage-time goals from Teddy Sheringham and Ole Gunnar Solskjaer turned defeat into victory as the soon to be knighted Alex Ferguson muttered his now famous phrase: "Football – bloody hell." It capped the greatest season by any English football team, a unique treble of League, FA Cup and European Cup. "Everything their hearts desire!" in the immortal words of Clive Tyldesley.

Then there was the knocking of Liverpool off their perch, with United assuming the mantel of England's most successful club. By the end of his reign he had also batted away challenges from Arsenal, Chelsea and Manchester City. By the end of his reign United were a title winning machine honed to perfection to pump out result after result, even if at times the football was less than scintillating.

Sir Alex might have wanted to sit on his decision for a few days and announce it to the fans first, after he and his players had collected the Premier league trophy in the home game with Swansea at the weekend. But news of his decision was leaking out and speculation grew, especially when the Old Trafford press office refused to deny the story. The story originally emerged late on Tuesday evening, with reports that United's player versus coaches golf day at Dunham Massey had been overshadowed by the expectation of such an announcement, with many expecting a big announcement at the Swansea game. It could only mean one thing; bookmakers had taken a lot large bets on David Moyes being next United manager. Again hardly surprising, all the clues were there with Sir Alex's fellow Scot out of contract at the end of the season at long-term employers Everton.

While it might not have been entirely unexpected, nevertheless, in a contradiction in terms, it was still a huge shock when it was officially confirmed. As the BBC put it: "It was an announcement that came as a seismic shock to football's system, coming so soon after a series of bullish statements from Ferguson hinting at exactly the opposite."

From No 10, as Sir Alex occasionally dabbled in politics as well as horse racing, to The League Managers Association, where the United manager was a very active and influencial member, there was a deluge of reaction to Sir Alex's announcement, and as you'd expect it was 100 per cent praiseworthy.

The LMA issued a statement, "We would like to congratulate Sir Alex Ferguson CBE on a truly remarkable and fantastic career following his announcement today that he will retire at the end of the season." Chairman of the LMA, Howard Wilkinson observed, "today's news draws to a close the career of a man and a manager, the likes of which we will never see again. His public face was always that of the ultimate professional with a fierce pride and determination to do the very best for his club. His frighteningly competitive nature has never nor ever will be equalled. He is the epitome of the mantra 'Survive, Win, Succeed'. But, in private, with those he trusted, he was the very best sort of friend you could ever wish for. To say his presence on the bench will be sorely missed in no way begins to describe the massive hole he will leave behind. He always said he was too old to retire, let's hope he manages to enjoy the retirement he deserves."

Richard Bevan, chief executive of the LMA, remarked, "Sir Alex has left an indelible legacy not only at Manchester United but on the art of football management itself. 36 major trophies in 26 years in charge of the Club is a record that simply speaks for itself. It's not just his longevity in the game, at one of the world's biggest and most demanding clubs which is remarkable, rather it has been his ability to consistently deliver the highest levels of success throughout his 40 years and over 2150 matches in football management. What Sir Alex has achieved personally with both Manchester United and Aberdeen, where he broke the Old Firm stranglehold in winning 10 trophies in seven years before his appointment at Old Trafford, is unrivalled. At the LMA we are also extremely grateful for the amount of time and dedication he has willingly provided to our association and our members since he first joined in 1986. His input as an Executive Board member and Trustee has been invaluable in the development of the LMA. As he retires as the most successful manager in the history of the British game we congratulate him on a magnificent career and wish him all the very best for the future."

Bryan Robson, at United from 1981 until 1994 and still an ambassador at Old Trafford and one time captain of club and country, commented, "It is unbelievable to change around probably four different squads and have the success he has. Ferguson is probably the greatest club manager ever." Legendary goalkeeper Peter Schmeichel said, "It's come as an absolute bombshell. I'm sad and disappointed. I was really, really hoping he was going to stay for another couple of years." Schmeichel's treble-winning team-mate of 1999, Dwight Yorke, added, "Regaining the Premier League this season, he's managed to do that, so in many respects that's the reason, with the hip operation and David Gill leaving, I just feel it's the right time for him to go."

Paul Ince played under Sir Alex for six years between 1989 and 1995. The former England captain now a manger in his own right, knows there will never be another manager to replicate Ferguson's achievements, "You will never see anyone of his kind again. His standards were so high. He was so demanding. Yes, we had our ups and down. The way he treated me was like a son." Former England striker Michael Owen played under Sir Alex at United from 2009 until 2012, remarked, "He is arguably the greatest manager to have ever lived and to say I played under him for three years is a proud thing to say."

Ruud van Nistelrooy was one of several high profile superstars who fell out with Sir Alex, yet he tweeted, "2001-2006, 219 games, 150 goals under the most successful manager in football history. It was a unique privilege." Now manager of Norwegian side Molde, and tipped to be a future manager at Old Trafford, Ole Gunnar Solskjaer spent over a decade at United, playing over 200 games from 1996 until 2007. He told MUTV, "I will never forget the loyalty he showed me. Everything I have learnt I have learnt from the boss." Richard Scudamore, Premier League chief executive, added, "The Premier League has had the privilege to witness many great players, managers and teams. No one has made as great a contribution to the Premier League than Sir Alex Ferguson." While Stuart Lancaster, the England rugby coach commented, "His longevity and what he has achieved as a coach I think is unparalleled in world sport. I admire him hugely for what he has done." Rory McIlroy, remarked, "An end of an era today! Sir Alex Ferguson, the greatest of all time! United will have a tough time trying to replace him!"

But the fall out from Sir Alex's departure was immediate. The truth about Wayne Rooney's position quickly emerged, for example. Rooney had told Sir Alex he wanted a new challenge two weeks before the managers retirement. Rooney wanted a fresh challenge after nine years at the club, but the club were adamant that their forward was not for sale as Rooney was set to be reunited with his former Everton manager David Moyes. Yet, Moyes and Rooney have had their differences. In 2008, Moyes accepted substantial libel damages over claims made in Rooney's book about their relationship at Everton. Since then the pair have reconciled. In September 2012, Rooney wrote on Twitter: "Everton are playing brilliantly. David Moyes has done some job over the last 10 years."

Rooney left Moyes and his hometown club Everton at the age of 18 in August 2004 in a deal worth an eventual £27m, scoring 197 goals in 402 appearances for United, winning five league titles, two League Cups and a Champions League.

Rooney had scored 16 in 37 appearances in helping United to their 20th league title, 12 of those coming in the league. Yet there had been persistent speculation in the second half of the season that Rooney may leave, especially after being sitting out the Champions League second-round tie against Real Madrid with Danny Welbeck preferred in attack. He was no longer leader of the attack following Robin Van Persie's arrival from Arsenal. Days later as the speculation about Rooney's future escalated Ferguson promised that he would stay at the club, saying: "He'll be here next year. You can have my word on that." The manager later said Rooney would be given a new deal but that was before the truth emerged about the manager's retirement.

Rooney first asked to leave Old Trafford in October 2010 when he pulled out of contract talks, questioning assurances about 'the future squad.' Fergie responded at the time saying he was "dumbfounded" and 48 hours later, Rooney signed a new five-year deal. United went on to win the title that season, and Rooney later said it was the best decision of his career to stay. This time Rooney did not submit a formal transfer request, but personally asked Sir Alex to leave.

Hours before Moyes announcement as manager and just 24 hours after Sir Alex's retirement, United chief executive David Gill told MUTV, "It is a dream job. The new manager will inherit a great squad and infrastructure off the pitch, with a great staff. He will be walking into a difficult situation in terms of the number of trophies, but the positive of also having the support of the Manchester United family."

Moyes quit Everton after 11 years in charge at Goodison Park, the 50-year-old Scot agreed a six-year deal. Sir Alex commented, "We unanimously agreed on David Moyes. David is a man of great integrity with a strong work ethic. I've admired his work for a long time and approached him as far back as 1998 to discuss the position of assistant manager here. There is no question he has all the qualities we expect of a manager at this club."

Moyes described it as "a great honour" to be appointed. "I am delighted that Sir Alex saw fit to recommend me for the job. I have great respect for everything he has done and for the football club. I know how hard it will be to follow the best manager ever, but the opportunity to manage Manchester United isn't something that comes around very often and I'm really looking forward to taking up the post next season."

Moyes paid tribute to Everton. "I have had a terrific job at Everton, with a tremendous chairman and board of directors and a great set of players. Between now and the end of the season, I will do everything in my power to make sure we finish as high as possible in the table. Everton's fantastic fans have played a big part in making my years at Goodison so enjoyable and I thank them wholeheartedly for the support they have given me and the players. Everton will be close to me for the rest of my life." In a statement, Everton said, "The chairman, on behalf of the club, would like to place on record his thanks to David for the massive contribution he has made to Everton since his arrival in March 2002. He has been an outstanding manager."

So not The Special One but The Chosen One. Sir Alex has enjoyed a close relationship with the new boss throughout his managerial career and even considered appointing him as his assistant when Moyes was manager at Preston. While Moyes has worked on a tight budget at Goodison Park, he failed to win a single trophy and has very limited experience in Europe, which is a big gamble for the United board, but the key to his appointment is that he is a safe pair of hands, he will continue in the Ferguson mould and retain the stability that Sir Alex created by his sheer longevity in the job at Old Trafford.

Much has been made of the error in the United board's judgement in retaining Sir Matt Busby in 1971 as a succession of his successors tried and failed while his larger than life figure was retained in the back ground. Many of the remaining players felt that Busby was their father figure and he was an intimidating force behind the scenes, the reverse is likely to be true in the modern ear, as the game has changed unrecognisably.

When Busby left the United hot-seat, they were already an anachronism. Poor training facilities, outdated training methods and non-existent tactics were glossed over by the geniuses of Law, Best and Charlton. The 1968 European Cup triumph allowed supporters to believe that the United way was superior when in fact, it was probably the last flourishing of an approach to football that died out in the late fifties. The years following Busby's retirement saw United decline. George Best, once hailed the greatest player in the world, typified the depths to which the club sank. Relegation just six years after that European triumph seemed inevitable.

The modern United by contrast is a well run, forward thinking institution. The care of its players is first class, how else to explain the apparently endless career of Ryan Giggs? Yes, the club has been dominated by the patriarchal Ferguson for the past few decades, but he leaves behind an incredible legacy that stretches from boardroom to canteen staff.

Back in 2011 two former Manchester United managers Tommy Docherty and Wilf McGuinness told me that Sir Alex Ferguson was the greatest manager of all time in British football. Sir Alex surpassed Sir Matt Busby's record as the longest serving Manchester United manage, and in the opinion of the Doc and McGuinness he was now the undisputed No 1. In fact the Doc goes as far as to declare that with Lionel Messi the best player in the world, Sir Alex is the best manager in the world.

United's record 19th English League title was his 12th League honour at the club. Little wonder he was named Manager of the Year by his fellow League managers and also picked up a special merit award for having passed 2,000 matches as manager. Speaking at the LMA awards dinner in London via video link from Old Trafford, Ferguson said, "It's a wonderful honour – it has been a fantastic season for us in the most difficult league in the world." Ancelotti, sacked by Chelsea the same day, attended the dinner and Ferguson said to him: "Carlo you are a fantastic man and you have showed great courage in coming to the dinner, well done."

In a chapter on the title victory in 1956, McGuinness declared that Sir Alex has established his credentials as the all-time No. 1 Boss in British football. The Doc, as you would expect, is far more colourful in the way he describes Sir Alex.

The Docherty era at United lasted five exciting and enormously entertaining seasons from December 1972 until July 1977. Weeks after his greatest feat, defeating Liverpool 2-1 at Wembley to lift the FA Cup, the manager with the most one liners in the game was sacked following his affair with the wife of his physiotherapist, Laurie Brown. Many believe that, had he survived, he would have built a title winning team, but the ever irrepressible and irascible Doc isn't so sure.

"I never got the chance to win the League, and might never have in any case even if I stayed because I needed a goalkeeper and although they were willing to pay Stoke £200,000 for Peter Shilton, they wouldn't pay him £200-a-week in wages. I am not saying I would have won the League, but we were always good to watch, it was always a pleasure for me to watch such an attacking team, and who knows we might have gone on to win it. I was sacked, and we all know why, but it was hypocrisy, there were things going on that we now know about too. The game has changed immensely and I don't like the present game - the money, the salaries, the players, it's not as I knew it. The game has gone as far as I am concerned. Yes, I resent what happened to me at United. Chelsea are wonderful to me, they sent me a £200 Harrods hamper every Christmas, but when I asked for a couple of tickets to take my daughter on her 21st birthday to Old Trafford, they sent me two tickets and invoiced me for £88."

Sometimes it is hard to separate the jokes from the facts, but the mind seems as sharp as ever, and the wit as pointed. Even so The Doc loved his time at Old Trafford and despite a fall out with Ferguson when he was Scotland manager, he has nothing but praise for the United boss, the highest possible praise. "He has got to be the greatest manager of them all. He is world class. Messi is the best player in the world at the moment, and Fergie is the best manager in the world at the moment. Cloughie did fantastic with a small club like Forest, Revie and Bill Nicholson were among the very best, but Fergie is the best."

The Doc, being a former manager, cannot register a vote in the Players' Player poll, but for the record he selects a trio of players in his own era as his personal favourites, Martin Buchan, Steve Coppell, Gordon Hill, Lou Macari, Jimmy Greenhoff and Stuart Pearson, but added that "Roy Keane was world class."

Gordon Strachan knows how Liverpool are feeling in pursuit of an elusive first title for 12 years as he suffered similar frustrations with United. It took United 26 years to break down the barriers for a title triumph, although it eluded Strachan's' era. Liverpool will be anxious that it isn't such a long wait as that. Strachan told '20|13', "It drags on each year, and each year it gets worse and worse, you know it's a long time since the last one and you get the feeling its never going to come. You know you are at a great club, as we did during our time at United without a title, but you rely on the other players, you rely on reputations and you end up living off the legends, the names of the past, and the longer it goes on the more you feel you are never going to win the League. I was at a great club and delighted to play for United. But it's like putting badly at golf and sometimes you need a complete change, a drastic change to solve the problem."

Sitting sipping a coke at the 18th hole at Celtic Manor, it was typical of golf loving Strachan to use a golfing analogy but when it comes to assessing United's 19th title, he goes for the driver and gave the subject some welly, "United have proved they can win in style in the past, they've proved they can win hanging in there. Whatever anyone says about playing this style or that, if you ask any manager the first thing they will tell you they want to do is to win, than nobody can touch you. United like to play to a certain standard, apparently they have this philosophy about style, but so too does a club like West Ham, but ask them whether they would stick to their philosophy or stay in the Premier League, the same goes for Nottingham Forest. Ok the United team that won the 19th title might not have had the flair of the past teams, but their home record was phenomenal."

With his own vast managerial knowledge, Strachan knows the values and virtues of Sir Alex, and his worth to United, "While some clubs have a lull in their trophy cabinet and use that time to rebuild, Fergie tends to re-shape his teams when they are winning trophies, and buying the likes of Ashley Young who can play anywhere in the front four or off the main striker, is one of the typical Fergie signings, a player who can give the team more flair when it needs it. Having said that, United won this title with a home record that was phenomenal, not great away from home, granted, but it's no fluke that Fergie keeps on winning.

"Ask anyone who built the best team at St. Mirren, and they will tell you Fergie did, ask anyone who built the best team at Aberdeen, and they will tell you Fergie did, and this legendary period at United is down to the manger, a terrific manager, the best manager, to do it once is good, but three times at three clubs is just ridiculous."

Born in Glasgow to a Protestant, working class family, Sir Alex's leadership skills first came to the fore as a shop steward in the Clyde shipyards, when Ferguson led an unofficial walk-out over a pay dispute. Ferguson cut a reasonably impressive figure with Rangers as a player but was made a scapegoat following the team's humiliating 4-0 defeat against arch rivals Celtic in the 1969 Cup Final. He switched to management, first with St Mirren and then, from 1978, at Aberdeen. His tough-talking, hands-on approach enabled him to smashed the Celtic-Rangers "Old Firm" monopoly, winning three championships, four Scottish Cups and the European Cup Winners' Cup in six years. Known for his fiery temper, he also won the reputation of a fiercely loyal coach who invests time and effort in star players and apprentices alike.

Appointed as successor to Ron Atkinson in 1986, the Scot took time to adapt to English football. Following a first full season in which he guided United to a runners-up finish, United struggled, the nadir coming in September 1989 when United were hammered 5-1 by bitter rivals Manchester City. A few months later, during a 2-1 home defeat to lowly Crystal Palace, a banner was unfurled which read, "Three years of excuses and it's still crap - ta-ra Fergie." Yet despite relegation form he was saved by a 'make or break' cup run that took United all the way to a final victory over, ironically enough, Crystal Palace. From then Fergie's United career blossomed – Cup Winners' Cup and League Cup successes were capped with the coveted league title 7 years into the Guv'nor from Govan's reign. Now, with 12 Premier League crowns, five FA Cups, four League Cups, two European Cups, a European Cup-Winners' Cup and a career total of 47 trophies in 37 years, Sir Alex has a medal haul beyond comparison.

Yet he is forbidden to keep a single piece of silverware inside his house by his wife, Cathy, who was not even impressed with the knighthood he received in 1999. Ferguson said in an interview with the LMA's The Manager magazine, "I prefer to think about what's ahead and what I can achieve next and I think that has kept my feet on the ground quite well. I've never got carried away with it. My wife, Cathy, is fed up with the whole thing. When Alastair Campbell phoned her about my knighthood she said to him, 'Do you not think he's had enough rewards?' You'll not find a thing about my career in the house at all. She's unbelievable. I can't even take a football book home or she'll say, 'What are you doing with that?'"

Stability has been the key to keeping control over players. Compared to rivals such as Chelsea who continually to change managers, Sir Alex says, "I would never have expected to achieve what I have achieved. There have been periods where there have been sudden leaps. Going to Aberdeen took me to a different level and it was an opportunity I grasped. When we won our first trophy at Manchester United there was that sudden leap of confidence and a sense that I was safe in the job. That stability is important, not for me, but for the players, because when they know who the manager is going to be every day it makes an immense difference to the structure, the confidence and the power base of the club, there's no doubt about that."

THE GREATEST

Sir Alex is "terrified" at telling his 'Ferguson Babes', the players at the start of his phenomenal success, that their time is up. Dreading the day he has to tell Giggs it's time to go, or when Paul Scholes quits. "It's a horrible thing to say, but you can't be sentimental in this job. I love the players that I've had and I've been very, very fortunate to have had great players who have come through my career with me. At Aberdeen there were the likes of Miller, McLeish, and Kennedy, who were a bunch of players that were very loyal to me. At United I've had Giggs, the Nevilles, Scholes and Butt, who represent the spirit of the club. All of the players that I have had here have played a part in my success. So when I see something happening, as in the cases of Nicky Butt and Phil Neville, I've had to release them to other opportunities. It was getting to the stage that I was terrified of talking to them and telling them they weren't playing. It wasn't fair to them because they were good players and played a big part in the resurrection of Manchester United. When the time came for me to let them go I knew I was cutting really important, loyal strings and I didn't enjoy it.

"My job is to manage United, to produce results and I am no different from any other manager. I'll not be regarded in the same way if I'm not successful. Everything to do with me is black and white; if it's on the football field and I see something that I feel is a retrograde step for the club I have to act and make decisions, which is something that I have always been good at. I can make quick decisions and I am lucky that way. In management you have to be able to make decisions; sometimes you're not right, but that doesn't concern me too much because the important thing is being able to do it."

David Moyes hails from a similar background to Sir Alex, and has many similar traits, but its typical of Sir Alex that he has not recommended a big name like Mourinho or one of the 'flavour of the month' candidates favoured by other clubs. Instead he has nominated another Scot, who will no doubt rely on the advice and guidance of his predecessor, warming to it, rather than fearing it.

Many have believed that when Sir Alex goes, United will finally lose their grip on their dominance both domestically and fade as a force in Europe. Much responsibility lies with Sir Alex for taking the brave decision to opt for 'stability' over 'style' while a few critics have claimed that United will tread water now, content with a top four place and the odd cup run.

Anyone who sincerely believes this does not understand the legacy of the greatest of them all.

SIR ALEX FERGUSON HONOURS

ST MIRREN (1)
1 SCOTTISH FIRST DIVISION (SECOND TIER) TITLE 1976–77

ABERDEEN (10)
3 SCOTTISH PREMIER LEAGUE TITLES: 1979–80, 1983–84, 1984–85
4 SCOTTISH FA CUPS: 1981–82, 1982–83, 1983–84, 1985–86
1 SCOTTISH LEAGUE CUP: 1985–86
1 EUROPEAN CUP WINNERS CUP: 1982–83
1 UEFA SUPER CUP: 1983

MANCHESTER UNITED (38)
13 PREMIER LEAGUE TITLES: 1992–93, 1993–94, 1995–96, 1996–97, 1998–99, 1999–2000, 2000–01, 2002–03, 2006–07, 2007–08, 2008–09, 2010–11, 2012–13
5 FA CUPS: 1989–90, 1993–94, 1995–96, 1998–99, 2003–04
4 LEAGUE CUPS: 1991–92, 2005–06, 2008–09, 2009–10
10 CHARITY/COMMUNITY SHIELDS: 1990 (SHARED), 1993, 1994, 1996, 1997, 2003, 2007, 2008, 2010, 2011
2 CHAMPIONS LEAGUE: 1998–99, 2007–08
1 EUROPEAN CUP WINNERS CUP: 1990–91
1 UEFA SUPER CUP: 1991
1 INTERCONTINENTAL CUP: 1999
1 FIFA CLUB WORLD CUP: 2008

FERGIE'S FAREWELL

HISTORY AND TRADITION, the very ethos of Manchester United, were unashamedly rolled out, as one might have expected, for Sir Alex's special 'farewell game'. It was Sir Alex Ferguson's 723rd match at the Theatre of Dreams, turned into a virtual testimonial dressed up as a Premier League game.

Sir Alex's Old Trafford debut was a 1-0 win over QPR 26-and-a-half years earlier, watched by a crowd of 42,235, remarkably 14,000 shy of capacity. 'The Farewell' was full to the rafters all right. A crowd of 75,572 will long be able to say "I was there" on such a momentous occasion for the club, and British football history.

1986 was a life-time ago but it is worth reflecting on the changes Manchester has undergone under Fergie's reign. Back then, English clubs were still banned from Europe following the Heysel stadium disaster and Liverpool were the dominant domestic force having become only the second club in the 20th century to win the League and FA Cup double. Meanwhile supporters still had the option to watch a match from the terraces at a reasonable cost while football in general still seemed at the fringe of national life – live matches had only just began to appear on national television and the skill level quite often left a lot to be desired. Foreign imports were rare and the sport didn't have its own dedicated TV channels. Attendances were falling and supporters were often treated like animals with an openly hostile government openly discussing how to shut football down if hooliganism persisted. Fighting on the terraces was almost a sport within a sport and a common sight on the news.

26 and a half years later the Premier League is one of

England's greatest exports with the city of Manchester gaining so much tourism through the popularity of United that it has become the UK's top destination outside the capital. Of course Sir Alex Ferguson, more than any other, is responsible for this economic boom in an area once synonymous with post-industrial urban decay. When he arrived in 1986 the city was falling to pieces, he leaves it as a place confident of its status on the world stage. If an academic could do a study on Sir Alex's economic impact on the area, I am sure he would be up there with the Victorian businessmen and benefactors who helped turn the region into the world's first industrial city.

Of course, it could have been very different had the club not won the FA Cup in 1990, as the first four years were trophyless, and a day of destiny arrived with his side struggling in the League. That unexpected at the City Ground, Nottingham in a third round FA Cup tie against Brian Clough's high-flying Forest team is popularly though to have saved his bacon. Mark Robins was the kid who emerged through the ranks to score the vital winner - whether Sir Alex's successor David Moyes is afforded the luxury of such time in an age of instant success, remains to be seen, although a six year contract was a statement of intent. It's interesting to note that across Manchester another overseas owner afforded Roberto Mancini a new lucrative six-year contract upon wrestling the championship crown from United, and that lasted less than a year with the Italian appearing to be on the verge of dismissal at the end of the season.

Michael Laudrup, manager of the incidental opponent on the day, Swansea City, observed that filling Sir Alex's boots was the toughest job in world football. Good luck David, you're going to need it, and Sir Alex made the point of actually asking the fans to back his successor.

In his final programme notes, Sir Alex wrote, "To the fans, thank you. The support you have provided over the years has been truly humbling. It has been an enormous honour and an enormous privilege to have led your club and I have treasured my time as manager of Manchester United."

FERGIE'S FAREWELL

There is always curiosity and fans hanging around waiting for the star-studded team bus to arrive at Old Trafford, but this time, three hours before kick-off, thousands of fans were already assembled. The small barricaded area set aside for the arrival of the team coach was a mass of people at 12.30pm, eager to be at the front to take pictures of Sir Alex leaving the team coach for the final time at Old Trafford. The fans queued to buy their programmes or fanzines featuring Fergie's Farewell.

Inside the stadium the atmosphere was naturally one of celebration and sentimentality, the mood captured as Frank Sinatra's "My Way" and Nat King Cole's "Unforgettable" got the fans in the mood for the tribute to the departing boss. There were plenty of banners in amongst the swarm of red flags; one read "Sir Alex - Immortal", another "Thanks Gaffer. From The Stretford End." , "Fergie rules" read another; but no longer.

Walking onto the pitch, 70,000 red flags with the word 'Champions' waved as Sir Alex was announced as "the man who made the impossible dream possible". Even Sir Bobby Charlton was waving one of the red flags standing in the directors' box. The music, well, The Impossible Dream, of course. Cue massive applause when the departing emerged from the tunnel. No red and white scarf tied fashionably like Roberto Mancini, nor designer gear like Jose Mourinho or Andre Villas-Boas, instead the uniform of an archetypal old fashioned British coach, that of dark overcoat worn against the Mancunian rain, covering the usual favoured black fleece zipped up, against the cold. Yes, it was still peeing down and chilly in the middle May in Manchester.

United's electric scoreboard cut through the gloom and rain to beam brightly "26 years – 38 trophies. 'Champions' was spelled out by the fans cards in white against the red background on the stand which bares his name. He received a guard of honour from both teams. He smiled and applauded back. He gave a thumbs up to both teams as he headed to his position on the sideline, signing a profusion of autographs before the kick off. By the way, the fans also gave a tremendous reception to Paul Scholes. But this was only going to be about one man.

As for the match itself, United won 2-1, with Rio Ferdinand scoring a late winner in the 87th minute, heaven sent, another late goal. How Sir Alex thrived on late goals. He loved them. At least it was a few minutes before the end rather than in Fergie time, a new addition to the football vocabulary invented by Sir Alex's desire to extract every possible second of over time to gain any kind of advantage he could. The whole event on the field was irrelevant in the sense that this was Sir Alex's Day, the result didn't really matter, but better a win to sign off with. The fans sang 'Champions' naturally, but also mocked City 'We Won Our Trophy Back and Now You've Got The Sack'. And of course, there had been rumours in the media for weeks that Mancini was a Dead Man Walking, and would have been sacked regardless of the FA Cup Final defeat to Wigan the day before Sir Alex's big day.

Javier Hernandez opened the scoring, and another cacophony of sound as the fans bellowed "Stand Up for Alex Ferguson', and of course they all did. Michu equalised, and the fans joked 'You're Be Sacked In The Morning!" Again it seemed part of the script that one of the central characters of the season, whose future was under constant review, Rio Ferdinand, should pop up with the late winner. It was Rio's first goal in five years. Here's another one for the stats freaks, Sir Alex won 514 of 723 home games at Old Trafford. Quite some record, but just one of many stunning stats that Sir Alex leave us all with.

But it's not just records Sir Alex has broken. He has broken some of the biggest egos in the game. Wayne Rooney was not included in the team, he wasn't even in the United squad. After the game, Sir Alex confirmed Rooney had asked for a transfer and it "made sense" for him not to play, even though the request was turned down. Asked whether the Rooney will stay at the club, Sir Alex smiled, "It's not my decision now!" Rooney had played under Moyes as a teenager at Goodison Park before joining United in August 2004, and although they fell out over Rooney's autobiography, they had since repaired their relationship. That, though, didn't necessary mean a healing of the rift between

Rooney and the club, but with Sir Alex gone, it might mean another chance with Moyes.

Although Rooney did not play any part against Swansea he did join his team-mates in the Premier League title celebrations after the match when United were presented with the trophy. Rooney watched in his tracksuit from his executive box, holding his baby and with his very pregnant wife Colleen, but changed into full kit for the title presentation on the pitch, where he was noticeably jeered by some supporters when collecting his winners' medal. He did manage a cursory embrace with his departing manager, who was by the podium to greet all his players before receiving the trophy, but it was far from convivial, and it was clear Rooney was upset about being on the bench for the big Champions League tie with Real Madrid, and equalled fed up at being hooked so many times. Sir Alex later explained, "I don't think Wayne was keen to play, simply because he has asked for a transfer. I think he should go away and think it over again. He wasn't happy about being taken off a few times this season but a Wayne Rooney in top form wouldn't be taken off."

Even Rooney's future was little more than a side show to the main event, and nothing was going to detract from that, not even a sulking superstar, irrespective of how big the headlines that had created, Sir Alex's farewell inspired whole pull outs

As a fitting farewell Sir Alex received a standing ovation. Sir Alex addressed the fans, microphone in hand, something he had done at the end of each season reviewing the past season giving a rallying call to the next. This was vastly different, as he told them, "I have no script in my mind. I'm just going to ramble and hope I get to the core of what this football club has meant to me. Thank you to Manchester United, not just the directors, medics, staff, players, supporters, all of you. Thank you. You have been the most fantastic experience of my life."

As the rain fell he implored his loyal fans to "stand by your new manager". David Moyes could not have got better backing, "I'd like to remind you that at the start, the club stood by me, the staff stood by me, the players stood by me and now it is your job to stand by our new manager."

He thanked fans and supporters, and his family, ahead of his trophy presentation. Managing the club was the "most fantastic experience of my life" he said and that he was "very fortunate" to manage some of the country's best players. It was "not the end" he told the fans. The next time he takes his seat at Old Trafford it will be in the directors' box, "I'll be able to now enjoy watching the team rather than suffer with them."

Sir Alex praised Paul Scholes, who was chosen to play after announcing his retirement the day before the game. He told the fans, "Before I start blubbing, I want to pay tribute to Paul Scholes who retires today. He is an unbelievable player, one of the greatest players this club will ever have. Paul I wish you a good retirement, though I know you'll be around, annoying me! And I wish Darren Fletcher a speedy recovery for the club."

He went on, "I wish the players every success for the future. You know how good you are, the jersey you are wearing, and all the people here. Don't let yourselves down. I'm just going inside now. Thank you once again, from all the Ferguson family. They're all up there – 11 grandchildren. Thank you. Thank you."

The stadium erupted in applause at the comments, and then the rest of the Ferige Show was the thing that epitomised his reign more than anything – delivering the silverware. Two of Sir Alex's most tried and trusted former captains, Steve Bruce and Bryan Robson carried the Premier League trophy out to the middle. "Albert give us a wave" was the chant as kit man Albert Morgan, also due to retire at the end of the season, emerged from the tunnel.

Later, in his media conferences, he disclosed the time table for his big decision. "I decided to retire last Christmas. Things changed when my wife Cathy's sister died. She has lost her best friend, her sister. Also, I wanted to go out a winner. It was very difficult [to keep it under wraps]. There were times when we sometimes blurted it out to the family. We told our sons in March. My brother didn't even know until Tuesday." He doesn't know where the leak came as news filtered out of the club 24 hours ahead of his retirement announcement. He explained, "This club is a sieve".

Sir Alex added, 'The most important achievement was winning the first league and the door opened after that. We just grew and grew and grew. We had some fantastic teams. He insisted he won't be bored, "I've got a lot of things to do. My son Jason's been organising things. I won't be sitting still." As for his big day, he said, "It's fantastic. What a send off. I was bubbling there for a bit. The atmosphere was unbelievable. I'm very proud of my fans, they were great. I've had a few days of wobbling a bit but you have to gather yourself. I wanted the fourth official to put up seven minutes! I was going to kill him!"

"What will you miss most?" Sir Alex was asked. "Those last-minute goals," he said. "I love those."

The players were full of praise for their departing manager, as you might have expected, led by club captain Nemanja Vidic, "I think it is a special day, in one way we are happy to get the trophy but in another we are sad the manager is not here another year. It will be strange not to see him in the dressing room. This is a big club and will always be a big club but it is sad after so many years, without him is going to be sad."

Rio Ferdinand commented, "It is phenomenal what he has achieved. It speaks volumes about the type of man he is, and his desire to win, that he leaving the club behind in a healthy state." Michael Carrick observed, "It's been an emotional day for everyone. It was a strange feeling and it's been like that all week. It was a special, special day. Even in the changing room he tried to keep it as normal as possible but in the back of your mind you were thinking this is the last one. With the reception he got, it was amazing."

Robin van Persie revealed the lure of working with Sir Alex was one of the chief reasons he chose United over City. He explained added: "It's an unbelievable day but a sad one as well. I had the honour to work with him for one year and it's been an unbelievable year. He's made such an impact on me. He may be the greatest manager ever and he's such a nice person. Before the game, he couldn't see anything about him retiring. All week he's been focused on what to do and what to expect. It's a massive honour for me to say I've worked with him for a year."

The evergreen Giggs added, "Sir Alex just said play the game and not the occasion. He wanted to win the game, wanted it to be an entertaining game and for us to do the things which he has wanted us to as a manager. The memories of him that stick out are when I was younger. When I was 13 playing for Salford Boys and looking to the sidelines and there was Alex Ferguson watching." Retiring Paul Scholes remarked, "It's been a good day. We've won the game, that's all that matters. We'll celebrate tonight and hopefully in more years there will be more trophies for these players. Today it was just nice to get through the game. I thought Sir Alex handled it well, he spoke really well and he has done a fantastic job here. I know it's the right time for me to go. It's not been the season I would have liked personally, but we've won the league and it's a great day."

Phil Jones added, "It's been incredible [working under Sir Alex Ferguson]. He's a fantastic manager. What he's done for me has been fantastic and I can't thank him enough." Jonny Evans said, "Obviously with the manager retiring, the atmosphere here is even more emotional. It's a great day to be involved. He's had a big effect on my career. It's hard to put into words. We probably won't notice it until a few years down the line when he's not here anymore. I think he's always had the ability to get the most out of his squad, with rotating the team and motivating players."

Michael Laudrup recognised the match had been overshadowed as he pointed out in the immediate post match interview, "It is a special day. It is one thing that a manager in a big club stops, but this is a lifetime not a small era. It is incredible. I have a lot of respect for Sir Alex to have so many years in the same club, so unique. It is a lifetime. I said before and just after, it is a celebration. For us it is a game in which we could relax. We did what we have done this season, finish ninth and we will stay there, we won the League Cup also."

Not too far away, and a touch earlier in the day, over at

FERGIE'S FAREWELL

Goodison Park, Sir Alex's chosen successor, David Moyes received heart felt applause from Everton fans as his team concluded their penultimate match before he departed for the managerial role at Old Trafford. Moyes was moved by the reception he received both before, during and after the 2-0 win over West Ham in his final appearance at Goodison. Moyes was highly emotional from the moment he arrived at the ground, applauded in by stewards, until at the end when he was awarded a guard of honour by his own players prior to the post-match lap of appreciation. Moyes would have sympathised if some supporters, who sang his name throughout, were not happy with his departure. He commented, "I am a football supporter and if I had been on the terraces today I would have clapped the manager – I might not have liked what he was doing but I would have certainly applauded. I think just by the reaction from most people in the last few days I thought it would be okay but if you are a football supporter you are entitled to support your team and if someone is not on your team you don't know what will be the reaction.

"It was really emotional from the moment I came in: all the stewards were standing clapping me and I didn't know what to do. I came here 11 years ago and it was really emotional walking out on to the pitch, a lot of people didn't know who I was I don't think. I got off to a great start (winning 2-1 over Fulham) so I am really fortunate I had a reception like I did today. I am gobsmacked, very thankful and humble for what the people of Everton have shown today. What I will miss is what you saw in the middle of the second half – the supporters were not cheering David Moyes, they were cheering their football club and standing up for it. I thought that was the toughest part for me today – it was a difficult time – because the crowd showed how big Everton are and what it means to them. More important for me was how well Everton played today. I thought they played like a top team today – I don't mean a team in fifth or sixth, I mean a top team. I think we would have been a match for any side: the players were terrific in showing a level of professionalism just to make sure they couldn't get caught up in anything." David Moyes was applauded out of his final press conference at by the media.

After a quarter of a century of unbridled success, a big down turn was predicted with bookmakers lengthening their odds of Manchester United retaining their Premier League title, with City installed as firm favourites, although that was prior to their shock FA Cup Final defeat by Wigan! One bookie commented, "No one knows how to build a title winning side like Sir Alex and for that reason we have had no option but to ease the price of the Reds winning the League next season."

However, after the emotionally charged long farewell at Old Trafford there was a deep feeling that this was not just the end of an Old Trafford era, the end of a United dynasty, but the possibility of one of British sports greatest institutions hitting a dramatic downward turn, very much the way Liverpool dominated English and European football when no one could see that ever ending. Has United's time come to an end? As Micheal Laudrup pointed out in the BBC studios as a first time guest on Match of the Day, Sir Alex's boots are pretty big and will take some filling. One of world football's biggest legends as well as now a success with Swansea, Laudrup stressed that this was now the biggest job to fill in world football simply by the extraordinary duration Sir Alex had held office at Old trafford and with such unparalleled success. Little wonder Sir Alex wanted his fans and Board to back the new manager.

THE VICTORY PARADE

Sitting in the Sky studios commenting on Manchester United's victory parade and the second Fergie Farewell, it struck me that, just like his favourite crooner Frank Sinatra, would we ever see a Sir Alex comeback? My view to the manager that enjoyed a melody of songs including 'My Way' at his final game at Old Trafford is that he won't be able to sit in the stands for too long watching before he gets itchy feet.

As he prepared for his third farewell with the final game of his managerial tenure at West Bromwich Albion, there was a suspicion that Sir Alex won't be able to keep his hands out of the fun and excitement of recruiting players as he, for so long, manipulated the transfer market to such devastating effect with his contacts, knowledge and personal charisma which was a lure for many players to join United.

Sir Alex had seen plenty of victory parades in his time, but never one like this. When handed the microphone on the open top bus before it departed Old Trafford, the emotion of the day before came flooding back.

I felt it was indicative of his inner self that he wore that emblem of a football manager, a thick padded puffer jacket emblazoned with the United crest and his initials. My point is that he has yet to get the 'coach' mode from his psyche, perhaps understandable as he will be in the dug out for one final time.

As one might have anticipated, the United bus was decked out as a Thank You to Sir Alex, but shortly after the joyful victory parade with around 150,000 in the streets of Manchester, the taxi arrived for Roberto Mancini. It was a vastly different goodbye for Sir Alex to the one afforded the City manager, who lost the

Premiership crown to United.

United supporters in party mood gathered at Old Trafford as the open-top bus tour got under way, and the parade travelled towards the city centre and arrived at Albert Square, where the bus was greeted by more fans. Many who had turned up early to secure a good vantage point suffered a down pour and thunder and lightning, but as current and former players arrived for the parade, sunshine broke through. With 20,000 fans packed into Sir Matt Busby Way, roads were closed prior to departure.

Speaking from the bus, Sir Alex thanked fans for their support over the years, telling them that his farewell match at Old Trafford the day before had been "a day I will never forget – it was wonderful". He added, "It was something all my family enjoyed and the grandkids will never forget it."

Talking of the phenomenal turnout for his retirement party, the manager added, "I thought that '99 could not be beaten but you've beaten it today. Thank you for the fantastic support. I hope we're here to win this many times again. You always think about it [whether you are doing the right thing]. But I think it is the right time. I really do. We have a young squad, with a lot of good young players, who are going to get better. The big test is to win it three times in a row. I hope the boys can do it." As I pointed out on Sky..."no pressure then", on successor David Moyes.

The bus left the stadium via Sir Matt Busby Way, with fans lining every part of the route from the stadium through the suburbs to Deansgate and finally Albert Square. Vantage points as precarious as scaffolding and one storey shop fronts were taken over and police refused entry to any more fans after the streets near Manchester imposing town hall filled to capacity. Some supporters let off red flares, several climbed lamp posts for a better view of the bus, others leaned from windows and stood on rooftops. Health and Safety officers must have been having kittens.

Once they got on stage the players were in a typically celebratory mood. Ashley Young ditched the crutches he was using to nurse an ankle injury that ended his season and Paul Scholes was coerced onto centre stage for a rare interview. The ginger haired midfielder, hailed as the best English footballer of his generation by opponents and colleagues alike, said "It [winning the league] means everything. We set out each year to try and win the league and most of the years we do it. It is great to see this turnout and I'm so proud to play for this club." Jonny Evans was asked by MUTV interviewer Helen McConnell, who also happens to be his fiancee, whether he was going to have a good summer. "Yes," Evans replied. "I am getting married, to you Helen."

For many of the United stars it was business as usual being involved with celebration parades. But this was a first for Robin van Persie. He was clearly enjoying his first piece of silverware as he said, "It's incredible. It is even nicer than I expected – there are so many people. It [his winners medal] didn't leave my neck since yesterday. It is a heavy trophy but it is great to win it. This is for the players, fans, staff, every single one here. It has made so many people happy and I'm very pleased to see that."

Michael Carrick added, "I've been getting a bit carried away. I've nearly fallen off three times. This turnout is just amazing, the whole week has been special. Celebrating winning the league but with Scholesy and the manager retiring it is a fitting send off. I never thought we would get anything like this. I have been singing quite a bit lately – you can probably tell by my voice."

So was Wayne Rooney still going? As I suggested on Sky, he had few options anyway. Chelsea? No, as United were unlikely to sell to a Premier League rival, after all they saw what happened to Arsenal after they sold Robin van Persie to them! Paris St. Germain? Can you really see Rooney abroad? I don't think so. Not for long, anyway. But anything is possible as Sir Alex often said. Yet, Rooney praised Sir Alex as a 'fantastic manager' despite receiving a mixed reception when he boarded the open-top bus. Speaking to MUTV, he said: "It is a fitting tribute to the manager after so long and so much success. As much as it is for the team, it's for the manager, for himself, what he has achieved and what he has done to this football club. He deserves everything he has got. He has been brilliant for us all. He is a great manager he is successful and he is a winner. To do it for so long is incredible, he is a fantastic manager."

"Manchester United have a bright future," Rio Ferdinand told MUTV. "The manager has left the club in great health and we are looking forward. We have a great number of good young players who are eager to win things and be successful and work hard. That is what the manager has instilled in these players. The work ethic has to continue if we are going to be successful. I would like to be part of that." Rio had tweeted pictures of him and his team-mates in the pub in the early afternoon prior to the parade. Rio has now won as many championships as Kenny Dalglish, "I dreamt of getting one when I turned up here. I remember looking at Ryan and the others when I arrived. At that stage they had five, six or seven. I just wanted one. I thought I would be happy with that. But once you get it, you want another. You continue striving to succeed, to achieve things and win trophies. To get six is unbelievable. But that is the main thing at this club, you want to be successful."

As for Sir Alex, Rio commented, "There have been a couple of emotional moments. The manager's announcement was like a bolt out of the blue. No one was expecting it. It disappointed a lot of us but I understand the manager's reasons. He has had a great stint and an unbelievably successful period. He instilled great qualities in the club and we must carry that on."

Ryan Giggs felt the reception topped the one in 1999: 'Thanks for coming out. I thought I'd never see anything like the treble again but this beats it. It is just brilliant. It gives us a chance to share with the fans a great achievement this season. It is an amazing atmosphere." As for Sir Alex, he added, Giggs said: "It has been tough, especially for the players who have known him for a long time. We are delighted that we were able to end on a high and win the league in his last season."

1,500 GAMES AND OUT

S IR ALEX EVEN SURPRISED HIMSELF. He was taken aback as he tried to take in his own incredible milestone as he bid his third and final farewell at the end of a marathon career in management.

"Quite incredible', is how Sir Alex described his remarkable longevity at Old Trafford. The 1,500th game of his Manchester United career; a simply staggering statistic, and one the football world knows will never be repeated at this footballing institution or indeed anywhere else around the world

As he prepared for the final Premier League game of United's championship season, effectively his third and final farewell following the Old Trafford goodbye, the victory parade and now the final farewell at The Hawthorns, he commented, "So my last game, 1,500 matches – quite incredible." Yes, quite right. Quite remarkable.

Typically, he wasn't looking for yet another party, although he was going to get one whether he liked it or not, but as usual he was seeking all three points, even though his team didn't really need them. "I want to win this one more than last week's even," he remarked, and whoever was digesting that comment would be wondering why he was bothering. But Sir Alex always bothered, it is in his DNA, when it came to winning football matches, he took that task deadly seriously irrespective of the circumstances.

There was a sense that Sir Alex had suffered sufficient emotional highs to live with him for the full term of his retirement, and that one more would be over the top. Sir Alex said, "Sunday was amazing and the parade on Monday, it was incredible, even better than 1999. I thought the scenes after the treble in 1999 couldn't be beaten but I think Monday probably did. I went home that night and got 10 hours sleep for the first time in my life. It was marvellous, really good."

Relaxed in his final press conference, the usual Friday morning before a weekend game, this meeting with the media was different, the last time under the usual circumstances, a match to preview; an uncomfortable chore usually in his love-hate relationship with the media. He used the media for his mind games, but deep down detested them for the damage that could be done when sensitive information leaked out of his dressing room, no matter how hard he tried to keep a lid on it. Now, at a time for reflection, he had a captivated audience. It was always going to be vastly different than the norm, and that's precisely how it began with Sir Alex was applauded into the room and given a bottle of wine and a cake, presented by The Sun's Manchester based correspondent, Neil Custis, who has the distinction of being banned by Sir Alex more times than anyone else, estimated at seven times, but it had occurred so often that the reporter himself had lost count.

So, on this rare, special occasion, there was not the usual tea or coffee at the training ground for his media briefing, but wine, served in plastic cups at nine in the morning. At his previous press conference, Sir Alex poured champagne for the media to celebrate the 20th League title and then suggested the Greater Manchester Police would be waiting with breathalyzers at the end of the single-track road that leads to the Carrington training complex. Of course, he was jesting. Or was he? Sometimes you couldn't tell.

Neil Custis is a nice chap, one of the newspaper pack I have known for some time, and one of those I can trust, which marks him out. Presenting the cake Neil spoke for the rest of the reporters by saying, "It's been a rollercoaster ride and it mirrors Manchester United for all of us. There've been highs and lows, but I think when Sir Alex has been on form with us anywhere from Carrington to Kansas, from Turin to the Temple of Doom he has brought drama he's brought colour to our pages. When he's been on form it's been gold. He has left us with phrases that will go down in the annals, and he has left us all with squeaky bum time on occasions! In years to come all of us will look back and feel privileged that we did this job at a time when this manager was manager of this football club, and for that, we thank him."

Sir Alex might have some private views about the media, and their attitudes toward him and his club, and the complexities of how his views have been interpreted over the years. This was not the time nor place to express them, rather to accept the cake in the spirit it was accepted, irrespective of whether he might have wished to splash that cake in some of the assembled faces, the way some of the more unsavoury headlines had been splashed across the back, and often front pages of their newspapers.

Instead Sir Alex put the media into perspective when he said, "Dealing with the modern media is difficult for managers and I've been lucky that I've integrated into all the different stages in my time here. It got me in a position where sometimes I don't accept what you write and sometimes when you write nice things, I tend to dismiss it also. I've always thought you've had a terrible job, a difficult job with the pressure you're under with modern television, the internet, Facebook and all the rest of the nonsense. But I've never held grudges. Even when I've banned people, I don't hold grudges as it's not my style. I react and then forget about it sometime later. Thanks for the kind words Neil, it was very good of you, and thanks for the time I've had here."

This was more a time for Sir Alex to reminisce, as he went on, 'Thirty nine years as a manager and from that day staring at East Stirling with eight players and no goalkeeper to today six 'keepers and about 100 players , if you count the academy. I remember the old chairman; he was a great chain-smoker. I asked him for a list of players he had and he started to shake, his cigarette was going 100 miles an hour. He gave me a list of eight players with no goalkeeper. I said: 'You know it's advisable to start with a goalkeeper'. That was an education that. It was fantastic. Anyone starting in management should start that kind of way but I don't suppose it is that way now.

"I'm driven to take on some challenges and some other things right away. I've got the league managers' meeting on Monday, Newmarket Tuesday and Wednesday. I'm going on holiday, it's the Derby on 1 June, then the operation, then the recuperation, then the season starts. It can't be a substitution, it's a different life.'

Following Sir Alex, and Scholes, David Beckham announced his retirement also going out on a high after his team Paris St. Germain won the Ligue 1 title becoming the first English player to win top-flight league titles in four different countries. He played 11 years for Sir Alex between 1992 and 2003 and his former Boss was eager to offer his tribute, quelling any lingering doubts about their mutual respect despite the dressing room big boot fall out. Sir Alex commented, "You talk about longevity and in many ways reinventing himself, it has been absolutely incredible. When he went to America there wasn't a person in this place who really thought he could have a career. Yet he went on and still played for his country, he played for AC Milan in European ties and he played for PSG in European ties, and I don't think anyone could have imagined that."

Sir Alex had signed the Leytonstone youngster as an 11-year-old in 1991 as Becks graduated from the 'Class of 92' along with Giggs, Scholes, Gary Neville and Nicky Butt, making almost 400 appearances under Fergie, winning six Premier League titles, a Champions League medal and two FA Cups. After a fall-out in 2003 following an FA Cup defeat by Arsenal when Fergie kicked a boot which hit Beckham in the face and inevitably Becks moved on to Real Madrid for £24.5 million. Sir Alex added: "The one thing he always had was unbelievable stamina as a kid. He had the best stamina in the club. He could run all day, and that has allowed him to stay in the game at that kind of level, playing for his country in his mid 30s. Coming from American football to do that is quite amazing, and he is an amazing person. I think he's picked the right time. He's won the league again with PSG and he is exactly the same as me, he has plenty of things to do. He's a young man, we know that fashion will be his role I would imagine but he will have plenty of things to do."

However the big issue in the back of everybody's mind was how new manager David Moyes would fill the big boots of Sir Alex, if indeed he could and how long would the United board, which now contained Moyes' biggest backer, Sir Alex himself, give him?   And how would Sir Alex ensure that the "Busby Factor' didn't repeat itself.

Sir Alex commented, "Sir Matt created Manchester United, he was the origin of what we are today, there's no doubt about that. He had the vision to take the club into Europe, he put the emphasis on younger players, we owe all that to him. I have just tried to carry it on. Now I am in the same situation he faced 40-odd years ago. I've got a good record but the past is the past. The future now lies with a new manager who will get all the support he needs. This is not the end of Manchester United as far as winning titles is concerned. I don't see any reason why we can't continue this success."

Sir Alex wisely advised going for an experienced manager, unlike, after the phenomenal Busby era, the United board chose relatively inexperienced coaches, Wilf McGuinness and Frank O'Farrell who had managed Leicester City but was totally unprepared for the pressure of the hottest seat in world football. Sir Alex explained, "Manchester United isn't a job for a young man, you need something solid behind you. I'm sure David Moyes has the character to succeed here. He's got good experience behind him, just the same as I had when I came down from Aberdeen. My eight and a half years there involved some big challenges, but we got through it because we had good people in place and we worked hard. If I hadn't had that experience from Aberdeen I don't know if I'd have done as well here. David has built teams at Everton, he has overcome the club's financial limitations to put out sides of great character, capable of great performances. When you think what he inherited, remembering that when Walter Smith was there Everton used to sell their best players every season, that took some doing."

Sir Alex's legacy is well documented and he leaves Moyes with a title-winning squad, a 76,000-seater stadium, one of the best youth set-ups in the world and a state-of-the-art training facility, but that doesn't make it easy for Moyes, far from it, much harder in many respects. Sir Alex recognises the fact, "I've always respected and admired the work David has done at Everton. Back in 1999 I interviewed him for the job and I've watched his progress. He has a work ethic about him and he's a serious football man. These are the qualities he's going to need. He's got perseverance about him. Eleven years without any tremendous financial backing but he's persevered with it and created some decent Everton teams. He's had to deal with a lot of financial constraints yet his teams have always been successful. They are the qualities he's going to need at our club. The one thing you have to do is definitely sacrifice and perseverance – it's not always a golden path of riches. You have hard days and difficult days, especially with the losses."

So can Sir Alex let go?. He says 'yes', but it won't be as easy as even he thinks. Yet, he is adamant he has learned from the post Busby failings, "I'm finished, done, I made the break last week. It's not an issue for me, I'll just get on with the next stage of my life. It is important to remain active, but health permitting I've got plenty of things lined up to be doing. I'd like to go and watch Boca Juniors play River Plate. That's one game I've always wanted to go and see. Now I've got a bit of time I fancy taking in the Melbourne Cup and the Kentucky Derby at some point too. There's a lot of things you can do, as long as you keep your health. The ambassador role at United takes up 20 days a year, so I should have plenty of time."

Sir Alex is no doubt whatsoever that he is leaving the club in better shape than when he started, unarguably better than when Busby himself left the dug out. He argues, "Football is a harsher environment these days, just look at the number of sackings, with Mancini being probably the biggest example. The owners are not English any more, they are American, Russian, Middle Eastern, and therefore remote to an extent. It's a different culture. Agents are another big change since I came into the game, and I'm not sure for the better. I used to talk to parents, that was part of the job if you had identified a promising youngster. I don't even know any parents any more. I just deal with agents all the time."

He leaves without looking back with any regrets, not even winding up Kevin Keegan! He said, "I have always thought that mind games and my supposed part in them were completely overrated. Sometimes I've said provocative things or tried to get my point of view across in advance of a game, because you try to get an edge wherever you can, but the Kevin Keegan incident was a complete accident. I was angry with the Leeds players because Howard Wilkinson was under pressure, and he's a mate of mine. I just made the point that Leeds should be playing as well as they played at Old Trafford all the time. I wasn't thinking of Newcastle at all."

Sir Alex advised his successor to keep on top of referees, as he had done so successfully over the years, as he explained, "That's been a part of it too, the pressure you try to put on referees, but I save mind games for opponents."

Reflecting on the next stage of the Manchester rivalry, Sir Alex reflected the stability David Moyes would inherit, in contrast to the apparent chaos down the road. "What happens at Man City won't have any bearing on David. He's got the structure here and he's got the experience. He's had to handle things at Everton that are more difficult probably. I don't think that matters. I think the enormity of the club will be the most difficult aspect, he will soon realise that anyway. The global brand and number of sponsors we have, he has to fit into that. I don't think that's an issue though and the most important thing is the team. He's got a good squad of players and he will want to add to that. He will have his own ideas and that's good. He will be fine."

Sir Alex added: "People used to say to me 'do you think this one will be a manager or manage United' about players who are not even in the job now. Football is that kind of industry. When you're assessing the job here you have to get somebody who has the longevity and the experience over a long time to manage this club. That is why David was above everyone else. I hope he can survive long term. It's the one club he could do that at. We've shown great loyalty to our managers."

Everton's American keeper Tim Howard worked with Moyes for seven years and knows that Sir Alex's infamous 'hairdryer' temper can be replicated by his successor. Howard gave an insight to Moyes work at Goodison Park, in work each and every day and "not taking any short cuts". Howard added, "He does not allow players to rest or slacken off. Look at a player like me, selected for damn near every game, so I think he has the utmost trust in me. But I can tell you with my hand on my heart that in training, when the goalkeepers get called over to work with the rest of the first team, I feel a bit of nerves. You might think it's only the training ground, but if I throw one in, it's not as if he looks the other way, he gives me a hammering from the touchline. After seven years you'd think a guy like me, who he trusts would get a break, but no, he is still on at you. That's his ethos, that's just how he is. He keeps you on your toes and believing you have to give more. United and Everton are in the same boat with having to replace the manager in terms of expectation and all the rest."

And so to Sir Alex's last game. It was an occasion not to be missed for the dedicated foot soldiers of United's Red Army. Most had probably seen his first game at Oxford in 1986. One fan bought 700 of West Brom's 20,000 special edition £4 programmes, a 144-page special edition, the biggest ever produced for a domestic fixture, with 38-pages devoted to the visiting manager, handing a programme seller £2,800. Another supporter bought 300 for £1,200. The programme detailed Sir Alex's life and time and contains a eulogy from one of Six Alex's greatest ever captains and players Bryan Robson 'to the greatest club manager in the world'.

Tickets for the game were in huge demand. Tickets ordered through Viagogo increased shortly after the announcement of Sir

1,500 GAMES AND OUT

Alex's resignation. Many ordering for home areas were United supporters. Albion had to call a halt to the sales through the exchange service which is used by season ticket holders to sell their seat to a fellow Baggies fan if they are unable to attend themselves. With United's help, Albion identified that the vast majority of these orders were lodged by United season ticket holders and members.

It felt like the end of an era as big names in the game hung up their boots – Jamie Carragher at Liverpool, Michael Owen at Stoke, Steve Harper at Newcastle, and Paul Scholes at United, surely glad to be out of the limelight once more. There were more managerial moves with Rafa Benitez and David Moyes managing their last games for Chelsea and Everton respectively at the Bridge and referee Mark Halsey who had battled back from cancer to enjoy a second career with the whistle.

Yet all of them were overshadowed by events at The Hawthorns. Typically, it was far from the expected as United were involved in a crazy 5-5 draw; one last blast of the 'hairdryer' for the lapse defending, or maybe not. United raced into a 5-2 lead just after the hour mark, but three goals in the last 10 minutes saw Albion snatch a point in a remarkable encounter, the first ever 5-5 in Premier League history. Half-time substitute Romelu Lukaku scored a hat-trick, the first against United, and his personal first.

Yet the football was a mere sideshow, the players doing their best to join in the party atmosphere reflected by home and visiting supporters alike. The banners were out in force. 'Sir Alex Ferguson + Paul Scholes "Legends" Thanks For All the Memories'. Another apt placard, read, 'FERG13" THE GR38T'....'For 26 years you gave us the world, thanks Fergie'

Sir Alex received a guard of honour and warm applause from around the Hawthorns before kick-off, shaking hands with referee Michael Oliver, who was only one year and eight months old when plain old Fergie had started his managerial reign at Old Trafford. Buttner and Lindegaard are guaranteed to feature in future pub quiz questions; name Sir Alex's final line up. Vidic, Ferdinand, Giggs, Evra and Scholes were on the bench, alongside

18-year-old Belgian Adnan Junzaj with Wayne Rooney given leave to join his wife Coleen who was expecting their second child.

At the end, the crowd rose to salute the great man. Ushered forward by Ryan Giggs, Sir Alex stood alone in the penalty area facing an army of deleriously happy United fans in the Smethwick End, raised both hands, then applauded the travelling support, and mouthed "Thank You".

With a broad smile, a final wave to his family in the main stand Regis Suite, he disappeared down the tunnel for the last time as manager, after 2,145 games that began at East Stirling in 1974, to mark, not just, an end of an era at United, but also for English football. Watching in the main stand was Ron Atkinson, his United predecessor at United, and Alex McLeish a reminder of the Aberdeen glory years, as well as England manager Roy Hodgson. Robin Van Persie scored again to finish Premier League top marksman for the second season running with 26 goals, having scored 30 the season before. Sir Alex departed with a 'no comment', explaining that he was feeling too emotional, not even a word for the in house MUTV. His sole words to the media were that was "very emotional". He saved his words for a farewell speech to his players and staff, telling them they must look forward to the new Boss.

Sir Alex was reported to have told his players and staff, "If all that we've been together means anything to you, there's just one thing I'd ask of you all. I don't want to hear you call me Boss ever again. You'll have a new boss then and he's the only one you should call that."

Michael Carrick, voted player of the year by his team mates, captained the side, and commented, "It's a bit funny in the dressing room because of the situation. We've thanked the manager for everything he's done and he's thanked us. We're ready to move on and there are new challenges for all of us. We're looking forward to it. The manager wanted to win but the job for the season is done. I'm sure he can retire very satisfied." Rio remarked, "5-5.....what a mad result! Lets be honest the boss was never going out with a boring 0-0!!" Javier Hernandez said, "I can't remember playing in a match with 10 goals. We're a little bit frustrated because we wanted to win it for the gaffer and Scholesy. The gaffer is certainly going to remember his last match in charge! He is going to remember this game. It's probably the first time United have been 5-2 ahead and not won. The gaffer has put the club on the top and we're going to miss him. I am going to thank Scholesy too. He's been an incredible team mate."

West Brom manager Steve Clarke shared a fine claret with Sir Alex and commented, "I've just had a quick glass of wine with Sir Alex. He's in good spirits. It's a game he'll certainly remember. Anyone who was in the stadium will remember that game for years to come. I think that's a good tribute. I'm not sure Sir Alex would say that it was a fitting way to end. He told me it's the first time that any team he's been involved with has given away a three goal lead, and they did it twice in one game. That's something for us to saviour. I think he's just ready for his retirement to be honest. He said it was a great game, he complimented us on the way we played. For Sir Alex, it's a great occasion, it's a great finale."

SIR ALEX FERGUSON'S FINAL RECORD AS MANCHESTER UNITED MANAGER

1500 games, 895 wins, 338 draws, 267 losses
2762 goals for, 1359 goals against
Win percentage 60%.

TITLE NO. 1 - 1907-08

"He was the Stanley Matthews, David Beckham of his day. He favoured a tooth pick which he chewed during matches and he became an inspiration when he won the Cup for United and went on to win the League. He was the icon of his age, a fantastic player, first for Manchester City and later United... and when he became a star he would still write about the shift down the mines in the early hours of Sunday morning..."

GORDON TAYLOR

ERNEST MANGNALL, Sir Matt Busby and Sir Alex Ferguson, between them, have won all 20 of the club's league titles. While Mangnall was the Sir Alex of the start of the Manchester United odyssey, the catalyst for United's on field success was Welsh winger wizard Billy Meredith, renowned for his union principles. Meredith's long running career puts Ryan Giggs' into perspective as Meredith was still turning out for Manchester City in the FA Cup in his 50th year.

When United won their first title they did so finishing an astounding nine points clear of runners-up Aston Villa and Manchester City. Memorably, their season included a 4-0 thrashing of rivals Liverpool.

Gordon Taylor, the Mancunian born boss of the players

union, paid tribute to Billy Meredith in an interview for '20|13'. Taylor, the PFA's long standing chief executive, says, "Billy Meredith was the Stanley Matthews, David Beckham of his day. He favoured a tooth pick which he chewed during matches, and he became an inspiration when he won the Cup for United and went on to win the League. He was the icon of his age, a fantastic player, first for Manchester City and later United. He took the bus from North Wales where he lived and when he became a star he would still talk about the shift down the mines in the early hours of Sunday morning after making an arduous journey to play football in places as far away as Newcastle.

"He was a fiercely proud union man from Wales and he campaigned for footballers who didn't even have a union, who were not professionally recognised, at a time when players' couldn't even claim for industrial injuries, under the law of the land. Meredith chaired the first meeting of the players' union as it is today on December 2nd 1907 at the Imperial Hotel, Manchester, with players from the north west, mainly from United and City. He would attend PFA AGMs into the 1950s and he would greet everybody at the door.

"The 1909 season didn't start on time because of the actions of the players who, led by Meredith, wanted to be recognised by the Football Association and wished to join the TUC. The FA wanted to ban any player who was in the union. There was a picture of these players looking to try and train privately and they came up with the idea of being typecast as The Outcasts. The name stuck and gave them much media prominence. While the 1909 season was delayed, eventually the FA caved in and recognised the players' union, which was a great victory for The Outcasts.

"In our Centenary year in 2007 we invited Bill Meredith's grandchildren to our celebration dinner. In our offices we have one of his caps, and one of his jerseys. He had the players' union printed on the shirt, which also had a players' union armband. In his last days, he called my predecessor at the PFA, Cliff Lloyd, to his home, and asked him to get for him an old battered suitcase from under his bed. When Cliff opened it up, it was packed full of international caps and medals. He told Cliff, 'Remind all your members, that those caps did not look after me in my old age!'"

It was a hard struggle to land the first title. Formed in 1878, originally as Newton Heath, the club was not considered good enough to join the inaugural Football League and had to wait until 1892 to join as a Division Two team. The start of the Manchester United story didn't really begin until John Henry Davies, a brewery owner, took control of Newton Heath in 1902. He cleared the club's massive debts and changed their name and retained an interest in the club until his death.

This led to a change of name and, after several alternatives including Manchester Central and Manchester Celtic were rejected, Manchester United was born in April/May 1902. Manchester United made the significant appointment of Ernest Mangnall, a manager from Second Division rivals, Burnley, as successor to James West, in October 1903. Mangnall was appointed secretary in September 1903 but is widely acknowledged as being the club's first manager.

Mangnall, the son of a joiner, was born in Bolton in 1866. He was educated at Bolton Grammar School where he played inside right for the school football team. Later he was selected for Lancashire County. A keen supporter of Bolton Wanderers, he eventually became a director of the club. He also served as the club secretary but had little success and the Trotters were relegated in the 1898-99 season. Mangnall joined Burnley as their secretary/manager but they were also relegated in the 1899-1900 season – hardly an auspicious start in management.

More serious than these failures, Mangnall's integrity was brought into question when Burnley's goalkeeper, Jack Hillman, was found guilty of trying to bribe Nottingham Forest players to lose the last game of the season in order to avoid relegation into the Second Division. Hillman was found guilty and banned for a year.

At the end of the 1902-03 season James West and Harry Stafford of Manchester United were suspended by the Football

Association for making illegal payments to players. Mangnall, who had failed to get Burnley promoted to the First Division, was appointed as United's new manager. This decision shocked the fans as he had achieved little success at his former clubs. Nor did he have a reputation for getting his teams to play good football. As the authors of 'The Essential History of Manchester United' point out: "Mangnall... preached a gospel of physical fitness and team spirit while maintaining that players should be given a ball only once a week".

John Henry Davies, the new owner of Manchester United, was a rich businessman and was willing to provide Mangnall with the funds to build a good team. Mangnall made several new signings. Probably the most significant was Charlie Roberts, who cost a record fee of £600. Other important signings included Charlie Sagar, George Wall, John Peddie, John Picken, Thomas Blackstock and Alex Bell. His side, including new signings like goalkeeper Harry Moger and forward Charlie Sagar, finished third in the Second Division in 1903/04 and again in 1904/05.

Season 1905/06 was to prove one of the greatest in the early life of Manchester United. The half-back line of Dick Duckworth, Alec Bell and captain Charlie Roberts were instrumental in the side which reached the quarter-finals of the FA Cup, but more importantly finished as runners-up in the Second Division behind Bristol City. Twelve years after being relegated, United reclaimed their place in the top flight. The club scored 90 goals in 38 games the top scorers being John Picken (20), John Peddie (18) and Charlie Sagar (16). Manchester United's defence was also impressive and only let in 28 goals all season. Charlie Roberts played at centre half and he was flanked by two outstanding wing halves, Dick Duckworth and Alec Bell.

Manchester City, who were playing in the First Division, also did well that season. City needed to beat Aston Villa on the final day of the season to win the championship. Villa won the game 3-1 and City finished third, two points behind Newcastle United. After the game Alec Leake, the captain of Aston Villa, claimed that Meredith had offered him £10 to throw the game.

Meredith was found guilty of this offence by the Football Association and was fined and suspended from playing football for a year. Manchester City refused to provide financial help for Meredith and so he decided to go public about what really was going on at the club: "What was the secret of the success of the Manchester City team? In my opinion, the fact that the club put aside the rule that no player should receive more than four pounds a week... The team delivered the goods, the club paid for the goods delivered and both sides were satisfied." This statement created a sensation as the FA had imposed a £4 a week maximum wage on all clubs in 1901.

In 1904 Manchester City had been the main force, winning the FA Cup that season, but they had aroused suspicion from the FA and an investigation found that the club had breached strict rules on the maximum wage – offering their cup winners a massive £7 in bonuses for their success. Each member of the City board was banned from the game for five years, Tom Maley was suspended from football for life and the club was fined £250. Seventeen players were fined and suspended until January 1907. As a consequence City arranged an auction for their star players, inviting rival club directors to Manchester's Queens Hotel to what can only be described as a fire sale. However many turned up realising they were too late, Mangnall had already bagged Welsh winger William Henry Meredith, for a mere £500, Herbert Burgess, Jimmy Bannister and Sandy Turnbull also crossed the city on free transfers. Once their bans were lifted, they were all free to play for Manchester United.

One of Mangnall's most controversial signings was John Peddie from Newcastle United. As Paul Joannou points out in his book, 'The Black 'n' White Alphabet', "Peddie... was often in trouble with the club's hierarchy for a number of misdemeanours; refusing to play, being absent from training and ultimately being suspended *sine die* in 1900 (later lifted)."

Over a four year period Peddie scored 73 goals in 125 matches. However, a local newspaper report pointed out that the fans had mixed views on his abilities: "Peddie is the most highly praised and roundly abused man on the club's books. A player of moods... his nonchalant ways and easy going methods are less inspiring than his shooting."

The key signing, though, was winger Billy Meredith, the superstar of this generation, a tobacco-chewing miner from Chirk, Wrexham, football's first superstar, the Ryan Giggs of his age, his career lasting for a remarkable 30 years – even Ryan has some way to go to match that. 'Old Skinny', as he was nicknamed, had a trademark toothpick in his mouth while he played to aid concentration, and was found guilty of match-fixing during his time with Manchester City prior to joining the Reds in 1906, which he strenuously denied until the day he died. In his early playing days he chewed tobacco, until the cleaners refused to wash the spit off his shirts.

Born in 1874, Meredith began his career playing part-time for local teams while working at Black Colliery. In 1894 he signed for City as a professional, where he enjoyed a successful career for more than a decade until he was embroiled in a bribery scandal. Meredith, who had joined the Reds in 1906, was the inspiration behind United's first major honour, the Football League Division One title - the first of United's record 20 league title wins.

United started off the 1907-08 season with three straight wins. They were then beaten 2-1 by Middlesbrough. However, this was followed by another ten wins and United quickly built up a good advantage over the rest of the First Division. United won 10 games on the bounce for the first time. This season also saw the first recorded crowd trouble at Bradford and Sheffield. In the autumn of 1907 United were top of the league with 14 victories in their first 16 matches. Losses to Middlesbrough and Sheffield Wednesday prevented them from a perfect run up to the end of November. Since that point United never relinquished top spot and their maiden League Championship had been achieved.

Although Liverpool beat United 7-4 on 25th March, 1908, Manchester United went on to win the title by nine points. Top scorers were Sandy Turnbull (25), George Wall (19), Jimmy Turnbull (10) and Meredith (10).

Mangnall had created an impressive team that was solid in defence and exciting in attack. The former Southampton player, Harry Moger, was a reliable goalkeeper who played in 38 league games that season. Dick Holden (26) or George Stacey (18) competed for the right back position whereas Herbert Burgess (27) was the left back. It has been argued that the half back line of Duckworth (35), Roberts (32) and Bell (35) was the heart-beat of the side. Meredith (37) and George Wall (36) were probably the best wingers playing in the Football League at the time and provided plenty of service for the inside trio of Sandy Turnbull (30), Jimmy Turnbull (26) and Jimmy Bannister (36).

The championship winning team included four players purchased from Manchester City at the Queen's Hotel auction in October 1906. Sandy Turnbull finished the season with 25 league goals in just 30 matches as United finished on 52 points. They had secured 23 victories, six draws and nine losses, finishing nine points ahead of second and third placed Aston Villa and Manchester City respectively.

United's website describes Meredith as the club's "first footballing legend". In a glowing tribute to the player, it adds: "They don't make them like this any more – but they didn't make many like this then, either."

Meredith was a spindly Welshman, wizard of the dribble, champion of players' rights and the game's first household name, who ruled the left flank in United's first title triumphs of 1908 and 1911, and the inaugural FA Charity Shield in 1908, as well as the 1909 FA Cup. Meredith was allowed to take the FA Cup to Chirk after United's victory. United beat Bristol City 1-0 in the final at Crystal Palace, with the winning goal scored by Sandy Turnbull.

In a fascinating article by Brendon Williams, from the BBC Wales News website, Nigel Roberts, author of The History of Chirk FC 1876-2002, states that Meredith remains a legend in his home town, where two commemorative plaques bear his name. He said: "The people of Chirk are to this day extremely proud that the one-time mining village played such an important role in the life of legendary Billy Meredith. His memory, even after a century, lives on in Chirk and even the younger generation are aware of the history of both Chirk FC and Billy Meredith. During the research for my book, the Billy Meredith era was probably the most interesting period as football moved from amateur status into professionalism and of course all the controversies that came with it."

Meredith's talents, and popularity among both sets of Manchester fans, saw him living the life of a "hero to the Edwardian working class," according to the National Football Museum. The museum's website says Meredith was, "celebrated and often caricatured in popular cartoons, Meredith gained popularity akin to that enjoyed by music hall stars. Like them, he revelled in entertaining the public and often chatted to spectators when play shifted away from his wing."

Mark Wylie, curator of Manchester United's museum, said Meredith was a man who "knew his own worth". Meredith believed his worth to be more than the £4-a-week wage ceiling for professional footballers in the early 20th Century. According to Mr Wylie, Meredith's match-fixing allegations led to Manchester City being punished for paying their players too much. As a result, key players had to be sold, and Meredith was among those who signed for United.

It was the start of a campaign by Meredith to gain better terms for footballers, and he was instrumental in re-founding the players' union. Such was his passion for the cause, he even went on strike during his playing days at United. Mr Wylie said: "It caused a huge furore. The Football League were saying they shouldn't wear Players' Union badges. Eventually the League came to recognise that a union should exist. Today, that union is the Professional Footballers' Association. He was an inspiration to other players to join the union, when they saw one of the best players of the day was a member."

Kenneth Allanson, a relative by marriage, agrees Meredith was a man who knew his worth, "He was a very direct man, very opinionated. He knew he was the best and he'd say so. I remember asking him his thoughts on Stanley Matthews in his prime. He said: 'Oh, Matthews, he's no good – how many goals did he score? Do you know how many I scored'?"

Recalling his only meeting with Meredith, Mr Allanson said: "Billy Meredith was my father-in-law's uncle. I do recall my father-in-law saying he used to train with Billy Meredith as a youth, and it was his job to put a handkerchief in the box so Billy could practise his corner kicks. He would get it there every time. It would have been some time in the 1950s when I met him. I was 20-something and I suppose Billy Meredith must have been about 80." Mr Allanson said Meredith was a "likeable chap" adding, "I remember him saying that if people think it's a dirty game now, they should have seen it in his day."

In celebration of their first League title, John Davies paid for the team to go on a tour of Hungary. After beating Ferencvaros 7-0 United were attacked by local fans, with the police having to get involved. Mangnall vowed that United would never return back there – and they didn't until September 1993 when a European tie saw them travel to face Kispest Honved.

As champions, United played in the first-ever Charity Shield in 1908. They duly won the trophy, beating Southern League champions QPR 4-0 thanks to a hat-trick from Sandy's namesake, Jimmy Turnbull.

According to the National Football Museum, Meredith fell out with management at Old Trafford by 1921, "leading to his transfer to Manchester City, whose supporters revelled in the return of their former idol. Now in his 40s, Meredith was still an automatic choice for Wales, as he had been for two decades. In total, Meredith won a record 48 caps for his country, culminating in a famous victory over England in his last match in the red of Wales".

TITLE NO. 2 - 1910-11

"Ernest Mangnall was instrumental in this milestone as he delivered the first of the nineteen league triumphs in 1908 and again in 1911. He helped to transform a poverty-stricken club, playing on a poor ground with mediocre results into a wealthy club with success in major competitions and a new stadium."

RICHARD BEVAN,
CHIEF EXECUTIVE OF THE
LEAGUE MANAGERS' ASSOCIATION.

MANCHESTER UNITED WERE already clearly one of the best clubs in England, yet its ground was one of the worst in the First Division. So not long after the club's first title success, owner John Henry Davies loaned the club £60,000 to build a new stadium with an 80,000 capacity. When it was completed the stadium had the largest grandstand in the Football League, including a gymnasium, massage room, plunge baths, bars, lifts and tearooms. United's previous grounds had been on North Road, Monsall 1878-1893 and at Bank Street, Newton Heath between 1893-1910. The former was a sports ground inherited from the original Lancashire & Yorkshire Railway company (for Newton Heath were descended from the L&YR works team). The latter provided better accommodation following Newton Heath's decision to abandon the L&YR moniker.

1910-11

The land on which the new stadium was built was bought by the Manchester Brewery Company (John Henry Davies) and leased to the club. Davies himself paid for the building work, which commenced in 1908 under the supervision of architect Archibald Leitch. By 1910, the club had moved lock, stock and barrel from their old home of Bank Street.

The first game at Old Trafford took place on 19th February, 1910. A crowd of 45,000 saw Liverpool beat Manchester United 4-3. This attendance record was beaten a few weeks later when 50,000 saw United beat Bristol City 2-1. The following season, 65,000 watched an FA Cup tie against Aston Villa. After the first fixture at Old Trafford, the *Sporting Chronicle* reporter wrote: "The most handsomest, the most spacious and the most remarkable arena I have ever seen. As a football ground it is unrivalled in the world, it is an honour to Manchester and the home of a team who can do wonders when they are so disposed." It turns out they moved venues just in time, as a storm blew down the wooden stand at the old Bank Street venue merely four days after their last game there!

In June 1910 Ernest Mangnall had purchased Enoch West from Nottingham Forest to replace Jimmy Turnbull in attack and he had a great season scoring 19 goals in 35 games as the manager repeated his championship success of two years earlier. United won the league with 32 points. 'Knocker' West formed a great partnership with Sandy Turnbull and together they scored more than half of the team's goals. West plundered 19 goals in the championship season. However the title was a tense affair. Going into the last game of the season Aston Villa led Manchester United by one point. United had to play third-place Sunderland at Old Trafford whereas Aston Villa had to go to mid-table Liverpool.

United won their game 5-1 with Harold Halse grabbing two of the goals but some decades before the advent of hand held radios, the destiny of the title remained a mystery. Charlie Roberts told the *Manchester Saturday Post*, "At the end of the game our supporters rushed across the ground in front of the stand to wait for the final news from Liverpool. Suddenly a tremendous cheer rent the air and was renewed again and again and we knew we were the champions once again." Aston Villa had lost 3-1 at Anfield and United had won their second championship under Mangnall.

This title victory completed a memorable pre-WWI period by the club, United having won the FA Cup in 1909 beating Brighton & Hove Albion (1-0), Everton (1-0), Blackburn Rovers (6-1), Burnley (3-2) and Newcastle United (1-0) to reach the Crystal Palace showpiece. Newcastle, who went on to be champions in 1909, were obviously disappointed by being prevented from winning the double. However, the whole of the Newcastle team waited for 15 minutes in torrential rain aboard an open coach so they could applaud their conquerors after the game. Jimmy Turnbull (5), Harold Halse (4) and Sandy Turnbull (3) got the goals during the successful cup run that got them to the final at Crystal Palace against Bristol City. As both clubs usually wore red, Bristol played in blue whereas Manchester United played in white shirts with a deep red 'V'. The game was disappointing, Sandy Turnbull scoring the only goal in the 22nd minute.

Charlie Roberts was born in Darlington on 6th April 1883. As a teenager he played football for Bishop Auckland. An impressive centre half, Roberts signed for Grimsby Town in 1903. After only playing 31 games for Grimsby, Mangnall paid a record fee of £600 for Roberts. At the time Mangnall was criticised for paying such a large sum for such an inexperienced player. However, it proved to be an inspired decision and it was not long before Roberts established himself as the keystone of the United defence. The form of Roberts was such that the 22 year-old won his first international cap playing for England against Ireland on 25th February, 1905. This was followed by games against Wales (27th March) and Scotland (1st April). But Charlie Roberts upset the FA by starting the fashion of wearing very short knickers. In 1904 the FA took action by passing a regulation that stipulated that football knickers covered the knees. Roberts and some other players ignored this regulation. However, it was one of the reasons that long baggy knickers remained fashionable until after the Second World War.

Following their league success United won their second Charity Shield at Stamford Bridge against Southern League champions Swindon Town – Harold Halse notching an incredible six times in an 8-4 victory. However United could not keep up their winning run and in 1911/12, the defending champions finished in thirteenth place. Secretary-manager Mangnall bore the brunt of the criticism.

In April 1911 Enoch West was involved in an incident at Aston Villa. As a result he was suspended for the first four matches of the 1911-12 season. Despite missing these games he was once again leading scorer with 23 goals in 38 cup and league games. However, his fellow strikers were disappointing and as United finished in only 13th position, in August 1912, Mangnall resigned from United and moved to Manchester City. During his nine years at the club, Mangnall had completely transformed United's fortunes before being replaced by J. J. Bentley, the former president of the Football League. City had a good start to the 1912/13 season and won every game in September, but could not maintain this pace and by the end of the season they finished 6th, two points behind United.

The 1913/14 season was a period of transition, while the following campaign was notable for a change of management – in December 1914, the roles of secretary and team manager were separated for the first time. Bentley became full-time secretary and John Robson was appointed to look after and select the team. Robson's team was a shadow of the one which had performed so well in the previous decade, as only Stacey, Meredith, Sandy Turnbull and Wall remained from the 1909 FA Cup-winning side. Not surprisingly, the club struggled, only escaping relegation by a single point.

Before United could form a plan for recovery, the outbreak of the First World War put football firmly to the back of people's minds. The Football League was suspended, and clubs resorted to playing in regional competitions. United played in the Lancashire

Principal and Subsidiary Tournaments for four seasons, but this was a less than successful diversion, the misery compounded by the fact that two of the club's players were found guilty of match fixing following a controversial 2-1 win against Liverpool at Old Trafford in April 1915 that helped the club avoid relegation. Enoch West was banned for life as was Sandy Turnbull, who joined the Footballers' Battalion to help Britain's war effort. Tragically Turnbull was killed during a battle in France in May 1917, to leave United without another of their early century heroes for their return to league football in 1919/20.

When the Football League resumed after the First World War, Mangnall made the surprising decision to buy the 46 year old Meredith from United. That year City finished in 7th place. Mangnall did even better in the 1920-21 season with only Burnley achieving more league points. In 1923 Mangnall arranged for City to move to Maine Road. It was popular with the fans and over 76,000 people watched City play Cardiff in the fourth round of the FA Cup. City won the game but was defeated by Newcastle United in the semi-final. At the end of the season it was decided not to renew Mangnall's contract. Mangnall died of a cerebral embolism on 13th January 1932.

Richard Bevan, chief executive of the League Managers' Association, paid tribute to Mangnall as the manager who began the United trophy haul.

"The 2010/11 campaign was significant for Manchester United as Sir Alex Ferguson guided the club to a record 19th league title. Ernest Mangnall was instrumental in this milestone as he delivered the first of the nineteen league triumphs in 1908. He helped to transform a poverty-stricken club, playing on a poor ground with mediocre results into a wealthy club with success in major competitions and a new stadium.

"Manchester United is a club with great history and tradition. A key factor to their prolonged success are the managers who have taken the helm. In addition to his success with Manchester United, Mangnall is significantly the only man to have ever managed both Manchester clubs, jobs he held over a period of

21 years.

"Interesting from the LMA point of view is that Mangnall was the first Chairman and Treasurer of the Secretaries' and Football Managers' Association – the forerunner of the LMA. He was also fully deserving of the long service medal he was awarded by The FA in 1921.

"The role of the manager has evolved and developed over the past century but it was shaped initially by the pioneers of the pre-World War era like Mangnall. So in addition to Ernest being such a major part of the history of Manchester United, he also led the way for the game and football management."

*

A lengthy period of decline followed the First World War, with United languishing in the lower reaches of the First Division until relegation in 1922. United returned to the top flight in 1925 but would continue to yo-yo between the top two divisions until the outbreak of World War II.

United's fortunes were to improve dramatically with the appointment of former Liverpool and Manchester City player Matt Busby in 1945 following a clandestine approach by legendary United fixer Louis Rocca. Busby, still registered as a player at Liverpool, was tapped up via a private letter while he still served in the army PE unit.

Busby, who had expected to take up a coaching role at Anfield, accepted the job at Old Trafford on condition that he had absolute control over transfers, team selection and wages - an unheard of demand. This unprecedented power effectively made Busby the first truly modern manager, responsible for all football matters.

Matt's United had verve and skill and, though they may have won the FA Cup in 1948, it was United's brand of football that won the hearts of fans up and down the country. The only thing that eluded this great team was a league title and, after finishing runners-up in four of the five seasons following the war, many assumed an ageing team had missed the boat...

TITLE NO. 3 - 1951-52

'The players would come to work on the bus, and go home on the bus. I lived about a mile up the road, which was about five minutes, seven stops...'

JACK CROMPTON

"WE WALKED TO THE GROUND, cycled, or took the bus" - the lifestyle of the players who won the title in 1952 is vividly portrayed by the oldest surviving Manchester United star.

Jack Crompton is the only man alive who can truly describe life under Matt Busby and the 1952 League title year. Jack is also the sole survivor of the 1948 FA Cup Final, on either side, as he celebrates his 90th birthday in December.

Still very sprightly, with a lively mind, Jack was delighted to contribute to this history of United through the key players in each of their 20 league title successes. "If I'm prompted, I can drift back to the past, and although very difficult, sometimes it's amazing what I can remember of those times," Jack began, "people stick programmes in front of you to sign, and they rekindle old memories. I can remember beating Burnley 2-1, I can remember winning the League in 1952, there is such a lot to try to remember, but I can dig it out of my memory, just need a bit of prompting."

Jack Compton was the United custodian between 1944 and

1956, when life as a goalkeeper was a far cry from what it is today, he explains why in graphic detail. So, too was the life style of the players in those days as you would expect, but he begins by painting a vivid picture of life in the dressing room and the managerial prowess of Matt Busby.

"When we won the League title in 1952 we were so pleased for Matt. We wanted to win the League for him, just the way we wanted to win the FA Cup in 1948 for him. Johnny Carey was a great captain, a great player, in a great team. The team was a team, a great bunch of lads, no prima donnas.

"The players would come to work on the bus, and go home on the bus. I lived about a mile up the road, which was about five minutes, seven stops, which meant I didn't have to come across Salford Bridge, which could be a rough journey if the steam ships were passing through and the bridge was raised. If I was ever late I would always say that I was held up by the steam ships and the bridge going up – that is until they realised that I didn't live in Salford and didn't come that route! I sometimes walked to work or would cycle, but the club stopped me cycling when they told me it was not good for my legs, as it shortened my hamstrings."

Following their league triumph in 1911, United roamed the footballing wilderness for nearly four decades before the arrival of Matt Busby in October 1945. Busby and assistant Jimmy Murphy led United to a runners–up finish four times in six years. In his seventh year, a dressing room upheaval saw the departure of several experienced players. United fans, though, were soon to be stunned by the impact of Busby's prodigious youth talent. Busby had a plan to ensure lasting success at Old Trafford as he and Murphy devised a junior set–up that would produce high class players, with the odd player bought to fill the gaps.

Yet back at the end of the Second World War, Manchester United didn't even have a pitch to call their own as their famous stadium had suffered severe bomb damage which had left it a blitzed wreck. There were no training facilities, no dressing rooms, or even offices, and it was only the generosity of their neighbours Manchester City, ironically one of Busby's previous playing clubs, which enabled United to continue. Busby relied on club captain Johnny Carey, who in his illustrious career even played in goal for United in a match at Sunderland, but was originally an inside forward, before his conversion to right back. His full back partner, Johnny Aston was another of Busby's conversions, and in time they established themselves as the best full back pairing around.

The 'Busby Babes' began with two youngsters promoted to first-team football in 1951-52. Jackie Blanchflower and Roger Byrne proved to be such a hit that United won the title and boasted a scintillating plus 43 goal difference — 18 better than their closest challengers! Although it was closer than that sounds, as the points difference was four. Busby called United's Division One victory in 1952 "most unexpected."

Jack has no doubts about the value of Carey as a club captain and inspirational figure within the dressing rooms during this period as he chooses Carey and Paul Scholes as his favourite all time players. Jack told me, "I am no long a regular at the first team games, mostly reserve games these days, as my legs are not what they were. The club is good to me, welcoming, they look after me. It is very difficult to pick your best players or a best United team as if you picked your best team, I could pick another one with what is left over and it would be arguably better than yours. Whenever I have sat down and written out my best United team I always find myself saying 'what have I done, leaving so and so out', so I have come to the conclusion that I would have to write to the FA to ask them to extend the 11 a side team to 28!

"But my favourite player is Johnny Carey, the Irish international, he was one of the best I have ever seen, together with Peter Doherty who also came out of Ireland and who played for City. Another player I admired was Stan Pearson who was very good on the ball and who scored in the 1948 Final. Paul Scholes is another favourite and it breaks my heart the thought of him leaving United, he has been a great little player, I love watching him, and I wish I could talk him into staying.

"I used to play up front, but I was useless, but I was

quite happy in the end to play in goal. The game was vastly different then, to what it is now. Present day football is great, I love it! The salaries are immoral, unfair to so many trades and professions and I believe there should be a limited wage. Perhaps the clubs should pass on some of their enormous wealth to children's homes instead of paying such enormous salaries to the players. £100,000-a-week, they don't need that. I am sure they would get by on £50,000-a-week! Players might be better without so much money, but it is conjecture, you just don't know.

"What I do know is that it is a different game, certainly for a goalkeeper, which has changed enormously, apart from stopping the ball going into the net! If a goalkeeper ventured outside his six yard box he was tackled by the opposing strikers, and when I say tackled I mean knocked about, charged into, roughed up, and very often that charging was not shoulder to shoulder but into your chest or back. If you tried to run with the ball bouncing it every three steps you were taking your life in your hands. Back then the rules were you had to bounce the ball after every three steps and if you didn't you would have a direct free kick awarded against you in the penalty area. I was always being pulled up for over carrying the ball but it wasn't easy when you had players trying to knock you over and take the ball off you.

"Goalkeepers had to be physically strong in those days to withstand the physical bombardment. I did a lot of weight-lifting to ensure I had the physical strength required. That would mean the entire team lining up on the goal line with me in front of them. Of course now the goalkeepers are wrapped up in cotton wall, you only have to look at them and they get a free kick in their favour."

Jack won the 1948 FA Cup with Busby's first great side. After his playing career finished he joined Luton Town as Assistant Manager before answering the club's desperate call following the 1958 Munich Air Disaster. He then served at Old Trafford as a trainer and a coach and was even, for a short spell, interim manager when Dave Sexton was sacked in 1981.

He says, "Matt was very popular with the players, you felt as though you wanted to do it for him. He was very similar to Alex Ferguson in so many ways – very, very similar. Alex is a bit more volatile, but otherwise they have similar ways. I knew Matt well as I worked under him for 14 years as a trainer. We once had a terrible year, and could have gone down very easily, but City lost to Leyton Orient and we were saved by a penalty at Maine Road from going down at the end of the season, but a few days later he told me to come into his office where I thought I was going to get my backside kicked.

"I walked into this office and he said, 'Jack, sit down'. He went to his drinks cabinet and poured out a whisky. I didn't drink whisky – until now that is. I said, 'no, thanks, not for me'. Matt continued to pour two drinks, one with a lot of lemonade for me, and he said, 'I will tell you a story about Bob McGrory (the former Celtic inside forward turned manager) who once called me into his office after a game we had lost 2-1. He said 'Jack, come into my office', and when I got there he poured two drinks. He said, 'this game drives either you barmy, or it drives you to drink... and we are not going barmy!' That was the type of person he was. He didn't say a lot, but he made you feel as though you wanted to play for him."

In 1945, Manchester United had an overdraft of fifteen thousand pounds and no stadium, but managed to extend their Bank Manager's patience by recruiting Jimmy Delaney from Glasgow Celtic, which enabled Busby to start the post-war football season in 1946-47 with a very experienced side generally consisting of: Jack Crompton, Johnny Carey, John Aston; Jack Warner, Allenby Chilton, Henry Cockburn; Jimmy Delaney, Johnny Morris, Jack Rowley, Stan Pearson, Charlie Mitten. United were runners-up, and with the crowds retuning, the club recorded a healthy profit of some sixty thousand pounds. Under Jimmy Murphy's guidance, the reserves won the Central League Championship, but Murphy reported to Busby that he felt none of them were good enough to step up so they would have to develop their own talent.

Having finished runners-up in 1946-47, United repeated

the feat in 1947–48, and also reached Wembley to play Blackpool in what turned out to be one of the finest ever F.A. Cup finals. Coming from behind twice, United finally triumphed 4–2 with two goals from Jack Rowley, Stan Pearson, and Johnny Anderson, a late selection in place of Jack Warner. The following year, Old Trafford was finally fit to accommodate First Division football again and United continued to excite their fans by going close to that elusive title, making it four times runners-up in the first five Championship years after the Second World War.

Jack recalls, "I was lucky enough to play in the 1948 FA Cup final, but I had an abcess on my back in the week leading up to the big game at Wembley. When the rest of the lads headed south to their hotel a couple of days before the final, Matt took me to see a specialist at the hospital. The specialist told us that it was not ready to be cut and if he did cut it then it would take a couple of days at least to heal, but we hadn't got a couple of days until the final. I told Matt that I would play at Wembley come what may, so I told the doc to cut it out, it wouldn't matter as I would play in any case. They operated on it, cut it out and I played in the Final and didn't feel a thing, although I had so much strapping I didn't need a jock strap!

"Matt stimulated you, even though he was not very demonstrative. He didn't say an awful lot. But you knew, if he gave you a squeeze on the shoulder, that you had done ok. After the Cup Final he put an arm around my shoulder, and he gave me a squeeze on the shoulder, then I knew I'd done my stuff. There were no words, though, and we knew what he was like, so he didn't have to say anything. That squeeze was enough."

With 1948 team ageing and the club diverting funds to re-build Old Trafford, United's network of scouts, under the supervision of Joe Armstrong were sent out to scour the country for teenage talent. The best were brought to United's Cliff training ground and the cream of that crop were honed by the likes of Jimmy Murphy, Bert Whalley and finally Busby. One of these scouts was Reg Priest, based in the Midlands, and he had helped to draw United's attention to a young player who had everything – Duncan Edwards.

The backroom staff organized the first team and reserves sides, plus three junior teams, made up of the 'A' team, the Colts, and the Juniors. The youth scheme that had started before the war as MUJAC (Manchester United Junior Athletic Club), with the express intention of one day having 11 local players in the first team, now blossomed into a direct route into the first team. Young stars therefore had plenty of opportunity to shine and eventually reach the standards United's first team finally achieved in 1952, just before Edwards left school and signed as a Manchester United player - Champions of The Football League.

The Manchester United squad of 1952 contained seven players from the 1948 FA Cup winning team; Jack Crompton, Johnny Carey, John Aston, Henry Cockburn, Allenby Chilton, Stan Pearson, and Jack Rowley. Roger Byrne had forced his way into the team and Johnny Berry had been signed to replace Jimmy Delaney. Names who figured in the Reserve side included Ray Wood, Billy Foulkes, Mark Jones, Jackie Blanchflower, Dennis Viollet and David Pegg. The Busby Babes were on their way.

A 16 match unbeaten run between November and March provided the backbone of United's third title triumph. Of the club's 95 goals that season, Jack 'Gunner' Rowley (30) and Stan Pearson (22) contributed more than half. Nevertheless United entered the final furlong nervously following unexpected reverses at Huddersfield (2-3), Portsmouth (0-1) and a 1-1 draw at Burnley. However four wins out of five against Liverpool (4-0), Burnley (6-1), Chelsea (3-0) and finally at home to title rivals Arsenal (6-1) secured Busby his first league title.

Jack Crompton had been replaced as first choice 'keeper by Reg Allen earlier in the season and consequently fell short of the 14 appearances required to win a league championship medal. Yet the majority of Jack's '48 peers would soon also find themselves superseded by the youngsters coming through the ranks...

Before the start of the next season, on 16th August 1952, Duncan Edwards appeared at Old Trafford for the first time in the club's junior public practice match, which took place before the senior game. An appreciative crowd saw the 'Reds' with Edwards at number 6, beat the 'Blues' 5-0. Other members of the winning side were Gordon Clayton in goal, Geoff Bent at left back, Ronnie Cope at centre half, and David Pegg at outside left. Playing opposite for the 'Blues' were Albert Scanlon at outside left, and a young Salford schoolboy who came on in the second half as a substitute, Eddie Colman.

Duncan was selected for the Colts the following week for his first competitive League appearance, playing against Heywood St. James in the Manchester Amateur League at the Cliff training ground. Another encouraging display helped United to a 6-1 victory and further victories in the following two matches, quickly earned Duncan a place in the 'A' team. The fixture was at Leek against the local team, Ball Haye Green, with Foulkes, Albert Scanlon and former club secretary, Les Olive, all in the same United team who ran out 4-3 victors. Olive turned out at outside right in this match, just one of the many playing positions he filled for United including, like Johnny Carey, even goalkeeper for the first team in later years.

After winning the league, the team suffered a reaction, being in the bottom five with a third of the season gone, Manchester City were bottom. United suffered a heavy 6-2 defeat at Wolverhampton Wanderers. Yet, at United's AGM in October 1952 Busby pointed out the way that the club would be going. Having cleared off the mortgage on Old Trafford, the purchase of the club's training ground at the Cliff was considered a masterstroke for the development of the many young players on the books. Busby commented, "Despite the marvellous achievement of finally lifting the League Championship in 1952, after four years of disappointments as runners-up, in my opinion the young players that are on United's books are worth hundreds of thousands of pounds. In a couple of year's time we shall have wonderful young material when it is most needed."

With his Championship side of 1952 off the pace at the top of Division One, and also suffering a 5th round FA Cup defeat at Everton, Busby moved to strengthen his hand early in March

1953, by signing centre forward Tommy Taylor from Barnsley.

Edwards was called up for his Football League debut at the age of just 16 years and 185 days of age. Jackie Blanchflower had been injured the day before, and with Henry Cockburn also on the injured list, it was up to Duncan to step in and fill the gap. The match was at Old Trafford and United's opponents were Cardiff City, who were making their first appearance at the ground since October 1928. The Welsh club surprisingly won 4-1. Duncan commented on that first team call-up from Busby, "The thought of making my Football League debut was not terrifying after having twice played at Wembley before I was 15. On leaving school I did not have to face the difficulty of finding a job, like some youngsters, as football was my future. I thought my future would be better away from the Midlands. United had a great reputation for giving plenty of opportunities to young players, and treating them in the best possible manner. The first time that I walked into the dressing room to meet other players I wondered if I was in the right place as there were so many youngsters there. I found it very easy to settle down and make friends, I went round one Friday morning and was called to Matt Busby's office. He quietly told me that I was selected for the First team. All I could think about was letting my parents know the news."

Alf Clarke of the *Manchester Evening Chronicle*, and also a contributor to the *United Review* the official programme of Manchester United, and in the *Evening Chronicle*'s Saturday *Pink* wrote of that 1-4 defeat to Cardiff, "The only ray of sunshine that filtered through the United gloom was the display of the boy debutant Duncan Edwards, who did all that was asked of him, including taking a shot from 30 yards that was only just wide." These words of praise were alongside an action picture of the debutant on the front page, while more encouraging words were written in the match report on the centre pages. In his report, Clarke continued, "Edwards had the right ideas when he tried another long range effort and was instrumental in setting United on the move with a glorious pass up the middle arising from which Berry forced a corner." This was just in the opening minutes of the second half and Duncan went from strength to strength.

The highly respected sportswriter Frank Taylor of the *News Chronicle* was another who witnessed the debut of Duncan that Saturday. He readily agreed with his fellow journalists that he looked a wonderful prospect, but looked a bit thick around the hips. Luckily, Duncan's size and weight were to be of no hindrance to him in the future, and he trained as hard as anyone which helped him develop an excellent physique. The final words on Duncan's entry into the Football League rests with Johnny Carey who said in the *Sunday Chronicle* the day after the match, "He's a good 'un, the best I've seen for his age."

In his PFA offices one of the most influential and long serving football administrators, Mancunian born Gordon Taylor recalled his childhood, as he talks with pride and passion of his boyhood heroes and those who dwelt at Old Trafford. The eight year-old Taylor would ride his bike the six miles to United's old training ground at The Cliff to wait patiently for the players to emerge to fill up his Charles Buchan gift books full of autographs.

He vividly recalls how the 1950s began with the break-up of Matt Busby's first successful United side, the 1948 FA Cup-winning team. Dressing room dissent led to Johnny Morris departing for Derby and Charlie Mitten exporting his wing wizardry to Colombia and so Busby promoted the youngsters he'd been recruiting and grooming in the late 1940's. Jackie Blanchflower and Roger Byrne were the first to emerge, labelled 'Babes' by the newspapers; and in their debut season 1951/52 United won the League Championship for the first time since 1911.

The memories of those early days came flooding back for Gordon as he told me, "As a seven and eight year-old I would wait eagerly for Charlie Buchan's Soccer Monthly. I had begun watching Manchester United and Manchester City, who won the FA Cup in 1956 with the Revie Plan as a deep-lying centre forward. Manchester United were a team that fascinated me as a boy with emerging young stars such as Duncan Edwards, they were simply remarkable.

"My parents would not have been very pleased if they had realised that, together with a gang of football mad kids, we would ride our bikes the six miles to The Cliff to wait for the players to sign our books after training. We always had the Charles Buchan books, and collected them every year. Our group would find out where the players hung out which was normally the Kardomah, in St Ann's Square, a tea and coffee house, and we would go there to collect autographs, then there was Paulden's in Piccadilly. We went to find the players and we would discover which hotels the visiting teams would occupy and we would chase teams like the Real Madrid side of the 50s. Di Stefano was my favourite player along with Gento and Puskas.

"I also watched Bolton quite a bit as my dad Alec knew George Taylor, no relation, but who went to the same school as my dad, and coached the Bolton Wanderers FA Cup Final team in 1953 and 1958. Because of my dad's friendship with George Taylor, we would often get tickets to watch Bolton, and I saw their cup games up to the final against Manchester United in 1957–58, Munich year. Eventually I signed to play for Bolton."

TITLE NO. 4 - 1955-56

'Winning the League is the pinnacle because it is achieved over the entire season, compared to a Cup tournament which is limited to the vagaries of the draw, key players injured at the wrong time, or suspensions which can turn a cup tournament such as the FA Cup or even the European Cup.'

SIR BOBBY CHARLTON.

"Nobody embodies the values of Manchester United better than Sir Bobby Charlton."

THAT IS THE ACCOLADE on the Manchester United official club web site, and it perfectly sums up this great man of Old Trafford.

In a 17-year playing career with United, having survived Munich at the age of 20, Sir Bobby played a record 754 games, scoring 247 goals, and went on to win the World Cup in 1966 alongside his brother Jack, and to this day holds the record as the nation's leading goalscorer with 49, one ahead of Gary Lineker. No-one symbolises English football more than Bobby Charlton. During the 1960s he was the most famous and popular Englishman in the world, a byword for sportsmanship and fair play.

Charlton won three Football League championships, the

FA Cup, European Cup and World Cup; was Footballer of the Year in both England and Europe; and scored more goals for Manchester United and England than any other player – quite simply he is England's mosr decorated footballer.

Charlton was forever affected by the Munich disaster that decimated an outstandingly vibrant team in which he was a rising star. Surviving that horror, he became the focus of his mentor Matt Busby's determination to rebuild a team that would honour the memory of those who had perished.

Busby said of Charlton, "There has never been a more popular footballer. He was as near perfection as man and player as it is possible to be." Sir Alf Ramsey, the only England manager to become world champions, put it like this, "He was one of the greatest players I have seen, very much the linchpin of the 1966 team. Early in my management I knew I had to find a role suitable to Bobby's unique talents. He wasn't just a great goalscorer, with a blistering shot using either foot. Bobby was a player who could also do his share of hard work."

The late George Best – a team-mate with whom Sir Bobby had an occasionally fractious relationship – summed up Charlton's ability succinctly, "I've never seen anyone go past players as easily as he did."

Knighted in 1994, in April 2009 he was further honoured when UEFA president Michel Platini presented him with a special award recognising his outstanding contribution to European football. Platini said it was a privilege to present the UEFA President's Award to an outstanding ambassador and role model who "represents everything that is good about the game of football; fair play, respect, and true loyalty, and is a good example for future generations, both on and off the pitch".

England coach Fabio Capello recently said Charlton was the one past player he would love to have in his current England squad. "He was a midfielder, a bit like Alfredo di Stefano. He had the same style. He ran a lot. He could defend and attack. Overall, he was a really fantastic player."

Charlton was born to play football. It was, quite literally, in his blood. His mother Cissie was one of the Milburns, a footballing clan from the Northumberland mining community. Charlton's grandfather and four of his uncles were professional players, one of them 'Wor' Jackie Milburn, the legendary Newcastle United centre-forward. Bobby grew up supporting Newcastle but was mesmerised by the wizardry of Stanley Matthews. The young Charlton represented England Schools and his potential soon attracted a host of scouts from leading clubs to the Charltons' Ashington home. He opted for United and turned professional with them in October 1954, winning the FA Youth Cup in 1954, 1955 and 1956.

Busby's ageing side that won the League in 1952 needed freshening up as Allenby Chilton was 34, Jack Rowley 32, Stan Pearson 33 and captain, Johnny Carey, 34. Busby had little transfer funds to replace his stars and had to find the replacements from the youth ranks. Busby saw the youth players developing under his tuition along with highly influential assistant manager, Jimmy Murphy. John Doherty, David Pegg and Dennis Viollet joined Jackie Blanchflower and Jeff Whitefoot as regular first team stars. Tommy Taylor was then brought in from Barnsley for the incredibly cost effective fee of £29,999 – £1 was given to the tea lady at Oakwell so not to saddle Taylor with the burden of being the country's first £30,000 player; something Bill Nicholson did with Jimmy Greaves, insisting on a fee of £99,999, so as not to make him the first £100,000 footballer. At just 23 years old Roger Byrne took over as club captain when Johnny Carey retired in 1953. The pieces were in place for United's next title triumph.

Since the 1952 triumph United had been in transition – finishing 8th in 1952-53, 4th in 1953-54 and 5th in 1954–55, just five points behind league champions Chelsea. Just 22,000 fans turned up to Old Trafford in November 1955 to watch them play reigning champions, Chelsea. United won 3-0 and never really looked back. Despite a shaky start to the season, winning just three games in their opening eight matches, they only lost one match between the 31st December and the end of the season.

Attendances towards the end of the season grew as United neared their fourth league title. 62,277 fans watched United beat second placed Blackpool 2-1 in their penultimate match at Old Trafford, the title decider against Stanley Matthews' team on Saturday, April 7.

The victorious United team that day read: Ray Wood, Ian Greaves, Roger Byrne, Eddie Colman, Mark Jones, Duncan Edwards, Johnny Berry, John Doherty, Tommy Taylor, Dennis Viollet, David Pegg. A week later 38,000 saw them beat Portsmouth 1-0 in the final game of the season. United won the league by 11 points. The Busby Babes had arrived. The squad had an average age of 22 and along with the prodigious Duncan Edwards, signings such as Tommy Taylor began rewriting the history books. Busby created a fine team with Taylor and Dennis Viollet spearheading the front line, scoring 25 and 20 league goals respectively. The youth team were also on form as they won the Youth Cup, featuring the likes of Kenny Morgans, Wilf McGuinness and, of course, a young Bobby Charlton.

As Sir Bobby recalls, "I was just a youngster when United beat Blackpool 2-1, and I was thinking even then that this was a club that was destined to win league titles, a club that should be winning league titles. Looking around at the talent there at the time; the team, the squad, it was clear to me that here was a team good enough to win the League.

"I will never forget the moment when we all knew United would win the League, in that game against Blackpool when Tommy Taylor's header just crossed the line before the keeper tried to get it out, it seemed to take a long time to get over the line." No need for any action replays, not that there were any in those days. "It definitely crossed the line", Sir Bobby insists and I for one would not doubt the word of this footballing knight, one of the most respected and influential ambassadors in the world game.

Charlton would go on to win his first League medal the following season, go on to win the coveted European Cup, and for one of the game's all time great players, winning the League title ranks as the number one achievement, "The hardest trophy to win in English football is the league title, by far the hardest, and the winning of the title back in the pioneering days of the European Cup was the only entry to the European Cup.

"The thing about the League is that everybody starts off at the same point, and no one can have any complaints about who finishes at the top at the end of a long season, and there is no feeling like it when you are crowned champions, winning the league is the pinnacle because it is achieved over the entire season, compared to a Cup tournament which is limited to the vagaries of the draw, key players injured at the wrong time, or suspensions which can turn a cup tournament such as the FA Cup or even the European Cup.

"Winning the old First Division or the Premier League as it is now, is the most difficult, and to see people start knocking the team that won the 19th league title for United, well, forget all that. United played everybody, home and away, and we have all seen the criticisms that the team didn't play particularly well at times. Ask the fans what they thought of their team, and they will tell you they played some fantastic football at times, and the season was packed with excitement, with all the twists and turns. You have to listen to your fans, and at the moment, they remain behind the team and committed to the team, and they are enjoying watching the team winning the title."

Wilf McGuinness played a dozen games in the 1956 title season and his everlasting memory of the early 50s was the emphasis United placed on promoting their young stars of the future as quickly as possible. He told me how he became part of the Busby Babes era, "I signed for United in '53 just after they had won the title, and at a time when the older players were being replaced by a succession of youngsters coming through the ranks. Johnny Carey, one of my boyhood heroes, was retiring, when I arrived, and Jack Rowley was one of the more experienced players who would need replacing because of his age.

"My dad used to take me to watch both the Manchester teams when they both played at Maine Road because Old Trafford was bombed during the war. By the time I signed for the club, they were back at Old Trafford. I signed on the same day as Bobby

Charlton. We both played for England schoolboys and we joined United together. By 1956 I was in the side and played around 12 or 13 games, enough to warrant a League title medal, and it struck me at the time just how many young players were being brought into the side.

"I can also recall winning the title in 1956 with relative ease, we were reasonably comfortable. Blackpool were a decent team and they gave chase, but we were the best team at the time, with Duncan Edwards coming into the side as a regular at the age of 19, 20. The future looked bright. It made me laugh when Alan Hansen came out with the view 'you can't win anything with kids' as we had proved him wrong many years before!"

The talented young half back, capped at every level by England, broke his leg at the age of 22, and eventually moved into coaching with United. At 31, he stepped up to perform the unenviable task of replacing his mentor, Sir Matt, as United manager. "Matt didn't want the everyday hustle and bustle that went with management. Out of loyalty to his staff, I was promoted to manager, which meant the coaches were not disrupted. Matt was still there to guide me. The problem as I saw it was that I knew too much about the players, and the players knew too much about me."

United reached three cup semi-finals, but indifferent league form meant Wilf's reign only lasted 18 months, before he reassumed his role of trainer. Wilf's passion for United remained unaffected and, after over a decade co-commentating for Manchester United Radio, he continues to provide expert opinion for the club's media channels. Wilf treasures one particular memory from his many years at Old Trafford, United's 3-0 win over Bolton Wanderers in September 1995 when Fergie's Fledglings reminded him of the Busby Babes. Refreshingly Wilf looks forward not back with any regrets, "My fondest times are now. I am chairman of the Association of Former Manchester United players, I get invited to games, talk to the fans in the hospitality rooms with others such as Norman Whiteside, Stuart Pearson, Alex Stepney and Paddy Crerand, it's the nicest time of our lives."

Having crossed so many generations as players, then manager, and now regular visitor to Old Trafford, Wilf has his firm ideas of which players constitute the appropriate recognition to be described as all-time Manchester United great. But he is more concerned about the players he leaves out of his list of all-time players than the ones he selects, "I don't want to insult them. I might not name as there are so many all time greats at Manchester United, so many of them, across so many generations. You could easily pick a great midfield, and in my opinion there would be, Robson, Keane, Ince. There were wonderful centre halves, two magnificent in particular in Steve Bruce and Gary Pallister, and the bald one, Jaap Stam. Then there is Eric Cantona! Defenders are plentiful in Denis Irwin, the Neville brothers and Duncan Edwards was the greatest of them all, better than anybody around at that time, and just 21 when he died, what would he have become had he survived Munich? He was immense. There is also Beckham, Giggs, Scholes, and of course, Bobby Charlton, Denis Law, and George Best, three European Footballers of the Year all in one team."

Wilf has no doubts about the best all time manager, not just at United, but in British football. "We have been blessed with two great managers in Sir Matt Busby and Sir Alex Ferguson, both were brilliant. But to land a record 20 league titles, what can I say about Sir Alex other than I would place him as the highest British manager ever, without doubt. If anyone wants to argue with that they would have to put up a pretty good case, because I cannot see anyone better in the frame."

TITLE NO. 5 - 1956-57

*'Rovers were top at the time we went to Old Trafford, having won
our last three games. When I got off the team bus, who was there to
greet me but none other than Matt Busby. He was waiting to greet
all the Blackburn Rovers team. He shook my hand and said 'How
are you, Dave?' I was flabbergasted that he knew who I was! I felt
really unnerved. I was in awe of the man but that was Matt Busby
for you, it was part of his tactics on the day and it worked. I froze
when I shook hands with him and probably hadn't recovered when I
walked out onto the pitch. United beat us 5-1, they battered us. It
served its purpose.'*

DAVE WHELAN.

ROGER BYRNE LIFTED the Championship trophy as
skipper of a great young side in successive seasons 1956
and 57 that included several more products of Matt
Busby's youth academy. Eddie Colman, Mark Jones and David
Pegg were all first team regulars, having cut their teeth in the
FA Youth Cup, which United won five years in a row from its
inception in 1953. Colman and Pegg were particular favourites of
the young Gordon Taylor.

Not all the young talent was home-grown, as Busby was
happy to plunge into the transfer market, as shown by the big
money signings of proven internationals Tommy Taylor and
goalkeeper Harry Gregg. Another young man who excelled for

club and country was Duncan Edwards. So powerful, talented and mature was the Dudley teenager that Matt Busby could not hold him back from United's first team. In April 1953, he became the First Division's youngest-ever player at the age of 16 years and 185 days.

Owner of Wigan Athletic he might be but Dave Whelan is a confirmed life long Manchester United fan, who played against his heroes for Blackburn Rovers. Whelan explained the mind games that Matt Busby employed to unsettle the opposition long before Sir Alex and Jose Mourinho became synonymous with trying to outwit their opponents with psychological tactics.

Whelan recalls, "Rovers were top at the time we went to Old Trafford, having won our last three games. When I got off the team bus, who was there to greet me, but none other than Matt Busby. He was waiting to greet all the Blackburn Rovers team. He shook my hand and said 'how are you, Dave?' I was flabbergasted that he knew who I was. Here was the famous Mr Busby asking how I was, imagine how I felt, really unnerved. I was in awe of the man and it was unreal to have met him as I stepped off the bus. But that was Matt Busby for you, it was part of his tactics on the day and it worked, as I froze when I shook hands with him and probably didn't recover when I walked out onto the pitch. Manchester United beat us 5-1, they battered us. It served its purpose."

Whelan has made no secret of his United affiliation, as he explained, "They are the best. You know how good they are, how massive a club that they are, there is just something about them. I played with Duncan Edwards and a few of the United players in the Army team. We all had to do our two years' national service in those days. Four weeks after I came out of the Army, the Munich disaster occurred and Duncan Edwards, among many others, was killed. It was awful, dreadful, a shock that was shared by so many, and it hit me hard at the time."

The Munich disaster had an equally devastating effect on Gordon Taylor, the long standing Professional Footballers' Association chief executive, "I used to watch the Busby Babes, as part of the crowd behind the goal, swaying at Old Trafford. Duncan Edwards was like a tank, such strong, big thighs, he would power through the surface, surfaces that were nothing like the perfect smooth grass ones you get nowadays. It was so exciting because of the quality of the football played, because they were my heroes. I was 12 at this time, and my paper round paid enough for me to afford the admission price, then after the games a group of us boys would play football behind the tram sheds until we were chased away. We would then go off to the cricket pitch because the surface was true but we would be chased off by the groundsman.

"You can imagine the profound affect it had on a young boy coming home from school, ready to do his usual paper round, to discover his idols in danger of losing their lives, it was the most traumatic time in my young life."

One match that epitomised the Busby Babes era was their last performance on English soil against Arsenal at Highbury on 1 February 1958. In front of a crowd of 63,578 the Reds beat the Gunners in a nine-goal thriller with goals from Edwards, Taylor (2), Bobby Charlton and Dennis Viollet. It was a fitting epitaph for one of the greatest sports teams this country has ever produced. From Highbury, the Babes headed off into Europe to play the second leg of a tie against Red Star Belgrade. Again they won 5-4, this time on aggregate, but on the way home - tragedy. After refuelling in Munich on 6 February 1958, the United aeroplane crashed, killing twenty-two people, including seven players – Byrne, Colman, Jones, Pegg, Taylor, Geoff Bent and Liam Whelan. Duncan Edwards died of his injuries fifteen days later in a German hospital. The club, the city of Manchester and the English game entered a long period of mourning.

Taylor told me, "The last game at Old Trafford before the Munich disaster was against Bolton, the team I would one day play for, and United beat them 7-2, and that was a good Bolton team. As there were no games delayed because of Europe, the United team went straight into that Arsenal match with more wonderful goals and looking the best side you had ever seen, then it was off to play Red Star Belgrade.

1956-57

"Many years later when England played Yugoslavia, I went to the Red Star Belgrade stadium as part of the FA's official party. It was my first time there. At first it looked as though the game might be called off because of fog in 1988 but it went ahead and England were two-up in next to no time. My over riding memory of that game in Belgrade, wasn't so much the England performance which was outstanding, but the tour of the stadium, where in the bowels of the stadium there was a football museum, the centre piece of which was a tribute to the Busby Babes, who had played their last game in that stadium. We didn't have anything like that in our stadia at that time. But on my return I worked hard and campaigned for football museums to respect the past and, I am proud to say, we now have a National Museum of Football Memorabilia and at Old Trafford there is one of the most popular memorabilia museums in the country and most clubs now have something similar. But the first one I had ever seen was in Belgrade, and I was very, very impressed."

It seemed inconceivable that United could recover from such an appalling loss. But as Busby defied the medics to recover from his crash wounds, the team bounced back and, patched up by Jimmy Murphy, they reached the FA Cup Final in May 1958. They lost at Wembley to Bolton Wanderers twelve months after losing the final to Aston Villa. To continue the theme of finishing a close second, the Reds were also runners-up in the League Championship of 1958-59.

Bobby Charlton was drafted into the Manchester United team in autumn 1956, appropriately enough against Charlton Athletic, scoring twice on his debut on 6 October despite carrying an injury. He didn't command a regular place until the latter stages of the season, notching 10 goals in 14 league appearances as the Busby Babes claimed their back-to-back titles and Bobby his first title medal.

United won the League by 12 points, scoring a staggering 103 goals. Sir Matt's side rapidly gained the attention of the footballing world, and began to be regarded as one of the best footballing sides in Europe. United lost only three of their 21 away games, winning 14. United won so comfortably that captain Roger Byrne had time to film an advertisement for a mud-wrestling competition before returning to lift the League trophy.

Bobby also played in his first FA Cup final, although Aston Villa controversially denied United the double. That summer United defied the Football League by entering the fledgling European Cup, progressing to the semi-final where they lost to Real Madrid.

In our interview Sir Bobby explains the motives behind Matt Busby's determination to lead Manchester United into uncharted European football, "I hadn't been at the club very long, mostly as a young player, but it quickly became apparent once I was in the first team, how much Matt Busby wanted to make Manchester United the best team in the world, and to achieve that he was determined to take the club into the European Cup, he saw it as a unique opportunity and a wonderful adventure. He made it plain that this year we had to go. It was a time where there was an explosion in the field of communication, airplanes could take you all over the world and Europe was suddenly far more accessible than it had ever been to go to play football. It was comparable to what has occurred in more recent times with computers and the internet. Back then, it was a similar big change in the way people were gong to live their lives, and the way football was about to evolve. Matt viewed it as vitally important that the club took part, even though the Football League were adamant that we couldn't go because we had far too many games already. But that didn't stop Matt, who said that we had never been before and that we had to be part of it.

"At that time, of course, you had to win the League to get into the European Cup, vastly different to the Champions League format of today and the club had won the previous year, and we were heading for a second successive league win. Matt's philosophy was simple - second best wouldn't do. We had to win the League, we had to conquer Europe."

★

The champions had sprinted from the blocks at the start of the 1956-57 season, winning 10 of their first 12 games before a shock 2-5 reverse at home to Everton on October 20th. But, for the first time, the League wasn't the be all and end all of the first half of the season, for now United had entered the European Cup. After accounting for Anderlecht, with a still record 10-0 home win, Borussia Dortmund and Athetic Bilbao to reach the last four, it was perhaps understandable that United's league form would suffer. Nevertheless by Easter United held their destiny in their hands, even if a 1-3 reverse in the Bernabeu meant that reaching the European Cup Final would be a stiff task.

United travelled to Turf Moor for a First Division game on Good Friday, April 19. This game would be was followed by Sunderland at Old Trafford the next day, Old Trafford again on the Monday against Burnley again, and then the "big one" against Real Madrid at Old Trafford the following Thursday. United needed four points to ensure retaining the First Division Championship title.

An account of how one fan took the football special steam train to Burnley was illuminative about fans' experiences at the time; ladies with flasks of Oxo and packets of sandwiches, men smoking Capstan Full Strength cigarettes, others drinking bottles of Jubilee Stout, the journey to Burnley taking just over an hour and 20 minutes. Another 15 minutes to reach Turf Moor, nine pence entrance and taking their places behind the goal at the 'open end' which was where the majority of United supporters congregated.

There was no pre-match chanting back in those days. Burnley appeared in their claret and blue shirts, with big name players; Colin McDonald, Jimmy Adamson, Tommy Cummings, Brian Miller, John Connelly, Jimmy McIlroy, Ray Pointer, Brian Pilkington, all internationals and an astute manager in the Geordie, Harry Potts. United came out and made their way to the 'open end' in their blue shirts, and lined up; Wood, Foulkes,

Byrne; Goodwin, Blanchflower, Edwards; Berry, Whelan, Taylor, Charlton and Pegg. United won comfortably that afternoon with a terrific display of attacking football that really entertained 41,000 plus fans. Billy Whelan was at his best and scored all three United goals, in a display of team power and flowing, attacking football. Following United's 3-1 win, they were now just two points away from retaining their title with Sunderland to play at home the following day.

When Sunderland arrived in Manchester there was a tremendous excitement and expectancy within the city that United would clinch their second title in successive seasons that afternoon. The city was abuzz with the imminent arrival of Real Madrid in town the following week for the second leg of the European Cup semi-final, in which United were trailing 3-1. Having to play three games in four days prior to a semi-final, seemed bizarre preparation for a game of such importance. Yet the Football League wouldn't countenance a postponement of a League fixture to help the cause.

Sunderland were also a team with many experienced internationals; Len Shackleton, Ray Daniel, Charlie Fleming, Don Revie, Billy Elliott, Billy Bingham, Stan Anderson and Colin Grainger among their number. United made just one change from the team that had played Burnley the day before, and that was Eddie Colman returning at right half in place of Freddie Goodwin. Almost 59,000 fans packed into Old Trafford that afternoon. Sunderland were no real match for a rampant United team and Whelan quickly added to his three goals from the day before by opening the scoring very early on. Sunderland's goalkeeper Johnny Bollands was injured in a collision with Tommy Taylor as he dived at the big centre forward's feet, meaning Sunderland were down to 10 men. Big Charlie "Legs" Fleming, their centre forward, took over in goal. United increased their lead when Tommy Taylor scored. Just before half time, the 'Big Fella' won the ball in midfield just inside the Sunderland half, drove forward and from 30 yards hit a tremendous thunderbolt with his left foot. A fourth goal from Billy Whelan gave the

Dubliner a tally of five goals from two games, and when the final whistle went, It was smiles and cheers all around as United retained their First Division title.

Busby now had the luxury of being able to rest a few players for the Easter Monday game against Burnley at Old Trafford. There was a real anticipation and excitement in Manchester that Sunday. The Championship secured, Real Madrid was now the target. The tickets for the Real Madrid game went on sale on Easter Sunday morning and thousands queued throughout the night to make sure that they got a ticket. At 5am there was already a queue down Trafford Road going towards Ashburton Road.

Busby made nine changes for the Burnley return game, only Wood and Foulkes played that afternoon from the team that had defeated Sunderland two days previously. Bob Lord, the autocratic Burnley chairman, made scathing comments about United, and considered it an insult to Burnley that United could put out a "Boy's Own" team against them as he put it. The Football League was incensed and there was speculation of punishing United for fielding a weakened team. Busby was unperturbed and went ahead as planned. Just over 41,000 fans turned out that day to watch Dennis Viollet lead out 'The Champions" and United lined up; Wood; Foulkes, Greaves; Goodwin, Cope, McGuinness;Webster, Doherty, Dawson, Viollet, and Scanlon. United had strength in depth and roared on by a partisan crowd, United displayed the same attacking ethos. They scored first through young Alex Dawson, and midway through the second half, the Welshman, Colin Webster, steamed in to power in a second goal. The game ended 2-0 to United. Bob Lord's Burnley team had been demolished by the young United reserves. The Football League could hardly charge United with fielding a weakened team after that result.

United failed in the European Cup against a tremendous Real Madrid team, drawing 2-2 at home, losing 5-3 on aggregate. United were on the receiving end of some poor refereeing decisions in the first leg, especially as Di Stefano should have been sent off in the first half of that game for a shocking foul on

Eddie Colman. Fixture congestion is nothing new as United had to play 10 games in the space of just 23 days and six inside a 10 day period! Nevertheless they comfortably retained the League title with an 8 point margin over Spurs.

Throughout the following season competition for a first-team spot was intense, but a hat-trick against Bolton Wanderers in January 1958 helped Bobby Charlton's cause, and Busby found it harder and harder to leave out the powerful young forward. A month later Charlton scored twice in United's 3-3 draw against Partizan Belgrade as the Babes sealed a place in the semi-finals of the European Cup. Nine months after winning his first title eight of United's champions had been killed in the Munich Air Disaster. Charlton was among those injured but his wounds were relatively minor and he was back in action within a month. Charlton proved an integral component of the post-Munich rebuilding, plying his trade across the field while the rest of the side was reconstructed. A permanent switch to a deep-lying forward role brought the best from him, and he was vital as United won the League championships in 1965 and 1967.

When the seriously injured Busby eventually returned to Manchester, 20-year-old Charlton became the key figure in his rebuilding plans. Charlton earned his first senior England cap two months after the disaster, scoring a sensational goal against Scotland. In May he was in the FA Cup final again, as a makeshift United side lost to Bolton. Then he was off to Sweden with the England squad for the 1958 World Cup. At this stage of his career he was playing on the left wing, though later he would move to inside forward and ultimately into the deep-lying centre forward role - essentially an attacking central midfielder - for which he is best remembered. Busby had said it would take five years to rebuild a winning team and in 1963 Charlton collected an FA Cup winner's medal as United beat Leicester. The following season, with the dazzling trinity of Charlton, Denis Law and George

Best now firmly in place, they finished runners-up to Liverpool in the League; and in 1964–65 were crowned champions again. They repeated the achievement in 1966–67; but in between was the little matter of the World Cup, hosted on English soil.

Those successes flanked international glory with England. Shortly before the 1966 World Cup, Charlton was named Football Writers' Association Player of the Year and European Footballer of the Year in quick succession. He went on to play a starring role as Alf Ramsey's side won the tournament, scoring twice in the semi-final win over Portugal. Charlton went on to win 106 caps – three as captain - and is still England's record goalscorer with 49 goals.

Bobby and his brother Jack forged an illustrious playing career with England and won the World Cup together in 1966. Although winning the World Cup is seen as the pinnacle of achievement in football, Charlton's finest hour at club level came in May 1968 when he captained United to European Cup triumph. For Charlton the victory capped the post-Munich rebuilding, and he famously missed the post-match celebrations – opting instead to conduct a solitary remembrance of absent friends.

Charlton hadn't played in 1958 but was a regular by 1962 in Chile, when England lost to eventual winners Brazil in the quarter-finals. In 1966 he and his team were destined to go all the way. They began inauspiciously against Uruguay, but in the second group game, against Mexico, Charlton lit the fuse of English expectations, firing home a stunner after collecting the ball from deep and running 30 yards with it before letting fly. It was vintage Charlton, a scorer of great goals. Further wins against France and Argentina took England to the semi-final, where Bobby produced possibly his best performance in an England shirt, unsettling Portugal's defence with his runs, spraying passes with precision and hitting both goals in a 2-1 win. In the final against West Germany, Franz Beckenbauer was deployed to try and shackle Charlton's effectiveness; the Englishman edged the contest, and his team lifted the World Cup. Bobby, already England's Footballer of the Year and European Footballer of the

Year in 1966, was also voted Best Player of the World Cup.

Sir Bobby continued to entertain as part of the famed Best-Law-Charlton triumvirate before he retired in 1973. He spent two years as manager and player-manager at Preston North End before resigning in August 1975. He briefly played for Waterford in the Republic of Ireland in 1976 before accepting a boardroom position at Wigan Athletic, where he took over as caretaker-manager during season 1982–83. In June 1984 Charlton became a director of Manchester United, a position he still holds today. Already awarded the OBE and CBE, he became Sir Bobby Charlton in June 1994. A respected ambassador for his club, English football and the game across the world football, he is a figurehead: a link with the club's past, present and future.

For all of these reasons Sir Bobby Charlton's view of the very best of the best Manchester United players down the ages has the greatest validity. Sir Bobby is often asked for his best ever line up and has always named Peter Schmeichel without hesitation. No longer. Step forward Edwin van der Sar to run the Great Dane so close, the Dutch master keeper might even have overtaken him…

"Sometimes I can change my mind, I suppose it's a privilege to change your mind, and when I am asked to pick my greatest United team, I find it impossible to do so without naming 15 players, there have been that many top quality players down the years showing so many different skills, in so many different positions it is virtually impossible to select a definitive team. I usually go for the players who stand out from the ordinary, those who could do things other couldn't. When it comes to selecting a goalkeeper, then I have never looked further than Pete Schmeichel as the best ever goalkeeper the club has ever had. Then Edwin van der Sar has had a fabulous final season, such a fabulous United career, and has been such a major influence on the club, his defenders, and even his strikers talk about the way he distributes the ball and maintains possession, the way he kicks the ball is unheard of.

"So, no, I am no longer simply going for Peter Schmeichel as the number one goalkeeper of all time. I would have to say he was more physically strong than Edwin, but Edwin van der Sar does everything that Schmeichel does; he is a great shot stopper, can save penalties if he has to, and comes out and catches the ball, dominating his area, but he is also very quick in distributing the ball. Peter Schmeichel was also a player with a big personality as well as a sensational goalkeeper. It's so very difficult to chose between them, but I now think that Van de Sar has been one of the greatest players ever in Manchester United's history, that's how highly I rate him.

"Of course there are so many forwards to chose from; Denis Law, George Best, Eric Cantona, Ryan Giggs, they all would be in my United team and what a fantastic team they would make. They all believed in good football, attacking football, exciting the crowds. The midfield is the same, with such quality players as Roy Keane, Nobby Stiles and Bryan Robson. Defence had a profusion of top quality players, but none better in the heart of defence that Steve Bruce and Gary Pallister and Duncan Edwards, of course."

TITLE NO. 6 - 1964-65

"In many ways George was very shy, despite his reputation. There are those who say he wasn't shy, but I thought he was shy back in those days, and he didn't change very much in the way he was shy. I always thought he was not that comfortable being in the real headlights, he never was. But the time was right for somebody like George to come along and turn football in something different."

DAVID SADLER

DAVID SADLER'S GREATEST CLAIM to fame is that he crossed the ball for Bobby Charlton to produce that wonderful flicked header against Benfica at Wembley which helped Manchester United lift the European Cup for Matt Busby ten years after Munich. From a personal perspective, the one time towering centre half informs me that winning his first England cap was the real highlight of this Manchester United legend's career.

Yet, perhaps, his greatest claim to notoriety is that he was actually George Best's room-mate when they shared digs with Mrs Mary Fullaway in Chorlton-cum-Hardy. Maidstone United and England amateur David Sadler turned 'pro' on his 17th birthday in 1963 and signed for Manchester United, leaving his Kent village for the big adventure at almost the same time that George Best left his Belfast home and the pair ended up together under Mrs Fullaway's roof.

1964-65

David had 11 seasons at Old Trafford, his cool-headed defending generally more valuable than his occasional periods as a useful striker. He helped United win the 1965 and 1967 League championships as well as the 1968 European Cup, leaving in 1974 after scoring 27 goals for the club to join Preston North End, then being managed by former teammate Bobby Charlton. David retired due to injury in 1977 became a building society branch manager in Hale, before becoming involved with Bobby Charlton in Old Trafford corporate hospitality. He is now Secretary of the Association of Former Manchester United Players.

After building one of the greatest teams seen in England, Busby had to start all over again at the start of the 1960s. The Munich air disaster had robbed him, and football, of some of the era's greatest players. But once the great man had recovered from his own injuries, he set about building another side to take the world by storm. Dennis Viollet was one of the leading names within this team. In 1959/60, the Munich survivor broke Jack Rowley's club record by scoring 32 goals in one league season. The team in total scored 102, but they conceded 80 and finished in seventh place. Viollet wasn't the only Munich survivor to enjoy a great Old Trafford career; others included Bill Foulkes and Bobby Charlton, who came through the club's youth ranks to break goalscoring records for club and country. Nobby Stiles also rose through the ranks, while Denis Law came via a record £115,000 transfer from Torino.

United's form was erratic at the start of the decade, while new names settled in, but then everything came together with a run to Wembley for the 1962/63 FA Cup Final. Busby's new-look team beat Leicester 3-1, with two goals from David Herd and one by Law. The next season saw United build on the foundations of FA Cup success to challenge for the title – finishing second, only four points behind the champions Liverpool, to whom they lost both home and away. The 1963/64 season was also notable for the signing and debut of George Best, the young man from Belfast who would become football's first superstar. His incredible skill, pace and control left opponents in knots, making him a hit with the fans, while his film star looks made him a hit with the ladies. In 1964/65, the famous trio of Best, Law and Charlton took United to new heights. They won the League Championship, pipping Leeds on goal difference, and reached the semi-finals of the European Fairs Cup and the FA Cup. Law plundered goals galore and was named the European Footballer of the Year.

Few know the real George Best better than David Sadler. He tells of those early days with George, how he himself failed to play enough games to earn a League title medal in 1965 but went onto to play a key role in that title two years later, and then the European Cup triumph.

However the title in 1965 will be remembered for the unveiling of the Belfast kid. As David Sadler recalls, "I signed pro at the age of 17 and played youth team football with George Best and came through the ranks with him. We shared digs together with Mrs Fullaway in Chorlton-cum-Hardy, two teenagers far from home, thrown together and having fun enjoying our adventure. Yes, it was a pretty fantastic adventure for the two us, George coming over from Belfast and it couldn't have been many times he had crossed the water, and I was away from home for the first time, hardly ever venturing far from my village in Kent. I think it would be fair to say that the pair of us were green behind the ears in every aspect of life, dumped into central Manchester, with very good jobs, the ones we loved. You could say we got out a bit!

"But Matt had an uncanny knack of knowing exactly what we got up to and exactly where we were getting up to it. He seemed to have his spies everywhere, he knew everything that was going on. We got into trouble, bit of trouble I would put it, not too much. We were living the dream, playing for Manchester United and having a great time. But Manchester United had a tried and tested method of looking after kids such as ourselves and Mrs Fullaway was one of the best landladies who was entrusted with looking after George and myself. They were nice digs, and Mrs Fullaway's family were a substitute for our own families while we were away, it provided a degree of stability, home life. It could have been a frightening experience for us, but it turned into a big adventure. Of course we made mistakes. But at Manchester United you didn't make the same mistakes twice. Mrs Fullaway had a son, a little older than us, and he would join us on nights out. We would go out and about with him.

"In many ways George was very shy, despite his reputation. There are those who say he wasn't shy, but I thought he was shy back in those days, and he didn't change very much in the way he was shy. I always thought he was not that comfortable being in the real headlines, he never was. But the time was right for somebody like George to come along and turn football in something different.

"I wasn't much older than George, maybe days or weeks in it, and while we both made our way through the ranks quickly, it was a couple of years later when I held down a regular place and that was when I won my first championship medal. You had to play 14 times for a medal, and I didn't quite make it in 1965, but George had made his big breakthrough. He started to make a real noise, although it was another year or two before his name jumped out at you when he crashed into Europe, especially the way he took Benfica apart, and became the Fifth Beatle.

"All the accolades coming George's way were perfectly understandable, first because he had this fantastic ability. The game in the 60s needed a soccer star like George, the game needed it. By 1967 George was a big star, really big star, he had changed the face of football, it had become part of the Rolling Stones, the Beatles, the show business of the 60s. Sponsorship, endorsements, and the things you now associate with football, were just starting to emerge, and it was brought about by a fantastic player such as George."

Sadler emerged into the limelight in time to make his bid for the title medal he missed out on in 1965. "I was fairly new, and didn't play enough games. My only championship medal came in 1967, and at that time I was playing fairly regularly in the team. We were all aware that winning the title meant qualification into

Europe, and the quest to win the European Cup. Of course at this time you had to win the League, not finish second third or even fourth to stand a chance of winning the Champions League. You had to win the title to get into Europe. The game has evolved and the Champions League is a fantastic competition just about the biggest probably in the world and we have all had to adjust to the way it has evolved to enable the top teams to be involved on a regular basis. For us back then it was a bit of a crusade to win the League as that crusade was to win in Europe.

"Oddly enough you didn't really know that, at the time, when you are actually doing it. You can sense it was special but it's only on reflection that you now appreciate the enormity of it all, of how much of a crusade it was for Busby to get back into Europe and win the European Cup. It was Matt who went against everybody's wisdom and better judgement to take United into Europe back in the mid-50s. It was bad enough travelling around Europe in the 60s, let alone the 50s, so I have no idea why Matt thought it was such a good idea at the time but of course he was eventually proved right. When you see the Champions League now, how could anyone have doubted him?"

The European Cup final at Wembley will be remembered for Best, Charlton and Kidd, but Sadler's cross for the Charlton goal was vital. He told me, "Bobby didn't score that many goals with his head, yet he was a terrific header of the ball. I must have put it on the right spot and he applied the perfect header and in it went. Naturally most people associate that European Cup triumph as the highlight of everyone's career who took part, mine included. But I am a bit old school and played quite a bit of international football at a variety of levels including amateur. From a purely personal point of view my first England cap was the highlight of my career, it was the biggest personal thing in my footballing life. Winning the championship with all your mates was special, of course it was, winning the European Cup was special, but playing for my country was the best. That is why, perhaps, it amazes me about the modern attitudes toward playing for England, players retiring at the age of 27. That all seems very strange to me, but I am from a completely different era."

Applying his 'old school' philosophy David Sadler doesn't follow the crowd in believing it was anything less than a magnificent achievement in winning the title in 2011, "Any team that goes for the championship and achieves it should be applauded, as it takes so much to do it. I don't believe any club wins a championship and doesn't deserve it. I know a lot of people have been saying this United team that landed the 19th title didn't deserve it... but not by me. There are enough matches over the course of the season for the best team to come out on top, enough time to sort out who is the best team."

When it comes to selecting his best ever Manchester United players of all time, without hesitation, David Sadler named George Best, "Yes, he would top my list. I know he was my pal, as much as anything, but that doesn't matter to me, he would top any list I'd compile of United greats. I was fortunate to play alongside him, as indeed I did with Bobby Charlton and Denis Law, and they too would be on my list, as the two runners up. It was a privilege to play alongside three European Footballers of the Year all in one team, sensational really. I watch United regularly as you can imagine and there have been many outstanding players since the days of Best, Law and Charlton. Bryan Robson and Roy Keane are very similar in many ways and while it would be a difficult decision to select one of them for say my ideal team, I would go for Robson. In even more recent times Eric Cantona was so fantastic when he came to Old Trafford that he took a team, a very good team without him, into a side that could win things with him, he was a major catalyst for big success for the club. Ryan Giggs and Paul Scholes have been without doubt incredibly long standing players for the club. Paul Scholes is a master craftsman, certainly in the Premiership era, and Scholes would be in my pick. So much has been said about Duncan Edwards, but it is difficult to select someone you have never seen play in the flesh. I have listened to lots of people I would respect who have told me how immense he was in a United shirt. With Scholes, for example, there is a direct relationship, seeing him at

Old Trafford, and with every game these days covered on TV, you can see his every game, his every move, that is where the game has changed so dramatically in the past 20 years."

David Sadler sampled this remarkable period from inside the Manchester United dressing room, admiration was universal, even inside rival teams dressing rooms. Now the highly respected chief executive of the Professional Footballers Association, Gordon Taylor retained his interest in Manchester United as he began to make his own way in his professional career. Gordon Taylor recalls, "I had become a professional by this time and at Bolton I was very much aware of the new Manchester United being assembled post Munich by Matt Busby. I was also very fortunate to have played at Old Trafford at this time, it was a fantastic experience for someone brought up on Manchester United as a kid. Everything was exciting about the experience, from the build up, to sitting their in the dressing room and listening to the team talk.

"Our manager, Bill Ridding, told us to make sure that our full backs covered inside, in the middle where United were most dangerous with Denis Law, Bobby Charlton and David Herd, that they were so dangerous that we shouldn't worry too much about a couple of young Northern Ireland wingers who were up against us for the first time, so unknown that our manager couldn't remember one of the winger's names. He mentioned Willie Anderson, but couldn't recall the other one, as he was so preoccupied with the threat from United coming down the middle.

"When we got onto the pitch, I was hyped up, desperate to do well as a nippy little winger out to impress, I went past the great Denis Law. He turned on me, 'Don't do that again, son!'..... he looked at me intently, 'if you do that again I will break your nose'. I went over to the ref, and complained 'did you hear that?' I thought the ref would do something about it, warn Denis, or something. Instead the ref told me, 'He was talking to you, not me, yes...'. Next time, I did it again, whizzed past Denis Law, and of course, he was true to his word, he broke my nose! There were no substitutes in those days, and we didn't even bring a doctor with us to Old Trafford, so the United club doctor, Alan Glass, came down to take a look at me. He told me I had two choices, I could grit my teeth and he would reset it there and then, and then I could go back on, or I could go to hospital. I was so desperate to keep my place in the team, and so anxious to get back on against United, that I opted to grit my teeth. The doc stuck his fingers up my nose and re set it there and then, and to this day I have the nose I was left with in that game.

"The manager came over and said; 'How are you feeling?'

"'A bit groggy but I want to go back on,' I told him.

"I was shocked when he replied, 'Maybe you shouldn't rush back on because we are 5-0 down, and it will look better if we only have 10 men!'

"I was a bit dazed and asked who had done the damage. It was George Best with two goals and he had laid the others on. The very player that the manager had not briefed us on. I came back on though, I was determined to continue playing. The next day I took my driving test. I failed. I must have looked a real state with two black eyes! It wasn't long before everyone knew the name George Best."

Rarely out of the top three from September onwards, United had vied with Leeds United and Chelsea for the title. When the Londoners imploded following an Easter Bank Holiday defeat at Blackpool, United beat Leeds at Elland Road to take pole position. A 3-1 win at home to Arsenal sealed the title. Nevertheless 1964/65 was the tightest of all 20 title successes as the top two were only separated by goal average.

The 1964/65 title-winning team seemed to be the finished article but they finished a disappointing fourth to Liverpool the following season and exited both the FA and European Cups in the semi-finals.

The season's focal point was the European Cup. United looked like hot favourites after a 5-1 thrashing of Benfica in the quarter-finals in Lisbon's Stadium of Light. George Best's contribution was such that he returned to England a hero and was quickly labelled 'The Fifth Beatle'. Yet injury and the aggressive attentions of United's semi-final opponents Partizan Belgrade saw the club miss out on the final once again.

TITLE NO. 7 - 1966-67

'I always felt we had a chance of winning the league. We had three Footballers of the Year and in Nobby a World Cup winner, the team was packed with internationals, and there was a real feeling that this was the time to win the league and go onto have good crack at winning the European Cup. It was a feeling rather than something the players talked about. We never spoke about Munich and how much it meant to the club to win the European Cup, but inwardly it was a feeling that was there with you all the time.'

ALEX STEPNEY

THE SHEER MAGNITUDE of winning the League and providing Matt Busby with the opportunity of winning the European Cup ten years after Munich has only now hit home to Alex Stepney, who lived through it but didn't quite realise the enormity of it all at the time.

Yes, of course, it was huge but the dawn of the Champions League and the manner of success in this tournament has made Stepney appreciate the way he and his team-mates fashioned such a significant piece of football history, let alone that of Manchester United.

The current generation of footballers are brought up on the excesses of the modern game and the sky-high rewards the Champions League. Back then the players basked in the glory of the FA Cup final at Wembley and the League title was the ultimate prize, European glory more remote, and they also kicked off routinely at 3 o'clock on a Saturday.

Such was Stepney's contribution to the title triumph that Matt Busby described signing him as "the single most important factor behind our championship in 1967." The highlight of Stepney's long career came a year later, when he starred in the European Cup final. His late save from Eusebio is still judged as important, if not more so, than any of the goals scored by United in the final. Not only is Stepney well placed, therefore, to assess the significance of the 1967 title year, but so sharp is his analysis that it also puts the entire campaign into historic perspective.

Stepney had heard from old friend Arthur Albiston about the task of analysing the 20 title years through the eyes of the key people who took part in each of the championships and he was eager to make his contribution.

Alex began his career as a trainee at Millwall, before moving to Chelsea for £52,000 in June 1966. But he should have been moving to West Ham, as he explains, "It was quite odd how I came about ending up at Manchester United in the first place. In fact, it was quite ironic that I did, and ended up with so much to look back on, when really I should have been playing for West Ham. It is uncanny the circumstances that brought me to Old Trafford. It was 1966 and I was leaving Millwall to join Chelsea, when, in fact, I should have been leaving Millwall to join West Ham. Ron Greenwood wanted to sign me, and I wanted to go there, and the move was going through smoothly, then Millwall sacked Billy Gray, who had won the FA Cup with Nottingham Forest in 1959 and despite taking the club through the divisions, they sacked him and in came Benny Fenton and the move to West Ham fell though. Maybe the clubs didn't like each other, maybe it was the change of manager, but whatever the reason it was called off.

"Then Tommy Docherty, the manager of Chelsea, stepped in and wanted to sign me. I wasn't so sure. Chelsea had Peter Bonetti, he was their No 1 and I wasn't going to a club where they already had a No 1. But I was told by the Doc that Chelsea planned to sell Peter Bonetti to West Ham. I wasn't convinced and I spoke to the chairman Joe Mears, who told me that it was a fact that they would be selling Peter to West Ham and I would be the No 1 goalkeeper at Chelsea. So, I signed for Chelsea believing that Peter would be signing for West Ham. Joe Mears died of a heart attack while he was away with England just before the World Cup and just as I arrived at Stamford Bridge. He was replaced by a Mr Pratt and aptly named I should say, because he refused to sanction the sale of Peter Bonetti. I ended up playing just one game for Chelsea."

After only three months at Stamford Bridge, Alex Stepney made the switch to Old Trafford, Sir Matt paying a then world record fee for a goalkeeper of £55,000. On his debut against Manchester City, he kept a clean sheet in a 1-0 victory and by the end of the season had won a League Championship medal to cap a wonderful first season. Alex takes up the story, "I played 35 games that season as we won the League without losing too many, just a couple of games, one against Aston Villa around Christmas time. In those days, of course, with two points for a win, one point for a draw, it was tight all the way through the season but eventually we overcame the challenge from Nottingham Forest. We drew at Sunderland we needed to win at West Ham to secure the league even though we had the final game left at home to Stoke. We won the League with a 6-1 win at West Ham, taking the title with a game to spare.

"I felt unbelievably proud as going back to the 50s as a kid I watched United, and my ambition was always to win the FA Cup and to play for my country, I always thought the league title was unattainable but here I was winning the title. When I joined United I realised the enormity of how much winning the League meant to the club because it meant another crack at winning the European Cup after Munich and it was felt it would be the last chance for Matt Busby. I always felt we had a chance of winning the League. We had three Footballers of the Year and in Nobby a World Cup winner, the team was packed with internationals, and there was a real feeling that this was the time to win the League and go onto have good crack at winning the European Cup. It was a feeling rather than something the players talked about. We never spoke about Munich and how much it meant to the club to win the European Cup, but inwardly it was a feeling that was there with you all the time. There was also an overwhelming feeling that existed that drove the club on to win the European Cup for Matt, Bobby Charlton and Bill Foulkes."

On that balmy May evening at Wembley, Stepney and his team mates earned immortality within the game, as well as icon status inside Manchester United, for their performance in the final to ensure United were European champions in 1968. As United and Benfica were level at 1-1, Stepney held on to a ferocious shot from Eusebio to ensure the game would go into extra-time. The additional half hour was illuminated by goals from George Best, Bobby Charlton and Brian Kidd, as the Reds ran out 4-1 winners but the importance of Stepney's save was lost on no-one. Jaime Graca had earlier equalised Charlton's headed goal to take the game into extra-time but further goals from Best, Kidd (on his 19th birthday) and Charlton gave United their first European Cup. Just ten years after Sir Matt had seen his dream team destroyed, he had performed the impossible. He was knighted soon afterwards.

Stepney recalls, "What a fantastic game, the first English side to do it. I suppose only now I look back and say to myself, 'yes, that was my greatest achievement'. I know it sounds a bit corny but there you go. I achieved the dreams I had as a kid, winning the FA Cup and playing for my country, but now looking back, it didn't compare to winning the European Cup, and I suppose it is the growth of the Champions League and how the game has developed into the direction of Europe that you now realise the importance of being the top club in Europe as opposed to being the top club in your own country.

"The other implication that has grown over the years is the importance of winning the European Cup 10 years after Munich, how much that means to everyone associated with Manchester United. I saw some of the Busby Babes and there is no doubt had they survived they were capable of winning the European Cup three or four times. For all those reasons it has been a great honour to have won the European Cup for the club."

For more than a decade Stepney proved a reliable, steady and efficient goalkeeper. He had excellent positional skills and during the club's ill-fated 1973/74 campaign was even employed as the club penalty taker. 'Big Al', as he was known, remains the club's top–scoring goalkeeper. In all he won one First Division winner's medal, an FA Cup, one Second Division winner's medal, as well as that European Cup. He joined the NASL revolution in 1978 when he signed for Dallas Tornado and later had spells as coach of Southampton, Exeter City and Manchester City.

Few are as well placed to assess United's greatest players of all time than Alex Stepney, "I have had the privilege to see George Best day in and day out, to train with him and to play in the same team, and there is no one better. He is without doubt my greatest player of all time for United. It was mind boggling to see what he was capable of doing on the training pitch and then so wonderful to see him repeat it in the matches at 3 o'clock on a Saturday, when we all played on a Saturday afternoon. To be in the same team as Denis Law and Bobby Charlton as well as Best, well, it doesn't get any better. Of the current generation my No 1 is Paul Scholes, a young guy I have seen mature and play for so long at the very top for the club. Often you are asked to compare players from different generations and it is quite hard. We played on mud heaps, now every game, every week, is played on pitches that look like Wembley. When I was growing up and watching United, Duncan Edwards was the player I admired most. Being a Londoner I had to wait for United to come to the capital and normally it would be Chelsea where I would watch them. For a man of his age, to play the way he did, Duncan Edwards is most definitely one of United's all time greats.

"I have generally gone for the British players. I am not opposed to the imports and United in particular have had some great players from abroad and we know who they are. But I am English, and I will stick with the English players, and the British players."

A series of managers tried and failed to recapture the glory of the previous era, and it was one of United's famous sons, Denis Law, who back-heeled the decisive goal for Manchester City that helped consign United to relegation to Division Two in 1974 following several seasons of decline. United bounced straight back to Division One in 1975 but were to be mainly a cup side for the next 15 years, winning the FA Cup on three occasions in 1977, 1983 and 1985. The Holy Grail for United remained the English League title and despite bringing cup success to the club, managers Tommy Docherty, Dave Sexton and Ron Atkinson all failed to mount sustained bids to win the League.

United turned to Alex Ferguson in November 1986, with his sole aim winning the League title for the first time since 1967. Ferguson was heavily backed by his board, with significant investment made for players to be recruited to ensure Manchester United could compete with Everton, Liverpool and Arsenal at the top of the First Division. Ferguson made a good start, finishing in second place in his first full season in 1987/88. The next two seasons were not as successful as United struggled at the bottom end of the First Division. Patience had worn so thin that by January 1990 it was rumoured that defeat to a strong NottinghamForest side in the 3rd Round of the FA Cup would result in Ferguson being sacked. In a watershed moment similar to Adrian Heath's goal for Everton against Oxford in 1984, Mark Robins scored the only goal for United in a game that was dominated by the hosts. United went on to win the FA Cup against Crystal Palace following a replay, when it was again rumoured that a defeat would have resulted in Ferguson being dismissed. Ferguson subsequently stayed, building upon his FA Cup success with a European Cup Winners' Cup victory the following season and they were hot favourites for the League title in 1991/92 before 'choking' at the sharp end of the season. United clearly needed something more to go that extra step to the title but in the summer of 1992, it wasn't yet clear who or what that was…

TITLE NO. 8 - 1992-93

"When I got to Old Trafford there must have been about 50 or 60 fans there, mostly youngsters, and it was good fun, but within, it seemed, a mere two minutes, there were something like 3,000 people gathered outside the ground to celebrate. Before I knew it, the fans were lifting me up in the air, then throwing me up into the air, and I was engulfed by this massive crowd."

LEE SHARPE

LEE SHARPE HAD A SPECIAL RAPPORT with the Manchester United fans to such a degree that he must be the only player ever to turn into a fan and travel far and wide to watch the team with the supporters, as well as being the only one of the players to celebrate that first League title for 26 years with the fans outside Old Trafford.

Lee also had a love-hate relationship with Sir Alex Ferguson; Sir Alex hated his swivel hip goal celebration to distraction and Lee loved to wind him up by continuing to do it every time he scored. For rebellious streaks, Lee Sharpe is up there with some of the best. Little wonder that the fans still remember the fleet footed winger/full back with such deep and everlasting affection.

Yet despite the historic significance of it, on a personal level, it wasn't the greatest season for Lee, as he confesses, "No, not massively great, I had my moments, my highs but also my lows, but what sticks in my mind was the end of the season and winning the title, and to be a part of that, was momentous for all the players concerned."

What was unusual about Lee was that he celebrated the League title success with the fans outside Old Trafford on a day when 26 years worth of frustration came to an end. Lee recalls, "Oldham had beaten Villa at Villa Park which gave us the title and I was desperate to have a celebration, I started ringing around the lads but couldn't get through to any of them. No doubt everyone was on the phone at the same time. I was around my mum and dad's and I heard that there might be something going on at Old Trafford, perhaps some of the players had decided to meet up there, I wasn't quite sure, but I thought 'let's go down to Old Trafford to find out'. When we got to Old Trafford there must have been about 50 or 60 fans there, mostly youngsters, and it was good fun but within, it seemed, minutes, there were something like 3,000 people gathered outside the ground to celebrate.

"Before I knew it, the fans were lifting me up in the air, then throwing me up into the air, and I was engulfed by this massive crowd. Security had to come to rescue me and take me into the ground, where I met up with my mum and dad, who were round at the other end of the ground for their own safety, and we were escorted to a back exit to sneak us out so we could make a hasty getaway. I found out the players had been pulling around to Steve Bruce's place for a celebration drink, but by now I'd had enough of celebrating! To this day there are fans who come up to me and tell me that they were in the crowd with me and were throwing me up in the air or witnessed it and couldn't believe it was taking place."

Lee recalls the moment that Sir Alex's leaders in the dressing room addressed the entire squad to galvanise them in the final push for the first title in 26 years. "That first League title is the one that sticks in the mind for me, especially the way we blew it the year before losing out to Leeds, which made everyone so nervous in the run in, not just the players, but you could also detect it in the manager, as everyone was so desperate to land the first time in so long a time. I am sure it is one of the reasons we blew it again and lost out to Leeds. We were all so uptight about landing that elusive title. We had about five or six games to go and it was either before or after a training session, that all the players were in the dressing rooms and 'Robbo' and Brucey had their say. 'There are big games coming up, we are close, within touching distance of winning the league, we blew it last year, but we won't blow it this year', that was the theme of their speeches, each in turn, and there was no question that this had an impact on the players.

"'Robbo' and Bruce were hugely admired and respected figures. 'Robbo' was different class and when he was in your side you knew you had a chance of winning, he did everything, a pure captain in every sense, a pure leader, a leader in everything, but because he had suffered with injuries, he wasn't playing so much, but Steve Bruce stood in as the captain. He too was a fantastic leader in the dressing room, a perfect replacement for 'Robbo' as captain, they both commanded respect, so the players listened intently about what they had to say, and they took it in. But there were other big time players, big characters in that dressing room at the time, such as Peter Schmeichel, Sparky and Brian McClair and they were all backing up what 'Robbo' and Steve had to say."

Another dressing room speech Lee recalls vividly was that of his manager in the first game following the championship win that illustrated his determination to win it again and again and again. "Sir Alex told us that we faced a different challenge, every bit as daunting as the first one, that it would be just as hard to win it again as it was to win it the first time. He then challenged all of us demanding to know that if we weren't up for that challenge, there was the door... no one stood up and walked out. It was the Rory McIlroy moment, he had blown it like we had blown it the year before allowing Leeds to win it, then he went on to win the US Open, and now our manager was making sure we all knew where we stood – win it again or we would be out of the door. However, having won it once, we were all pretty confident we could win it again, winning breeds confidence and it sure did with this group of players."

Lee can also recall another fan-related period, which would surprise most, if not, all the top Premier League stars of his day and any of the modern era. "The team were having a great run in the Cup and while I was injured, I wanted to see the game, but also wanted to travel with some of my mates who were mad United fans and it felt natural to join in with the supporters, jump up and down and celebrate with them. With my cousin Brian I travelled to Hereford to watch the team in the Cup. As a player, I could have gone into the dressing room with the rest of the squad, injured or not, but that would have meant turning up in my Manchester United suit, and I felt far more comfortable in jeans and football gear jumping around like a loon with the supporters and maybe that's why you might be right in saying I have a good rapport with the fans, as many of them might have seen all of that and it would have come as a surprise to them. I even travelled to Milan to watch the team play Inter and it was such great fun just being a supporter."

A pin-up boy of his time, Lee began his career with unfashionable Torquay. One of United's former scouts was living in retirement in Torquay and came to some of the games where he first spotted Lee, alerting Ferguson who, along with assistant manager Archie Knox, came to watch one of their matches on a Friday night. The story goes they attended in disguise to avoid being detected. After the match they took the Torquay manager, the late Cyril Knowles (a Spurs legend who had his own terrace classic 'Nice One Cyril') out for a drive and refused to leave the town until they had met the player, which happened the next morning. Lee signed from Torquay United in June 1988, aged 17.

Lee played against Newcastle at Old Trafford in the semi-finals of the Mercantile Centenary Credit Trophy on 21 September 1988, a competition to mark the Football League's 100th anniversary. The game went to extra time before United won 2-0. Three days later, Lee made his League debut in a 2-0 victory against West Ham, also at Old Trafford. But he really came to national attention in a League Cup fourth-round tie at Highbury on 28 November 1990. United beat Arsenal 6-2 and

Lee scored the only hat-trick of his United career. His favourite goal, though, was a backheel against Barcelona in the Champions League in the 1994/95 season. United were 2-1 down and the goal ensured it finished 2-2 and United's record, at that time, of having never lost at home in Europe was maintained. Paul Ince won the ball and played it to the right where Roy Keane's low cross took a deflection. The ball was going behind Lee and, as a defender slid in, he backheeled it into the bottom corner of the net.

Lee's finest moment was winning the European Cup Winners' Cup in 1991 again against Barcelona in Rotterdam. That competition was his first taste of European football, as English clubs were just back after the Heysel disaster. The stadium was three-quarters full of United fans and the atmosphere was electric.

Aston Villa fan Lee spent eight years at Old Trafford, helping the club to that first title for 26 years, the 1994 Double and that European trophy but he also suffered the lows of injury and not playing. "Of course I always look back with fondness at my time with Manchester United, there was plenty of success, breaking records; the first time winning the Double in the club's history is no mean feat, and the first European trophy since the Heysel ban. I've played alongside some unbelievable players. I had a great time. I realised the time had come to move on. I was left out for the last League game of the 1995/96 season at Middlesbrough where I wasn't even on the bench. We had clinched the title, but I was stuck in the tunnel in my United suit watching the lads celebrating on the pitch and felt really out of it and a week later we completed the Double but I felt a million miles away from the celebrations."

Lee looks back over his Old Trafford career with a deep respect for Ferguson irrespective of their remarkably tense relationship. "Even when Eric Cantona performed his infamous kung-fu kick, apart from one short comment that he shouldn't be doing that sort of thing, the manager spent much of the time bollocking all of us for a poor performance at Crystal Palace, telling us how he'd been playing rubbish. I had a bit of a difficult time with the manager, it must be said.

"He found me difficult at times, and perhaps there was a personality clash, if I was to be honest about it. Every time I scored, I would go off to do my daft dance by the corner flag, it was a bit of fun, the fans loved it and I enjoyed it. The first time I did it, the manager gave me the 'hairdryer' treatment in front of all the players, which I thought was a bit harsh. He could have let it go and called me in for a quiet word, but let rip in his usual style when we got back into the dressing room. He sure did bollock me, he called me every name under the sun but never actually gave me a reason why he objected so strongly, and I don't really know to this day, as we never actually discussed it in a calm environment at any time. Unfortunately I didn't stop with my goal celebration, and it seemed to wind him up, even though I never found out why he hated it so much. I suppose he wasn't mad at me that much, because I didn't score that many goals but I did it whenever I did score; the emotions take over at the time as it's special to get a goal in the Premier League where it means so much.

"I don't think I had a great relationship with the manager from the start, which didn't help. From the time I got to the club he was forever telling me to settle down and get married. I was only a kid, about 18 or 19, and my girl friend from my school days moved up from Birmingham and the manager agreed that I could move out of digs and into a house with my girl friend, but he warned me that the first sign of a dip in my form and he would have me back in the digs. Six months later I was playing really badly. That was it. He kicked me out of my house, and put me back in digs. I had to send the girlfriend home, yet every week he kept on at me about settling down and getting married and I told him, 'How am I expected to get married when you send my girlfriend home?' But he was adamant that he wanted me to have a wife and family and settle down. He didn't like a lot of the things I did. I would go out after a game with Pally and Roy Keane for a drink and he wasn't very keen on that. He kept on asking me why I couldn't go home and have a drink, rather than out on the town. But it wasn't as if we stayed out until two in the morning and got smashed, we had a few beers and went home at a reasonable time. We were all single lads at the time and it would be pretty sad to be sitting home together having a beer on a Saturday night. My best friend was initially Ryan Giggs, and latterly Roy Keane, Gary Pallister and Dion Dublin. We were always a close-knit group and a lot of the players would socialise, going out for meals with wives and girlfriends. But I am sure that's all forgotten with Sir Alex, he says 'hello' and I seem to get on well with him now."

Given his comments already about the influence of Bryan Robson, it is no surprise that United's Captain Marvel is listed among Lee's all time greatest United players. "I was too young to have watched George Best, but from what you see on TV, he was awesome. When I first got into the team, Paul McGrath, Gordon Strachan and Jesper Olsen were the players who made the biggest impression one me. Bryan Robson was simply outstanding in everything he did, he bossed everything including the referee and linesmen. Bryan Robson was an unbelievable captain, leader and person, as well as being the complete all-round player. If I was ever in trouble, you could guarantee he would never be more than three yards away to help out. He could create goals, score and was the boss on the pitch, controlling everything.

"Mark Hughes was one of the giants of the game who I played alongside, while Eric Cantona on his day was the best. Scholes, Beckham, Butt and the Nevilles were great youngsters coming through to provide the bedrock of teams to come for years, while Ryan Giggs is an absolute legend. When you look back you cannot ignore either the likes of Roy Keane, Paul Ince, Bruce, Pallister, Schmiechel, the players in the team that won the titles, one of the toughest group of players you are likely to come across. There was only Giggs, Andrei Kanchelskis and myself who couldn't kick any one up in the air, but the rest made up for it, there was a special bond between the players, a tremendous team spirit at that time."

Lee specialises in TV punditry in England, the Middle East and Far East. He also does after-dinner speaking, has a few other business interests and has his own charity, the Lee Sharpe Foundation to raise money for underprivileged kids in South Africa and also for children suffering from cancer and diabetes in Manchester.

Ryan Giggs personally savoured all 12 of United's Premier League titles, to rightly earn the tag of the most successful player in football history. Giggs agreed with Pallister that the most important championship triumph in United's trophy-laden era was the first one. As the evergreen 37 year-old told me, "To overhaul Liverpool is an incredible achievement by the players and further testament, if any was needed, to what a great manager Sir Alex Ferguson is. But I still think the first title in 1993 had more significance. To wait 26 years to win it was far too long for a club like United, and there was no doubt the pressure to secure it was unbearable at times and became a millstone around the players' necks. I think your first title is always special, it certainly was for me. I had grown up watching the great Liverpool sides dominate domestic and European football in the 70s and 80s. Despite all the rivalry between the two clubs you couldn't argue with their success. At the time no-one could live with them."

United's breakthrough in 1993 came a year after they had blown up in the final furlong and seen Leeds steal the 1992 crown – the last season of a 92 club Football League before the formation of the soon to become mighty Premier League.

Giggs never contemplated the success he enjoyed with United over the past 18 years, "After winning the first title there was a great sense of relief as if an enormous amount of pressure had been lifted. But at the time I never imagined what was to come. I just don't think you look that far ahead. Naturally you are hungry for more success but if someone had said to me you will eventually surpass the achievements of Liverpool I would have probably burst out laughing. It had taken the club 26 years to win their first title, so to go on and win another 11 and overtake Liverpool was not something you even think about in reality. The desire, ambition and determination to build on the success after the first title was always present. And I genuinely felt that after we got the first one out of the way winning the next one would come with less pressure."

Giggs has broken individual and collective records for United and played in great teams blessed with world–class players. Does one United side stand out above all others? "It's hard to compare them," he said diplomatically, "there are all sorts of arguments you could put forward for the merits of certain squads and the success they achieved. Each one was unique and special in its own right. I'm just grateful and fortunate I got to play in all of them."

Arthur Albiston played for United for 14 years without ever winning a title but the full back has nothing but admiration for Giggs and his achievements. Albiston now runs the United legends team and in an interview for '20|13', eulogised about the accomplishments of Giggs. "In my time we came close a couple of times, in fact, I once recall it went to the last game [in 1979/80] and we had to win at Leeds, never easy, and Liverpool had to lose at home to Villa, but it didn't happen, but for me the big breakthrough year, 1993, was the vital one, as it gave everyone belief that they could go on an do it again.

"When I stopped playing in the mid 90s, I went into radio and was fortunate to be able to watch the batch of youngsters coming into the side; Beckham, Scholes, the Neville brothers and watching them play has been a pleasure. You can talk about the great players down the years, the goalkeepers like Schmeichel and some wonderful goalscorers, but the player that stands out for me is Ryan Giggs. The amount of games, the amount of medals and to be at the top for so long, it just will not happen again in my lifetime, if ever. Twenty years at the top is just incredible.

"Of course you can pick out more skilful players like Ronaldo, but for me the players I have most admired are Denis Irwin, whom Sir Alex once said, pound for pound was the best signing he had ever made. Again, like Giggs, he played a huge amount of games and won so many trophies, and he scored a few goals as well, and could show David Beckham a thing or two about taking free kicks. Beckham was a fantastic footballer and goalscorers like Ruud Van Nistelrooy were outstanding while Ronaldo was eye catching and scored so many goals, but for me a player like Paul Scholes epitomises Manchester United.

"Of course players were bought in like Roy Keane, but there are so many home grown talents. Roy would be among my all time favourites, a fantastic leader, like the Bryan Robson of my time, and I count myself fortunate to have played alongside Bryan for so many years, but Giggs comes out on top for me, the way he has adapted to the modern game, from a flying young winger with long hair to a midfield player or someone who slots in behind the main striker. He is someone for young kids to look up to in the way he has handles himself, although a lot is down to his manager who shielded him for the first four or five years from the harsh realities of the media, until such time as he gained confidence, as Sir Alex didn't want him exposed to being labelled the next George Best." Of course the media intrusion, ironically, caught up with Giggs at the tail end of his career, but that is another issue for another time.

The dawn of the 1990s was a different era altogether when footballers were not quite yet at the level they are now, in terms of wages and celebrity status, although not far short. It saw Ferguson collecting his first silverware as United manager and Liverpool winning their last League Championship with an ageing team. The tide was turning.

Ferguson's first silverware came in that 1990 FA Cup Final following a fortuitous 3-3 draw with Crystal Palace in the first game. United had struggled in the League that term and lifting the Cup at Wembley that Thursday evening probably saved the Scot his job. At the time it seemed to be a blessing in its own right but as history now shows, Lee Martin's winning goal against Palace was the springboard for an explosion of unprecedented success.

Victory at Wembley allowed United to make a return to European competition after an absence of five years and they went all the way to the final of the European Cup Winners' Cup in Rotterdam where their opponents were Barcelona, the former club of United striker Mark Hughes. Two goals by Hughes sealed the match 2-1 in Fergie's favour, United's first European success in 23 years. It was an occasion that Garth Crooks picked out as one of the highlights that he looks back on, in the transformation of United, and the emergence of Hughes, "Hughes goal and that win in Europe was something special and marked the emergence of United as a real force again."

The other long wait, for that elusive League Championship, very nearly ended in April 1992. The Reds had already won Fergie's third trophy in March, the League Cup, and were in a two-horse race with Leeds. Liverpool were out of the running but they still had a say in the destiny of the title, beating United 2-0 at Anfield to ruin their challenge. The 1991/92 title is remembered as the title that United lost, rather than one that Leeds actually won.

By the start of the following season it was clear that Leeds' championship was a flash in the pan and their star quality was further reduced when they allowed one of their best players to join United in December 1992. Up until that point United had started the new season just as they had finished the last. While the defence was in decent shape, they struggled to score goals. Following failed summer bids for Alan Shearer and David Hirst, Ferguson had bought Dion Dublin. Unfortunately Dion broke his leg in an early away game at Southampton and the club was back to square one. Their form through autumn was disappointing and United were tenth, eight points off the lead by early November following defeat at Ron Atkinson's Aston Villa. The signing of Eric Cantona proved to be the steal of the century. The Frenchman brought that little bit of magic and arrogance that had been missing from United's previous campaigns and was an instant hit, scoring nine goals to help the Reds win their first title in 26 years. United lost only two more games all season as they took the inaugural Premier League crown ahead of Big Ron's men.

A key moment was Steve Bruce's two critical late, late goals (a pair of towering headers) against Sheffield Wednesday deep into injury time. On one of the most memorable days Old Trafford has ever seen (April 10th 1993) Bruce's double edged the Reds ever closer to a first title triumph under Sir Alex, whose on-pitch celebration with assistant Brian Kidd will live long in the memory.

Sir Alex was on the golf course when United were officially confirmed as inaugural FA Premier League champions following Oldham's 1-0 win over United's closest challengers Aston Villa at Villa Park on May 2nd. Cue the famous player party at Steve Bruce's gaff. Mark Hughes top scored with 15 league goals. At the time Sir Alex said, "The players knew they were the best and for the most part of the season they demonstrated it where it mattered, on the pitch."

According to the now Sunderland manager, Steve Bruce, the first title in 26 years really got the ball rolling for United's dominance of the modern game and all the players knew the significance of winning the clubs 'Holy Grail', turning them from Cup specialists into real Champions. Bruce holds United in such high esteem and speaks with enormous sincerity and emotion about his near 10 years at Old Trafford; "I am sure it is true for all the United players at that time, we were all aware the club hadn't won the League for more than 20 odd years and that United were a great Cup side of the 80s but that the Holy Grail was the League.

"To kick Liverpool off their perch was the remit of the manager, it was the remit of the players, that was the big thing inside the club, and it all has come about since that day we finally won the League title for the first time in 26 years. So, arguably that has to be the most important for me and for the club.   The year before that we blamed the Football League for forcing us to play four games in eight days at the end of the season. But by Christmas we had won it and then we let it slip and we ended up being pipped by Leeds. In all honesty we can make excuses about the deluge of games at the end, but the truth is that we choked, we bottled it, it caught up with us and we didn't cope. That made it all the sweeter when we won the title and that first title was without doubt the most memorable moment of my career. It had been a gradual process, winning the FA Cup and then the Cup Winners' Cup against Barcelona."

TITLE NO. 9 - 1993-94

"We achieved immortality winning that first title... but it wasn't good enough... Ferguson told us that winning one title was not good enough for a club like this and that really we had not done anything unless we go on and retain the title and prove we are worthy champions. He went further and made it clear that he would not tolerate any player sitting back and feeling content with themselves."

PAUL PARKER

PAUL PARKER IS ONE of the most articulate and bright ex-footballers you are likely to come across, so his choice of language is always something worth valuing. When he chose the word 'immortality' to describe the player's value to themselves and to others in delivering the Premier League title in 1993, it was not chosen at random, it was a careful analysis of the worth of the feat of those players.

But for Alex Ferguson that first trophy in 26 years was not good enough. Not good enough by a long way. He demanded more, and the following season he got more. The club's first ever Double; retaining the League at a canter and a 4-0 win over Chelsea at Wembley to land the FA Cup with two Eric Cantona penalties.

The importance of the first League trophy in 26 years, though, was a springboard to go on to win the title again and again, and the defender who joined Manchester United in August

1991 for £1.7 million from Queens Park Rangers in search of cups and glory and who ended up with three titles, reveals the challenge Alex Ferguson threw down to all the players as they set out to win more and more League titles on the back of the first for 26 years.

Parker told me, "I won three titles in my time at Old Trafford and naturally the first was the most important. The previous season we had come close but lost out to Leeds but my next season was just fantastic, winning that first title having come so close the year before and winning the first ever Premier League title. Of course, we could have won the last Football League title, but that might have taken the shine off the first Premier League title, somehow. The fact that it was the first Premier League title, the fact that it was United's first title for 26 years, every player achieved more than just silverware, they achieved immortality."

Parker made his debut in a 2-0 home win against Notts County on 17th August 1991 and remained in the side for the opening seven league fixtures during which time the team only conceded two goals. However, just as he was settling in, he was injured and missed over six weeks of action. He returned to the first team in a 3-2 defeat at Sheffield Wednesday and later that season picked up a League Cup Winner's medal following a 1-0 win over Nottingham Forest in the final. United looked favourites for the title with four games remaining, however injury again cost them the services of the highly influential Parker and the side lost three consecutive games to hand the title to Leeds United.

Parker returned to League action in October 1992 and soon re-established himself. Having come so close the previous season, United didn't make the same mistakes again and romped to their first Championship for 26 years. In the process, Parker scored his first goal for the club with the final effort in a 4-1 win against Spurs on 9th January 1993.

He was the final piece in the defence that gave United the platform for Premiership glory and his contribution was significant in laying the foundations for the success that has followed. Parker remained injury-free for the following season as

United retained their title and reached both domestic cup finals. A 3-1 defeat to Aston Villa in the League Cup was countered by a 4-0 victory in the FA Cup Final against Chelsea as United won their first ever 'double'.

The team virtually picked itself en route to an historic League and FA Cup Double, with Eric Cantona sporting the number seven shirt that had been Bryan Robson's property for so long. United were rapidly out of the blocks winning 14 of their first 15 games. And, despite a slight stumble that saw rivals Blackburn draw level, United romped to the title with an eight point advantage over Kenny Dalglish's men. With Cantona in his pomp, United then charged to the FA Cup semi-final against Oldham. Deep into extra-time and with the Latics leading 1-0, an incredible off-balance volley from Mark Hughes earned United a replay. The Reds then stormed to a 4-0 win at Maine Road to reach Wembley. The same scoreline saw United defeat Chelsea in the final to become only the third club in the 20th century to complete The Double.

"After winning that first title for so long, Ferguson was far from content, and he told us all soon after landing that title that he expected everyone one of us to be even hungrier to win it again and again," Paul recalls, "He repeated this challenge before the start of the new season. It was clear that he was not happy just winning one title. He told us that winning one title was not good enough for a club like this, and that really we had not done anything unless we go on and retain the title and prove we are worthy champions. He went further and made it clear that he would not tolerate any player sitting back and feeling content with themselves. He was putting more pressure on us. He wanted that type of mentality from his players, in fact he was demanding it.

"I liked that attitude. I had come to United to win trophies, suspecting that it might be cups rather than titles and United had come close in the past but seemed to lack an edge in the title race. I had reached a World Cup semi-final but had not won anything in my career, and the reason for my move from Rangers to Manchester United was to go in search of cups, but ended up runners-up in my first season and winning the title in my second. Retaining the title in my third season was another great achievement."

Injury plagued the final two years of Paul's United career as he played only a handful of games. He made his final appearance in a 3-0 win against Reading in the FA Cup on 27th January 1996, scoring his second goal for the club as a parting gift. He left on a free transfer in the summer of 1996. "I loved every minute of my five years at the club from 1991 to 1996, and my only regret was that it wasn't long enough. The only thing I didn't like about my time there was leaving. I would have wished for a much longer time there, if only that had been possible. I still have a real fondness for the club, I still go there whenever I can, although at the moment I am living in Singapore but I value the time I can spend at Old Trafford, whether it is doing some work for MUTV or the corporate side for the club.

"I love popping my head into the dressing room and heading off round the corner for a pre-match coffee with Sir Alex. He must like me because he never tells me to get lost! But I also know never to trouble him before a really big match, a game against Liverpool or a Champions League tie, I know him well enough not to do that. That's Sir Alex, and Manchester United. They have a manger still totally focused after all of these years and never one to sit back and enjoy his time, instead he wants to go further, win more."

Parker, though, has felt the wrath of Sir Alex. Well, everyone has. Has anyone actually escaped the infamous 'hairdryer'? I doubt it. Parker recalls, "I get on fine with Sir Alex, always have done, and I love the fellow, because you know precisely where you stand with him. He doesn't bear any grudges. You know when to speak up and when not to, you also know if he tells you what he thinks, he won't hold it against you.

"I did fall foul of Sir Alex once during my time at Old Trafford. We were playing a testimonial match against Celtic for Paul McStay, and he came into the hotel and found us up a bit too late after the game, but I thought it being a testimonial, it would be alright, but he fined us and I had the hump. I got the hairdryer treatment a few times as well. But when he is sounding off about your performance or the team's performance it is wise to listen rather than answer back. If you think you have a point to make, it is best made in private rather than in front of the rest of the team when he is sounding off, that never pays. If you go into his office to make your point, nine times out of ten, you will leave wishing you hadn't bothered, as he was invariably proved right. He would produce a video of your performance to prove his point (these days it would be a DVD!). You walk out of his office, though with a smile on your face, because he was very rarely wrong. If he was wrong, he would hold his hands up, and he would be the first to apologise. But you didn't go around shouting the odds that you had got the better of the Boss because he was wrong and I was right, that was not the way things were done at the club, everything was kept under control with Sir Alex."

When it comes to the tough task of selecting his all-time United favourites Parker has his own style of setting aside the players of his own personal choice. Firstly, he selects his contemporaries, explaining, "I would go with the players I played with, first of all, I suppose because you know and appreciate their worth more than anyone else. For that reason 'Robbo' is my No 1. When you walk out onto the Old Trafford pitch or behind him when he was leading out the England team, you never felt you would end up on the losing side. Steve Bruce was another in the same mould. Everything about Steve Bruce smacked of a player who relied on his physical attributes but you didn't realise just how good a footballer he was until you played with him, and that was my conclusion once I joined Manchester United, having played against him, and now was playing with him. You just did not appreciate how good he was on the ball, how good a footballer he was. I would go so far as to say I have not seen any better than Steve Bruce when it comes to a defender's ability on the ball. Denis Irwin was another who has not got the big name status but who was one of the best and most consistent players of his generation. In my book he was the best full back around for the past 20 years, without a shadow of a doubt. Ashley Cole is nowhere near as good. I know I am good mates with Denis, and I suppose people might say, 'well, he would say that wouldn't he?' I would say it, if I was his worst enemy. Denis was the complete full back, by comparison Ashley Cole has his weaknesses. Denis had no weaknesses, he could play on either flank, he was brave, tough, much tougher than he looked, he could score goals and had a wicked free kick, only losing out as the free kick taker when Eric Cantona came along.

"So many big names can be thrown up when discussing United's greatest ever players, and so many go for the obvious such as Eric Cantona, and who could blame them, as he was such a wonderfully gifted player. I just look at it differently when it comes to putting down my own favourites. Outside of those I played with, the United players I grew up watching and admiring would be the ones I would pick out, such as the Greenhoff brothers, those are the players I remember with most personal satisfaction, Jimmy Greenhoff was a wonderful centre forward to watch, Lou Macari was another I enjoyed watching, Arthur Albiston was a very, very good full back; United were the club I watched as a kid and always wanted to play for."

Steve Bruce is often asked about his best ever United ream. He has no doubts that the Team of '94 was the best. 1994 was the season the club mourned Sir Matt Busby's passing, United not only retained their Championship crown but went one better by completing the domestic double. Eric Cantona collected 18 league goals. Returning from a five-match ban, Cantona made his mark for all the right reasons as he fired the Reds to a crucial derby victory over City on April 23 with a calmly taken first half brace. United's victory at Ipswich on May 1st coupled with Blackburn's defeat to Coventry over the same weekend ensured back-to-back titles for the Reds. Sir Alex said at the time, "Winning the double was a fitting tribute to Sir Matt. We did it by playing the game in a way of which he would have wholeheartedly approved."

The former United captain recalls, "I am, of course, asked all the time to pick my best United team, and it's so hard, so many great players. My favourites players would have to be "Robbo" and Cantona. "Robbo" is the sort that any team would want him, he was such a great captain, such a great leader, such a great player. Eric brought something to the team just at the right time, a touch of arrogance, something that was missing, he was our missing link. How can you ignore footballing geniuses such as Law, Best and Charlton, when you look at that era they were truly remarkable players, all three of them. When you walk into Old Trafford you are in awe of the place when you think of such great players, the whole place is steeped in such traditions. Since the war, the club has been synonymous with entertaining football and how to win football matches.

"As for the best team, well, I can see that team now, Mark Hughes and Eric Cantona up front, Andrei Kanchelskis on one wing, Ryan Giggs on the other, Paul Ince and Roy Keane in the middle of midfield, and myself and Gary Pallister at central defence with the finest pair of full backs you are ever likely to come across in Paul Parker and Denis Irwin, and with Peter Schmeichel in goal. What a shame that we didn't play together for that long. After we beat Chelsea in the Cup Final to win the Double, Paul Parker didn't play a lot after that, in '95 Kanchelskis left, along with Ince and Hughes, I left in '96 and Robbo had already gone too. That's the beauty of Alex Ferguson, when one team comes to a natural end he builds another one. Everyone said he was bonkers to put the kids in when we lost so many experienced players, but it turned out to be a master stroke."

★

By the end of the season, Cantona was at the height of his powers, but his 1994-95 season was cut short by his king-fu kick at a Palace fan. Cantona gravely told a news conference that "when the seagulls follow the trawler, it is because they think sardines will be thrown into the sea". An official at the club disclosed that far from having a deep philosophical meaning, the quotation had a more humble origin.

The infamous incident had occured after Eric was sent off in a game against Crystal Palace. He lost control of his emotions as he walked to the dressing room and launched a martial arts–style kick at a fan he alleged had verbally abused him. Sentenced to 100 hours' community service for assault, Cantona's actions made worldwide headlines. But his only comment to the press after his conviction was that one sentence.

Many believed it was the work of a little known French philosopher; others thought that Cantona had shown himself as a deep and enigmatic thinker. But Michael Kelly, the former head of security at Manchester United revealed, seven years later, that the quotation had been assembled by a number of people including Cantona in a London hotel room.

Mr Kelly, Eric's bodyguard, was asked by Cantona and his agent for another word for fishing boat – hence trawler. He was also asked what small fish were called. His response was "sardines", and so the phrase "When the seagulls follow the trawler, it is because they think sardines will be thrown into the sea" was born.

Cantona's eight-month absence after January 1995, following his clash with a fan at Crystal Palace, proved to be United's undoing as they tried to defend their Double. They lost the title by a point to Blackburn Rovers and then lost the FA Cup final by a single goal to Everton. The former champions were hampered at Wembley by an injury to Steve Bruce, the brave captain who was a defensive rock in the early 1990s.

TITLE NO. 10 - 1995-96

*"Eric Cantona transformed Manchester United at the time. It was a
privilege and a pleasure to play alongside him, and appreciate what
he has done in football and for Manchester United."*

DAVID MAY

IT WAS THE SEASON an Eric Cantona–inspired Manchester
United proved you can win things with kids as the Reds
stormed to another double triumph. And didn't United love
it! Kevin Keegan's infamous 'I'd love it if we beat them' rant has
become part of football folklore as United completed a second
double with a young David Beckham coming to the fore, Eric
Cantona top scoring with 14 league goals, most of them 'winners'.

The turning point came on 4th March - having been 12
points behind leaders Newcastle United at one stage, the Reds
cut the lead to a single point thanks to Cantona's winner at
St James' Park on a night when Peter Schmeichel was simply
unbeatable. A series of single goal victories over Arsenal, Spurs,
Manchester City, Coventry and Leeds powered United to the top
as the Magpies faded.

One game summed up the manner of Newcastle's implosion.
On 3 April 1996 Newcastle lost 4–3 at Liverpool in one of the
most thrilling games played in the Premier League. The lead
changed four times, Newcastle were ahead 3–2 with 22 minutes
to go but were undone by a 90th-minute Stan Collymore

winner. The drama certainly got to Keegan as he slumped over Anfield's advertising hoardings after defeat. Meanwhile United ground out result after result, relying on inspirations Cantona and Schmeichel.

A last-day 3-0 victory, on May 5, at a canter, away to Middlesbrough confirmed the Reds as champions for a third time in four years leaving Sir Alex to comment, "Some pundits suggested we couldn't win the title with kids but they reckoned without the force of a rejuvenated Eric Cantona and the respect and admiration our 'kids' have for him as a footballer."

David May's medals for 1996 and 1997 are in the bank, safe and sound. "I treasure those medals," he announces with utter sincerity in this interview for '20|13', "I scored the first goal at Boro when we won the title in 1996. The whole day was something to remember for the rest of your life, all the build up, going there in anticipation of winning a game that can land the title. Scoring the first goal in the 3-0 win, and knowing you are the best team that year and no one could argue with that, those are the memories to carry around, I don't need to carry around the medal, that's in the bank.

"It was the year that Kevin Keegan was sounding off about loving it if he could beat us to the title, and the year Alan Hansen was sounding off about never winning anything with kids. I had missed out on the title the year before with Blackburn as I had left for United and that made me even more determined to win my first title with United and in the year that I was just establishing myself in the side, that first League medal was simply fantastic, there is no ample way of describing it, as it meant so much to me and to all the players. It was great travelling back down the A19 and A1 with all the lads signing their songs, and enjoying a few beers together, the likes of the Nevilles, Scholes, Butt, and also David Beckham's first season, and there was Eric Cantona singing with the rest of us and enjoying a beer with the rest of us."

David May eulogises about Cantona's influence on the field. For the man with a knack of getting in the picture himself, he paints a fascinating picture of the real Cantona off the field, much removed from the popular image of the aloof Frenchman. May makes clear that although he might have appeared to be full of arrogance and swagger behind the scenes his team mate's knew a man who just wanted to be one of the lads. "Eric Cantona transformed Manchester United at the time. It was a privilege and a pleasure to play alongside him and appreciate what he has done in football and for Manchester United. What he did on the field was absolute different class. He would always give you that extra bit of class that you needed at the time to turn a game. In 1996 and indeed the following year I cannot remember how many goals he scored but his contribution was immense.

"Of the field, he was equally surprising. He was a good lad...one of the lads. At the club's Christmas dinner and the club's parties with the wives and girlfriends, he was dancing away, having a few beers, I could see another side to him that I never expected to see. If we went out after training, after a game, he would also want to come along, always join us in a few beers. He would have a beer and enjoy the crack, and not a lot of people would have expected that of him but he was also a very funny guy, who enjoyed our company and loved to have a laugh. He was also a gentleman, nothing pretentious about him, he was not a Prima Donna, quite the reverse, in fact, he was the first in for training and the last out, a great example to all of us, especially all the young kids there at the time. Yes, he was just a decent bloke, and I am really glad to see that he is back in the game with New York Cosmos, football needs characters like him."

Needless to say, David May selects Eric Cantona among his all time Manchester United players, while also selecting Bryan Robson, "you looked to him as a player to inspire and he was an inspiration, not just on the pitch, but he was a mentor to the young players, and a truly great leader as captain of the team." His other choice will come as a surprise – Kevin Moran. "I played alongside him at Blackburn, and he taught me so much as a young kid coming through, that I owe him so much, as he was such a massive influence in my development as a player, and also when I joined United."

1995-96

David only appeared in seven matches of the 1999 Treble-winning campaign, yet his instantly recognisable blond hair and film star like features are prominent in all the celebration photographs around Old Trafford and Carrington of the Premiership title, Champions League and FA Cup triumphs. His dad had advised him "Get yourself in the pictures so nobody ever forgets you!" It was an instruction he took on board and has not regretted. He grabbed a chair on the winner's podium in the Nou Camp on that famous European Cup winning evening to ensure he was behind the huge trophy as it was lifted up for the world's photographers. "Yes, my dad did say that a couple of times", says David, "I always got myself near the trophy, that was the key, if you are by the trophy, you are guaranteed to be in the pictures and that is something to look back on for the rest of your life. Looking back on so much of Manchester United's history when you look at those pictures, you look at the changing hairstyles, but you look first and foremost for the trophy, and where you see the trophy, you will see me!"

However, David would swap his Champions League medal for a third title medal, having collected two, but missed out on a medal in the 1999 Treble Year. For the central defender the highlight of his Old Trafford career were his championship medals in 1996 and 1997 but not the 1999 treble year as he explains, "The club secretary then promised me it would be alright, that I would get a medal, but I never did. I would have loved to have got that medal. I believe I warranted the medal and I blame the FA for this as they insist that you have to play a certain number of games. But that isn't right. If you play one game you deserve a medal. Even in one game you might have helped the likes of Ryan Giggs or Paul Scholes get their hands on the title and their hands on a winner's medal. If you play five, six or even eight times and miss out on a medal, I don't see that as being fair if you've helped the Rooneys of this world in some way, you deserve your recognition."

David signed for Manchester United in July 1994 and stayed for nine years. May finally managed to establish himself in the team towards the end of the 1995–96 season. He was also in the starting line-up for the 1996 FA Cup Final victory over Liverpool. Oldham born David May was one of Old Trafford's true dressing room characters from the 90s. He says, "When I first arrived we won the Charity Shield and I was chuffed to bits because I hadn't won anything in the game. The lads thought it was nothing much, but for me, it was great. But there was much more to come in the first four or five years, but then I suffered quite a few injuries and the club signed Jaap Stam, then Henning Berg, and finally Rio Ferdinand, so I didn't play much in the last two or three years."

United won the championship at the Riverside, a special occasion for Gary Pallister. Born on the Kent coast in Ramsgate in June 1965, Gary grew up on Teesside and started his career with non-league Billingham Town and joined the Reds from his boyhood heroes Middlesbrough for £2.3 million in August 1989, then a record fee for a British defender, it was fitting that he should help United land the title back at Boro. Pallister was given a weight-training regime to bulk his skinny body up at the outset of his career but when he joined United it was one of the most significant signings for Ferguson and his quest for titles. The 13th-placed finish of his first season was followed by a remarkable run in which United finished outside the top two just once in the next eight campaigns.

"That was a bit special as I had started my professional career there," Gary explains, "I received a standing ovation from the Boro crowd, and I wasn't expecting that as I was expecting a little bit of stick, to tell you the truth, because of the way I had left the club. Winning the title there, and the reception I got felt like redemption, it felt good, it felt like forgiveness by the Boro crowd, it felt as if they were proud that one of their own was picking up the title. That for me was one of the most memorable moments of my Manchester United career.

"It was also another Double, and it certainly answered Alan Hansen's 'you won't win anything with kids' dig at us. It was true that for a couple of years we had played quite a few of the club's kids and usually it would take time for them to bed in as you would think they might fall a little short to start with. Instead they showed not only their abilities but also their mental strength to go and win the title, and there was no doubt that the team had such exciting young talent at that time."

After nine years at Old Trafford and 317 league appearances and a further title success in 1997 following Bruce's departure, Pallister's career went full circle, leaving United to return to the north-east with Premiership new boys Boro for £2.5 million in the summer of 1998. All that success, and a £200,000 profit! He is still a regular face at Old Trafford, popping up on MUTV as a pundit.

Steve Bruce missed the FA Cup final. Liverpool stood between United and a first-ever 'Double Double' and were holding out for extra-time when who else but Eric Cantona struck home a sublime shot in the 86th minute. United became the first team in the 20th century to secure two doubles.

TITLE NO. 11 - 1996-97

"I am not sure if I was supposed to be Dolly or Daisy, but neither are flattering. The only way to find out is to ask Fergie, he knows everything!"

GARY PALLISTER

THERE ARE CERTAIN Manchester United stars synonymous with the 20 titles. Certainly in that group of years 1993, 1994, 1996 and 1997 two players in particular stand out. Gary Pallister and Steve Bruce were referred to as 'Dolly and Daisy'. They are among that special elite group of title winning players who were at the heart of so much championship success. But which one was Dolly and which one was Daisy? It remains a mystery to this day. So to find out I tracked them both down, which was not really that tough assignment as I have known the pair for many years.

Gary Pallister and Steve Bruce were as solid a centre half partnership as it was possible to find. But they were not only known as 'Dolly and Daisy' as Pallister, that towering 6ft 4in giant told me, they were also known as 'that couple of old hens' and 'the sweetie wives'.

Pallister, who possessed real pace for such a big defender, formed half of "arguably the greatest central defensive partnership the club has known", according to United's own web site. The central defenders enjoyed a remarkable partnership in seven glory filled seasons together. Their rock-like presence yielded three Premiership titles (1993, 1994, 1996), two runners-up spots, the 1991 European Cup-Winner's Cup and Super Cup, three FA Cups (1990, 1994, 1996) and the League Cup of 1992.

By 1997 Bruce had departed after a hat-trick of titles but Pallister remained for one more title medal. The turning point of this season came on 19th April with two Pallister headers and another goal from Andy Cole thanks to some famous 'Calamity James' goalkeeping at Anfield. Just 24 hours after drawing 3-3 at home to Middlesbrough, the Reds were confirmed as champions on May 6 after Newcastle's goalless draw at West Ham and Liverpool's 2-1 defeat at Wimbledon.

So, to clear it up once and for all, which one is Dolly, which one is Daisy? "Sorry, I cannot answer that!" Pally told me, "I am not sure if I was supposed to be Dolly or Daisy, but neither are flattering. The only way to find out is to ask Fergie, he knows everything! Steve Bruce just came out with it, a flippant comment, but he also called us the sweetie wives and a couple of old hens. It popped out during an interview and stuck, it was a label that we have been lumbered with."

Pallister's brace of headers against Liverpool at Anfield all but clinched the 1997 title and burns brightly in any self-respecting Red's memory bank. It was a tumultuous season, make no mistake. United retained their title, David Beckham was voted Young Player of the Year, and Eric Cantona stunned the footballing world by quitting the game at the end of the season. For Pallister, it was a major final input at Anfield to enable him to clinch his personal accomplishment of a fourth title.

On the serious issue of Pally's four titles, he singles out the first one. "1993 was the special one, because the club had gone so long without winning a title. That was the one that mattered, it brought a huge sigh of relief over Old Trafford. Twenty-six years. It was a long wait for that title. That's why I enjoyed the first one the best, after 26 years of frustration and I also had the previous four years of frustration with United chasing the holy grail. It was especially pleasing having been denied the title the year before when Leeds won it. Nothing against Leeds, I might add, but we felt it was the FA screwing us up by making us play five matches in ten days in that title run in. It was unheard of. We played Thursday, Saturday, Monday, Wednesday, Sunday, it was ridiculous. Worse still we were labelled, totally unfairly, bottlers, that we didn't have the nerve to win it. So when it came we were all bursting with pride, it was a mixture of relief, pride, a real mixture of emotions.

"The best part came when we walked out against Blackburn Rovers having already been handed the title by virtue of Villa being beaten the day before at Oldham, which gave us the title. It was an unbelievable atmosphere. There are two such games where the atmosphere was really special in my entire time at Old Trafford, One was the Blackburn game when we finally received the title, and the day we played at Everton after Sir Matt Busby died and the piper led the two teams out – there were powerful vibes around the ground both times although for vastly different reasons when we walked out against Blackburn knowing we would receive the trophy that day. We felt justified in winning the title after what had happened to us the year before."

Pally was the backbone of an imposing backline, in which he was a permanent fixture, missing just one league game between 1992 and 1995, and this proved a cornerstone of United's success in this era. He was voted PFA Player of the Year in 1992 and was unlucky not to win more than 22 England caps.

Steve Bruce has no inhibitions in praising Pallister for being such a wonderful centre half partner, even though, Sir Alex once said that, pound for pound, as a £850,000 buy from Norwich two weeks short of his 27th birthday in December 1987, he was one of the best deals Manchester United have ever done.

The current Sunderland boss has the looks of a battling centre half – his broken nose hinting at an uncompromising style. The craggy defender feels his 'opposites attract' partnership with Pallister just clicked. "We were totally different types of players, but we got on very well socially, and still do to this very day. Although we are two different characters, they say opposites attract, and that's what happened here. Maybe not a lot of people appreciate that we missed only around three or four games between us in four seasons, we played week-in-and-week-out, others were getting the odd rest here and there bar me and him, instead we played on and on. If nothing else, that constant playing together breeds a partnership. I was lucky to have played alongside someone as good as Gary Pallister, that was my good fortune, he was a wonderful, wonderful centre half."

Remarkably, for all his honours at Old Trafford, Bruce was never selected for a full England cap, though he did lead the side at 'B' level. When I mentioned Sir Alex's tribute to him about being pound for pound the bet ever buy for the club, he responded, "Coming form Sir Alex that is a compliment indeed. All I can say is that I enjoyed a wonderful nine and a half years at the club. It is a fantastic club and I consider myself fortunate to have played for such a big club, fortunate to have got there at all, when you consider that the club were linked with some of the best centre halves around at the time, and I thought at any minute they were going to buy either Terry Butcher, Mark Wright, Alex McLeish or Willie Miller, but instead they bought me. And, of course, I ended up as captain when Bryan Robson left, and that is the ultimate honour to captain Manchester United, and I did so for the best part of four or five years.

"I left 15 or so years ago but I still hold the club in such high esteem, yes I do, and if I ring up and say I am coming along, they still make me most welcome, it's that sort of club. When I walk through the door it is as if nothing has changed in the last 20 years, but of course it has, life has changed, football has changed and Manchester United are even more huge now than they were then and that is saying something, but they are now such a massive club, yet they can still maintain that family atmosphere I remember when I was a player there."

Bruce was a product of the famous Wallsend Boys Club that developed talents such as Alan Shearer, Peter Beardsley and more recently Michael Carrick. He represented Newcastle schoolboys, but was rejected at 16 by his boyhood idols, as well as Sunderland,

Bolton Wanderers, Sheffield Wednesday and Southport because he was perceived to be too small. He subsequently got a job at the Swan Hunter shipyard as a trainee plumber but a week before he was due to start was offered an apprenticeship with Gillingham. After making his league debut for the Gills at the start of the 1979–80 season while still just 17, he went on to make more than 200 league appearances for the Kent club before Norwich paid £135,000 for him in August 1984.

At Carrow Road, Bruce won a League Cup winner's medal in 1985 and the Second Division Championship medal the following year. He left United on a free transfer for Birmingham City in the 1996 close season after nine years, 414 appearances and a prolific 51 goals. Assisted by his accuracy from the penalty spot he had remarkably finished as the club's joint top scorer in 1990/91 with 19 goals in all competitions. In 1998 he started out on the management trail with Sheffield United as player-manager, and has also been in charge at Huddersfield Town, Wigan Athletic, Crystal Palace and Birmingham City. The current Sunderland boss has no doubts about Sir Alex's standing in the game, "Sir Alex is the best, there will never be another like him. He has such a huge appetite for achievement."

Bruce's vast experience now as a manger gives him an insight into Sir Alex as a manager, but with a decade playing under him at Old Trafford, he also has got to know the real Fergie. "There is a humility about him that few actually see or are aware of. He has the common touch that he is as appreciative and approachable to the cleaning lady as he is to his captain. He has a way about him that makes people want to play for him. He also has a sensational appetite for the game, and his motivation comes from within. Nobody is going to repeat what he has done, not in my life time. Just to be Manchester United manager for 20 odd years is an achievement in itself, let alone all those trophies and honours he has won."

A season that started with David Beckham's half-way line stunner ended with an even greater shock as King Eric bid farewell to Old Trafford after skippering the Reds to yet another

H. Moger, J. Picken, W. Corbett, R. Holden, H. Burgess, J. Clough, W. Meredith, G. Boswell,
G. Wall, A. Turnbull, C. Roberts (Captain), T. Coleman, R. Duckworth.

THE OUTCASTS FC

*Above: Banned from football for forming a prototype players'
union, these players, most of them from Manchester United,
attempted to train privately calling themselves The Outcasts.*

ERNEST MANGNALL

*Left: A managerial failure at Bolton and Burnley before he
arrived at United, Mangnall made a reputation as a shrewd
operator in the transfer market. By hi-jacking a 1904 player
auction of Manchester City's finest he poached Burgess,
Bannister, Turnbull and Billy Meredith, key players in
United's 1907/08 inaugural league title winning team
(below).*

HOLLYWOOD FC

*Following their 1951/52 title success, United embarked on a US Tour with a difference. P̶
pictured with crooner Bing Crosby, the team were feted by the rich and famous.*

THE INCOMPARABLE BABES

*Captain Roger Byrne collects the 1955-56 trophy, a championship won by 11 points. Joh̶
Berry, Duncan Edwards, David Pegg and Eddie Colman join in the celebrations.*

THE SIXTIES

ᴏᴘ Lᴇꜰᴛ: *United stalwarts Jack ᴿ ompton, John Aston senior d Wilf McGuinness celebrate ᵉ 1964/65 title secured by (top ᵗ) Denis Law's double against ᵣsenal.*

ᴳʜᴛ: The Holy Trinity celebrate ᵉ 1966/67 title in the final ₋ gue game against Stoke City

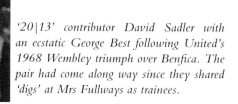

'20|13' contributor David Sadler with an ecstatic George Best following United's 1968 Wembley triumph over Benfica. The pair had come a long way since they shared 'digs' at Mrs Fullways as trainees.

ROBBO IN HIS POMP.

LEFT: *The health of Bryan Robson quite often dictated the fate of United during the 1980s when overcoming Liverpool appeared to be an impossible dream.*

AT LONG LAST!

BOTTOM LEFT: *Steve Bruce 'crowns' Bryan Robson following United's coronation as league champions in 1993.*

DOLLY AND DAISY

BOTTOM RIGHT: *Gary Pallister and Steve Bruce formed the bedrock defensive partnership on which United's title ambitions were laid.*

THE CLASS OF '92

Top: *It was United's great fortune to foster the youth team containing Scholes, Beckham, Butt and Gary Neville that later went on to form the nucleus of United's double-winning side of 1995-96.*

THE KING HAS HIS CROWN

Eric Cantona holds aloft the 1996-97 trophy shortly before he announces his retirement. Cantona's influence on United's young team was vital.

UNBEATABLE

Peter Schmeichel transformed goalkeeping during his spell between the posts at Old Trafford. His performances helped the club land the Double in 1995/96 and the Treble three years later.

STRIKING A POSE
ABOVE: *Dwight Yorke and Andy Cole formed a deadly partnership during United's Treble campaign - here they celebrate the club's last gasp victory in Barcelona*

THE GREATEST?
LEFT: *Sir Alex with the three trophies that formed the Treble. He has since won a whole trophy room more including (below) the 2001 title that gave him his first hat-trick of league titles.*

CHAMPIONS 2001

BECK AND CALL

Left: *David Beckham holds aloft the Premiership trophy following his final league triumph at the club in 2003.*

VETERANS

Gary Neville (bottom left) and Ryan Giggs (below) lift back-to-back titles.

THE DEADLY DUO

Below: *Cristiano Ronaldo and Wayne Rooney formed a deadly partnership that secured United a second hat-trick of titles.*

Sir Alex Ferguson and the last of the 38 trophies he won as Manchester United manager.

Signing off after 1500 games in charge, Sir Alex claimed he knew they'd win the title on Au 17th the day before the start of the season, "If you'd seen our dressing room at Sunderland, day we lost the league to Man City, you had a feeling about them... I felt we had a great char

title. At the end of this season, just seven points separated the Premier League's top four, the most competitive title race in Premiership history due to results against United's rivals. United finished with 75 to top the table, followed by Newcastle, Arsenal and Liverpool on 68 points. Home-and-away victories against both Arsenal and Liverpool inflicted psychological damage from which neither could recover, although, the Gunners did recover to win the League the following season. Autumn was particularly traumatic as United crashed to three successive League defeats; 5-0 at eventual runners-up Newcastle, 6-3 at Southampton and 2-1 at Chelsea. Crisis, what crisis, was Sir Alex's response to the media frenzy, as the team embarked on a 16-match unbeaten run, stretching from 16 November to 8 March and included 12 victories. The highlight of this sequence was December's 5-0 home win over Sunderland during which Cantona, in what would prove to be his last season for the Reds, scored twice, his second (chipped over the keeper's head) being remembered as much for the casual celebration as the stunning technique. Ole Gunnar Solskjaer, in his first season at United, also hit a double that day and was to finish the campaign ahead of both Cantona and Cole as top scorer with 18.

Eric Cantona is described by Pallister as "the catalyst to winning titles" and he helped the club to its fourth League Championship in his five seasons at Old Trafford. It was to be his last, as he surprisingly retired from football later that same month. The shock waves of Eric's decision seemed to last for a whole year, as the Reds went empty-handed in 1997/98 as Arsenal won the Double under new manager Arsene Wenger. United did a 'Newcastle' this time, streaking 13 points clear by early March only to fade in the closing stages to a rampant Arsenal, who then went on to beat Newcastle in the FA Cup Final. Again, injuries to key players, especially Ryan Giggs and Roy Keane, were cited for United's downfall but most suspected the loss of their talismanic Frenchman was just as critical. As Sir Alex commented at the time, "Eric Cantona's contribution to the Manchester United cause can never be underestimated – I doubt that I will ever be able to spend £1 million like that again!"

*

Eric Cantona later reflected on his United career in typical style. Cantona, now an actor, scored 82 goals in 185 games at the club and won four league titles.

He confessed that he found it so hard to leave in 1997, and that is why he has found it so difficult to return to Old Trafford. He even struggles to watch them on TV and now has other interests. "If you are a heroin addict and you've gone through the agonies of withdrawal, you don't go back and start hanging out with your dealer," Cantona told *GQ* magazine.

"It was, as I say, like quitting a Class A drug. Psychiatrists have demonstrated that the body of a retired professional footballer can replicate the kind of symptoms that you get with abrupt opiate withdrawal. And that's why I've avoided going back."

TITLE NO. 12 - 1998-99

"Andy Cole and myself had a fabulous understanding and to score 35 goals between us just in the League was astonishing. My relationship with Andy was spectacular, and it all came about without working on our partnership a great deal in training."

DWIGHT YORKE

DWIGHT YORKE AND ANDY COLE collected 35 League goals between them as Manchester United won the League by a point ahead of Arsenal in what was, unequivocally, the club's greatest-ever season. Little wonder then that the Trinidad & Tobago striker has no doubts that landmark year stands out in his career as he finished top scorer with 18 league goals.

Dwight moved to Old Trafford from Aston Villa in 1998 for £12.6 million, and with such a big price tag, so much was expected. He expected much of himself. He delivered, immediately. He won three successive League titles in 1999, 2000 and 2001, scoring 64 goals in 151 appearances.

It is as a free scoring forward at Old Trafford in partnership with Cole, that he looks back with such deep affection, as he tells me, during a train ride from London to Manchester, "Without doubt the Treble winning season is the landmark year for every one of the Manchester United players in that team. There is no doubt in my mind, that making history in a season that will never be forgotten, cannot be beaten. We won our first Premier League trophy together in the last game of the season, then went onto win the treble, the best moment in any player's career."

For so many Andy Cole remains a mystery; he seems aloof, even shy, often defensive, even making an issue about whether he should be called 'Andy' or 'Andrew' and his long running feud with Teddy Sheringham. When the truth finally emerged, it was discovered they wouldn't even pass the time of day with each other. There was an edge, an attitude, that for most people, it was hard to penetrate, it seemed so difficult to know the real Andy Cole. None of this existed for Dwight Yorke. He knew the real Andy Cole both on and more importantly off the field.

"Andy Cole and myself had a fabulous understanding and to score 35 goals between us just in the league was astonishing. My relationship with Andy was spectacular and it all came about without working on our partnership a great deal in training, it has to be said. For the first few games I was paired with Teddy Sheringham, and the forward line included Giggsie and Ole Gunnar Solskjaer. There were plenty of strikers at the club at this point, plenty of options, and after three or four weeks, the manager decided to make changes, and it kind of just happened that he put the two of us together and I was hoping to get a chance alongside Andy as we had become very close friends during that period.

"Andy was also very highly motivated to prove himself as, at this time, there was constant speculation about him leaving the club. Yet, when I arrived there, no one did more than Andy to help me settle into the new club, helping me find living accommodation, showing me the best areas, inviting me to his home."

As for the internal personal conflicts, they seemed to go over Dwight's head, as he explained, "I really had no idea what was going on. I was just thrilled to be at such a great club, playing with such great players. And, I am a happy go lucky type of fellow, and it was two years into my time at Manchester United before I realised something like this was going on, because I wasn't clued into anything else other than the fact that I was having so much fun playing for United, and also taking my football very seriously; winning trophies, winning the Treble, I really hadn't a clue who was getting on with who, and who wasn't getting on with someone, I didn't see that type of thing going on, and I didn't have an issue with anyone, and I didn't see any kind of issues going on, and they certainly didn't disrupt the team. Later, it came to light that there had been a lot of wrangling between Roy Keane and Peter Schmeichel, but it was petty stuff, and the dressing room harmony was intact which was the most important point.

"People have very differing views of Andy Cole, different takes on what sort of person he is. When you don't know someone, and they are so much in the public eye, there is always going to be plenty of speculation. Knowing Andy the way I did, there is no doubt in my mind that he is a great guy. When you really get to know him, certainly as well as I did, then you find someone completely different to the way he has been portrayed – he was really a very fun loving and funny person to be with, someone who loves to have a laugh, a private person, yes, he was, but someone who loves his family and loved being with his family. He was different to me, I am more out going.

"When we went out onto the pitch together, we seemed to link up with the same unity that we shared off the pitch, it was uncanny. If you ask all the top strikers, Alan Shearer, Kenny Dalglish and Ian Rush, they were out to score as many goals for themselves but they all measured success with their clubs and were desperate to win trophies. To win those trophies, you need your strikers firing on all cylinders, and there can be no bigger incentive for a striker than the challenge of other strikers, and good ones at that, so you want to be in the team and you want to be scoring in a winning team. We had four top strikers, four unbelievably good strikers, and the competition was intense, but extremely healthy for the club and the team. As much as you want to score the most goals for yourself, the most important aspect is that you play for the team and a winning team. Naturally you want to be top scorer, win the Golden Boot, but when you go out and play for Manchester United there are a multitude of challenges, to win the trophies and to win the individual awards. The only way to succeed is to have confidence in your own ability and to deliver, the only way is to deliver.

"For me, playing for Manchester United was everything I could have wished far and far more, as I came to Manchester United as the record signing, with such high expectations to deliver on such a huge stage and to end up as part of Manchester United's rich and long history, and be one of the integral players in the Treble season was something to treasure. I played alongside some great players and under a great manager.

"Not only did we win the Treble, but the following season we won the League by an incredible 18 points from Arsenal. No one should under estimate what we did in 2000 by winning the League by such a huge margin, a record margin for the Premier league. The League was over by the end of March, beginning of April, our league season was over because we were so far ahead. But because we had won the Treble, what we achieved the following year was, to a large degree, overlooked. We had a disappointing season in Europe, and of course we went off to Brazil for over a week to take part in the World Club Championships, which at that time, had little significance, and it denied us the chance to participate in the FA Cup and possibly win another trophy."

As an aside here, I accompanied the United party to Rio for the World Club Championship, running a campaign in the *Daily Mirror* at the time trying to force the football authorities to make the club take part in the FA Cup. Personally, I was concerned at the time that the FA Cup would never be the same again if the country's leading club turned its back on the oldest and most prestigious knock out tournament in the world, and so it has transpired. Now global tournaments such as the Champions League, with all the world's best players now concentrated in Europe, have become so important that it has dwarfed the FA Cup and made finishing fourth in the Premier League more important than winning it – as it gives the club a crack at the

Champions League.

My stance on the *Mirror* wasn't popular with the United faithful at the time but I knew their participation was politically motivated, designed to help England's cause to win votes to stage the World Cup. That also proved to be a flawed policy as FIFA were never in the FA's camp, and were never going to award England the World Cup Finals, as Germany were awarded the tournament. I was berated by some United fans who made the trip to Rio intent on seeing their team try to win the World Club Championship. But abandoning the FA Cup has turned it into the second rate tournament it has now become. Players such as Dwight Yorke have come to appreciate that, in retrospect, it was one of the worst decisions ever taken on behalf of the most powerful and influential club in English football.

Dwight told me, "Of course we all had a good time out in Rio for a week or so, but the decision to go to Brazil didn't involve the players, and looking back I can now see it was such a bad idea. We were all were happy to go to Brazil for a break from the winter and to have a bit of fun and we all had a great time but in retrospect it was a wasted opportunity to win the FA Cup and for that I will always be bitterly disappointed that we went, but we had no option, it was a decision taken by those who ran the football club at the time.

"The media and everyone else thought it would be detrimental to our chances of retaining the League title, but as it turned out when we returned we stormed away with the League. I suppose the reason was that we were so confident after winning the Treble, but the Treble remains the season everyone focuses on, and winning the League by a record 18 points is rarely mentioned by comparison, and for me this is indicative of the way sometimes people don't give credit where credit is due. Winning the League is an indication that you are the best, winning by such a big margin indicates you are the very best, and we won the League three years in a row, the third year by another impressively big margin.

"It's very similar with the team that has just won the 19th

League title, too many people have been too quick to cast aspersions, to criticise, but they are wrong. When you are so successful as winning the League title you deserve the rewards that go with it. In today's football, players are rewarded without achieving true success, and for me this has become a major issue. I have been out of the game only a short while, but already I have seen big changes and I don't like what I am seeing. Money comes into the game in vast quantities, and this naturally distorts aspect of it. I am not going to criticise players for earning such vast quantities of money today because the playing career is short. But it is a reminder that the game has become distorted in a variety of ways, where success is not justly rewarded.

"For example, it does aggravate me that I never won Player of the Year in the season where I did so well for Manchester United, winning a Treble and scoring so many goals to win the League and FA Cup. Instead David Ginola was voted the Players' Player of the Year, and then by the football writers, the Footballer of the Year. I would question this, as indeed I would question why Scott Parker was voted Footballer of the year in a season when West Ham were relegated. Ok, Scott Parker is an excellent footballer, and I would not dispute that, but he cannot surely be regarded as having a good season when his club are relegated, it cannot be justified, certainly by comparison to a season in which United won their 19th League title with some outstanding individual performances. My point is that relegation cannot be rewarded in any shape or form and how can players who did so well for United be overlooked?

"Nani had a great start to the season while the youngster Chicharito scored 20 goals in his first season and was a brilliant goalscorer. Instead there were moans that it was not a vintage United team. How many times have your heard that one? How many times have people underestimated the achievements of United teams in the past? I would have thought if you were champions, you deserve to be recognised as such, and it is not realistic to suggest that you have to play like champions every time you take the field, as the measure of true champions is to win when you are not playing well.

"You cannot expect any team, irrespective of how talented, to be spectacular in every game. That is how you win the game, in some games you have to win ugly. You cannot be great in every game, sometimes it is a question of winning the best way you can, and that is the hallmark of a team that wins the League."

The hallmark of Dwight's playing career, which began with a 10 year spell with Aston Villa, was that he played with a smile on his face, something often lacking in the modern day footballer. He still has that smile as he concludes, "When I joined the club I hadn't won anything, and went there aiming to win the title within a year or two and in that first season I ended up with the Treble – I didn't see that coming! It was simply a fantastic year, and I was fortunate to be part of it. I had an opportunity to represent a highly successful and great club, and to be part of that historic Treble, and three back-to-back titles. The history books don't lie, and what we achieved will never be forgotten."

Yorke joined Aston Villa in 1989 enjoying a successful career with Villa, and after United, he moved to Blackburn Rovers in 2002 and Birmingham City in 2004. A short spell in Australia with Sydney FC was followed by a return to England with Sunderland in 2006, where he played mainly as a holding midfielder. Yorke captained Trinidad & Tobago at the 2006 World Cup.

As for Dwight's all-time greatest Manchester United player, he doesn't hesitate when he names Paul Scholes, "Without doubt", he says, "from the day he started out he trained every day with great intensity, and his attributes were that he is such a great passer, great finisher, his all-round game was incredible. I could name Giggs, Beckham and Keane as they were great players, people talk about Eric Cantona, but for me Scholes is my No 1. Scholes was apart from them all because there was something about him that I liked more than any other United player I played with or saw over the years. If I was to do it all over again, I would model myself on Paul Scholes."

★

United and Arsenal had vied for the title throughout that 1998/99 season but entering the run-in Arsenal seemed to have stolen an advantage – coming from behind to win at White Hart Lane while United tossed away a two-goal advantage at Anfield to finish with a draw. Yet the tables turned the following week as Arsenal lost at Elland Road and United took advantage one night later with a goalless draw at Ewood Park that condemned Blackburn to relegation. Going into the final match of the season, United had to beat Tottenham at Old Trafford to secure the title. Anything less and Arsenal could steal it with a win at home to Aston Villa.

Les Ferdinand threatened to spoil the title party giving Spurs an early lead in the decider. However United were never going to be beaten; David Beckham swerving in a leveller before the break and substitute Andy Cole chipping the keeper in memorable style in the second half to secure United the League.

However the League was only one aspect of the club's rivalry that season. The epic FA Cup semi-final replay victory over the Gunners gave Sir Alex's men the psychological edge in that run-in, especially as Arsenal 'choked' at the vital moment on a night of high drama; Sheringham scored, Bergkamp equalised, Keane was sent off before Schmeichel saved Bergkamp's injury-time penalty. In extra time, and down to ten men, Giggs broke away, beat most of Arsenal's back four before scoring high past Seaman's right hand.

Just as epic was United's Champions League semi-final against Juventus when, after a 1-1 draw, Keane inspired the team to fight back from 2-0 down in the second leg despite picking up a booking that meant he would miss the final himself.

So with League and Cup tied up in successive weeks, United attempted to complete an unprecedented treble in Barcelona the following Wednesday. The omens looked bad as Bayern took an early lead through Mario Basler and defended it with typical German resilience. But then, in injury time, the Reds produced one of the most stunning revivals in sporting history – Sheringham equalised and moments later his fellow substitute Ole Gunnar Solskjaer flicked home the winner to make the score 2-1. United had won the Treble; their manager Alex Ferguson was subsequently knighted as fans around the globe basked in the glory.

★

"And Solskjaer has won it!" – Clive Tyldesley's screamed commentary is synonymous with the night that Ole Gunnar Solskjær became the world's most famous Norwegian. Nou Camp, Barcelona, 1999 and two minutes into extra time... Beckham's corner, Sheringham headed flick and Ole Gunnar stuck out his right foot and finished a goal that was to mark the most important moment of his career. The evening after the Champions League victory in Barcelona, Ole Gunnar has a picture of himself and Ferguson. They stand there with a bottle of champagne in the midst of all the congratulations. "I look at that picture, and I remember exactly what I thought at the moment. 'You deserve this, after all you have done for this club.' The only thing I could think about was how much Ferguson deserved this. Yes. I am proud of what I have done as a player."

In a home game against Everton in 1999, United won 5-1 and Ole scored four goals, but the striker nicknamed the 'Baby Faced Assassin', who played for Manchester United for 11 years, number 20 on his back, collecting 126 goals, will always be remembered for completing United's famous Treble. When he retired it was suggested that grown men openly wept. Sir Alex called him "a fantastic person" and he still has his own song sung regularly at Old Trafford. Ole suffered torn knee ligaments and his career was cut short after 366 games, although he made a brief, telling comeback in 2006 to help United to another title in another era.

The 'Baby Faced Assassin' was nervous about telling the manager about the doctor's verdict. As he arrived at Carrington

Ferguson walked across the parking lot. He stopped the car. "I can't keep playing, I need another operation. I have to retire," he said to Ferguson. Ferguson looked at him. "You have had a fantastic career," the manager said, "you have done your family proud, you've done me proud and what you did for the last few years was great. Why don't you coach my forwards?" It was an offer Ole couldn't refuse.

For Peter Schmeichel, Manchester United's victory over Bayern Munich marked the end of an era. The game was Schmeichel's last for the Reds and brought the curtain down on a career spanning more than eight years at the club. For the Dane, who captained his side in the absence of the suspended Roy Keane, the match was the perfect finale. "Not even Hans Christian Andersson could have written a fairytale like that," Schmeichel said after the game. "Of course you believe you have a chance until the final whistle goes and I never stopped believing we had a chance – although I admit, not much of one. But the late goals exemplified our team spirit. One thing I have learnt throughout my time at United is that we never give up and we proved that tonight."

The Great Dane had announced the previous November that he was quitting United at the end of the season. At the time few were surprised. He had made a poor start to the campaign and the club were rumoured to be interested in Aston Villa's Mark Bosnich. Since Christmas, however, the Dane had been back to his best, helping United end the season unbeaten in 33 matches. Ferguson paid tribute to Schmeichel, saying: "It is sad that he is leaving us but he could not go out in a better way. We wish him well – he's the greatest goalkeeper Manchester United have ever had." Schmeichel's final act as a United player was to lift the European Cup. "This is absolutely fantastic for me and I just feel on top of the world," he said at the time. "When I announced I was leaving at the end of the season I vowed to myself I would do all I could to help the club finish at the top – and you cannot get higher than this. I do not want to talk about other clubs now. Tonight is the night for Manchester United –

Manchester United and champagne."

Immediately after the game, Ferguson confessed he thought his side had thrown it all away. Substitutes Sheringham and Solskjaer snatched two last-gasp goals to secure a 2-1 victory over Bayern Munich, who had looked the better side for nine-tenths of the game. Bayern had led through Mario Basler's early free-kick and the trophy Ferguson longed for appeared to be slipping away. "My players never give in," he said at the final whistle, "you always expect they can do something, but this time I thought we were beaten. The team spirit is just unbelievable. Everyone works together and is in this together." Thirty seconds into injury time, Sheringham stabbed home the equaliser, before Solskjaer sent the 40,000 United fans in the Nou Camp, and the millions around the world, into raptures with the winner; a goal which ended 31 years of European heartache for the Reds who lifted the trophy for the first time since 1968 and the days of Sir Matt Busby. "I thought it had gone going into the last few minutes," Ferguson admitted.

The United boss hailed his players as "incredible human beings" and warned that their hunger for success would lead to more trophies in years to come. "The future is to keep playing with such pride and the players won't rest on that because they're young. It's fantastic. They never give in so you always expect something from them. They are incredible human beings. You can talk about tactics all you like but that spirit is unbeatable at times. Tonight they just never gave in. We got off to a bad start but kept at them and got our reward. In the last 20 minutes we got caught on the counter attack but you've got to gamble in a European final. I don't think we've played as well as we have done but Teddy's come on and then Ole, and they've repaid the faith I showed in them."

★

The Treble became a quadruple later in the year when Sir Alex Ferguson's men travelled to Tokyo to compete for the Inter-Continental Cup. Keane's goal against Palmeiras of Brazil bestowed upon United the title of World Club Champions.

Officially, at the end of the millennium, the biggest football club in the world had also become the best in the world!

United's spectacular victory in the European Cup, sealing an unparalleled Treble secured their manager a place in soccer sainthood, a knighthood was just a matter of time. Ferguson conceded, "You can't top this because this is the pinnacle. You can equal it and we can try to maintain our high standards."

Fergie established himself as a British footballing icon to rank alongside Sir Matt, who established United as a world class outfit in the 1950s, and whose reputation every United manager since had tried to rival. His sides had topped the Premiership in five of the last seven years.

A close friend, Richard Greenbury, a former chairman of Marks and Spencer, called him the "best man-manager in Britain today". The soon to be Sir Alex commented at the time, "I have a group of players who never cease to surprise me and I'm convinced they are capable of virtually anything. The final weeks of this season will remain with me until the day I die."

TITLE NO. 13 - 1999-2000

"In 2000 and 2001, we won the League by lots of points and we only had Arsenal to worry about really, but now you've got one of four to worry about or even all four.'

SIR ALEX FERGUSON

THIS WAS UNITED'S MOST DOMINANT championship season, the rest of the field inflicting just three Premiership defeats. The gap at the top had been just one point over the Gunners the previous season. Now the gap was a devastating 18 points over their north London rivals as United landed an impressive sixth title in eight years. Ending with a record 91 points, their dominance was comparable to Arsenal's 2003/04 championship in which the Gunners went unbeaten and Chelsea's title triumph in 2004/05 when Mourinho's men suffered just one League defeat.

As Sir Alex looked back while on tour in Seattle ahead of his assault on title number 19 back in 2011, he looked at the challenge of Arsenal, and Chelsea, and the new thrust of noisy neighbours City and observed, "In 2000 and 2001, we won the League by lots of points and we only had Arsenal to worry about really, but now you've got one of four to worry about or even all four. So I think Arsenal have got caught in the draught that Chelsea created and, of course, them not winning the title for six or seven years has put a pressure on them. But it's cyclical. The

Barcelona team is a team of its time and it's a cycle for them, a fantastic cycle, and you can't really see it changing for the next two or three years. That happens in football. We went 26 years without winning the League and hopefully we don't have to wait 26 years for the next one."

As he examined the big challengers for the 2012 title, he warned Kenny Dalglish the League remains a "difficult league to win", despite forecasting a "big improvement" at Anfield. Arsenal's hopes of ending their six-year trophy drought were compromised by the uncertainty surrounding the futures of Cesc Fabregas and Samir Nasri, but Arsène Wenger's problems run deeper; "Look, you thought Arsenal were going to have a real chance last season. They got to the very brink and that means they're going to be challengers this season. But it's not easy to win the League. We waited 26 years at one point and it's 20 years since Liverpool last won it. It happens sometimes." Are Arsenal at the cross roads? "That's one way (of looking at it), but honestly, you've got to remember the way, when Jose Mourinho came, Chelsea all of a sudden just won their first six games in a row and we were all chasing our tails. I think Arsenal got caught in the draught that Chelsea created. And of course not winning the title for six or seven years has put a pressure on them. We generally always took our time at the start of the League and usually waited until around February or March, but it changed our attitude after they won the two leagues. It became far more competitive."

He believes Liverpool are now "back on the radar" after two years outside the top four. Liverpool have not won the League in 21 years and finished sixth last season, as United overtook them as the country's most successful club. However, under Dalglish, Ferguson concedes they are a club to be wary of again. "Liverpool went off the radar for a bit. They are now back on it," he said, "long-term, you know they are going to be there." Speaking of Liverpool in the same breath as Arsenal, Chelsea and Manchester City, he added: "Let's be honest, you hate losing to any of them. One of those four will always be a thorn in our flesh. They are our immediate challengers. History doesn't change. No matter where it comes from, somewhere along the line we are going to be faced with a big challenge from one of those four great clubs." Another challenge for United will be to end the dominance of Barcelona. Despite being so obviously outclassed by Pep Guardiola's side in the 2011 Champions League final, Sir Alex refuses to accept they cannot catch the Catalans. "Barcelona are the team of the moment. It is a cycle. It is the same players. They can dominate any game and could have probably done that to any other team. But it is not the kind of thing that makes you think, 'Let's not bother with European football any more, we are never going to beat Barcelona.' Manchester United are bigger than that. We have a better philosophy than that. The challenge will be can we improve enough to get to the final next season – and win."

Back to the turn of the new decade and there was absolutely no Treble hangover from United. Inspired by "Captain Keano", United cantered to title glory with a record 18-point margin and Dwight Yorke collecting 20 League goals. The team was largely unchanged from the previous year, except in one notable respect. Peter Schmeichel, the club's best ever keeper, left the demands of the Premiership to play in Portugal. He proved difficult to replace. Six different goalkeepers were used over the next six seasons. For the 1999-2000 season, Mark Bosnich and Massimo Taibi arrived to join Raimond van der Gouw.

In the Premiership, United looked comfortable. They won six of their first seven games and all of their last eleven. They won the title with four matches still to play and, in the end, way ahead of runners up Arsenal. They endured only one major reverse; a 5-0 defeat at Chelsea in October. United trailed Leeds by four points at the turn of the year but Andy Cole's predatory opportunism ensured United left Elland Road on 20th February with a vital win over their rivals which proved to be the turning point of the season. By mid April it was all over. David Beckham, a Francis Benali own goal and yet another from Ole Gunnar Solskjaer ensured an early end-of-season party at The Dell as a

3-1 win over Southampton on April 22nd confirmed United as the runaway champions.

Sir Alex commented, "Some people suggested it could have been difficult to motivate the lads after the Treble. It could, but it hasn't. They are as keen to succeed today as they have ever been."

Such was the massive gap between United and the rest of the Premiership, it caused some pundits to wonder if the club's financial dominance was developing into a problem for the English game. Ironically, this question was to be answered within four years with the sudden emergence of Chelsea as the new financial superpower in England, and now continues with City's even great financial muscle. While, at one stage, the top four were so predictable that I was constantly on the media outlets answering questions whether English football had become too similar to the Scottish version in its predictability, it has now swung back to a far more open concept.

*

One bizarre aspect of the season was United's absence from the FA Cup. The fact that the holders didn't defend their trophy was something of a scandal in my opinion and contributed to the devaluing of the world's oldest cup competition. As winners of the previous season's Champions League, United were invited to participate in a FIFA World Club Championship in Brazil in January. The FA wanted them to take part, believing it would help England's ultimately failed bid to host the 2006 World Cup. Being in Brazil in January meant they would miss the fourth round of the FA Cup in England and so it was agreed they should withdraw. It wasn't a popular decision, with United accused of being disrespectful to the FA Cup. When they got to Brazil, they didn't progress beyond the group stage.

There was a great deal of debate at the time that the January jaunt to Rio would leave the players open to burn out and return unfit to mount a proper challenge for the League. As it turned out, it provided valuable relaxation time in the sun. Rejuvenated, United raced ahead of their rivals in the title race when they returned to England, achieving their sixth Premiership title early in April, and still without a convincing replacement for Schmeichel.

For all their domestic success however United were undone in the Champions League. They reached the quarter-finals where they faced 1998 champions Real Madrid. After a goalless game in Madrid, United looked favourites to progress but an incredible Spanish performance at Old Trafford combined with a nervy home display saw them crash out 3-2 – an own goal from Roy Keane summing up a desperate night for the Reds. Later Jaap Stam admitted losing in the quarter-finals took the shine off winning the Premiership title.

Roy Keane, Manchester United's captain, signed a new contract during the season. He also won both the Football Writers' and the Professional Footballers' Association's Players' Player of the Year awards. He did this despite featuring in one of the season's uglier moments, when he and other United players chased referee Andy D'Urso around Old Trafford following a contentious decision. At the end of the season, United's Chief Executive Martin Edwards retired and was replaced by Peter Kenyon.

All was not well within the squad particularly between Sir Alex and David Beckham. After Beckham missed training to look after his family, the manager claimed the player's life-style was interfering with his football. Sir Alex went public on his bust-up with Beckham at the end of the season and explained why he dramatically dropped him. United's manager revealed how he 'blew up' at Beckham and why he banished him from the team for a crucial Premiership match at Leeds in February, in an updated version of his autobiography Managing My Life. Although, he wrote that the row proved beneficial in that Beckham agreed to spend more time in the north-west and less at his Hertfordshire home, which had become a major irritation to the manager. As Ferguson writes in the book "[Beckham] made me lose my temper badly" by missing a Friday training session before the Sunday game at Leeds and then refused to apologise when reporting back on Saturday. The player claimed he had missed training because he had to look after his son Brooklyn, who was unwell. Ferguson writes that the explanation "would normally have made me totally sympathetic. But when it was well known that Victoria was out in London that Friday I had to think David wasn't being fair to his team-mates." The manager continues: "It doesn't matter to me how high a player's profile is. At first he simply refused to accept that he had anything to answer for, and that made me blow up... from time to time somebody in my job is confronted with the situation which must be handled in a manner that he had anything to answer for, and that made me blow up... from time to time somebody in my job is confronted with the situation which must be handled in a manner that signifies control."

Twenty-four hours before Leeds were due to entertain United, Leeds United had announced that Brian Kidd, seen by some as the likely successor to Sir Alex, had been promoted to head coach at Elland Road. The immediate reaction was that Kidd, who left Manchester to pursue an ultimately unsuccessful management career at Blackburn, was being put in place to eventually succeed O'Leary. Leeds, though, acted quickly to quash such speculation, contacting the BBC to insist that Ceefax, their news-text service, drop a report claiming O'Leary was stepping down at Elland Road. Following Kidd's 11 months at Ewood Park, he spent six months working in the media before returning to the game the previous May as director of the youth academy at Leeds. It was the first time Kidd had faced Ferguson since the Manchester United manager criticised his former assistant of eight years in his autobiography. In the book, Managing My Life, Ferguson questioned Kidd's coaching ability and claimed he was a moaner who could probably not have succeeded him as United manager. Kidd responded by claiming Walt Disney wanted the book as a sequel to the film Fantasia. The spat occurred in the summer of 1999, just months after a goalless draw at Ewood Park between United and Blackburn resulted in Rovers being relegated to the First Division. "Whatever happened between

Alex and Brian is no concern of mine," then Leeds manager David O'Leary said, "That's for those two people to sort out. As far as I'm concerned, I don't think there is a much better coach in this country, or in Europe."

Kidd had became assistant to Sir Alex in 1991 and helped the club win four League titles. Spells with Blackburn, Leeds, England and Portsmouth preceded his return to Manchester City in 2009, as coach and later assistant to Roberto Mancini. Having made his debut as a teenager in the 1967/68 season, Kidd was in the United set-up when they faced City at Old Trafford in March 1968, the last time the two sides had competed for the title. Brought back as assistant, Brian has never stopped calling Sir Alex "the Boss" as Kidd was in the United dugout when their 26-year wait for a title ended in 1993. Kidd's debut season as a player was a dream as United went on to win their first European Cup under the charismatic Matt Busby with Kidd scoring one of the match winning goals at Wembley. He went on to make over 200 appearances, but the highlight for the tall striker was scoring in the 1968 European Cup final.

Kidd worked alongside Sir Alex for nine years. Kidd and Ferguson enjoyed unprecedented success together at Old Trafford, guiding United to their first League title in 26 years before winning two Doubles in three seasons in 1993-94 and 1995-96 and a further Premier League crown in 1997. But after Kidd left to pursue an ultimately unsuccessful managerial career with Blackburn - his Rovers side were condemned to relegation by United in 1999, four years after they had won the League - Ferguson gave a stinging assessment of his former colleague in his autobiography. The Scot described his former assistant as a "complex person, often quite insecure", and claimed that the board viewed him as a person "with a natural inclination to complain". Ferguson also accused Kidd of going behind his back to moan about training and questioned whether he could cut it as a manager. But Kidd insists there is no animosity between the two. "I've never even talked about it with him because I don't think there's ever been a cause to," Kidd told *The Guardian*, "and

I will always appreciate what he's done for me. You can't buy those wonderful memories. I'm relaxed about it all. As I say, I know how I feel; that's all I can say. Other people might feel differently. There's life before Old Trafford, there's life after it. You get on with it, don't you? It was my decision, no problem. I've been very, very lucky and blessed in my football career. No regrets at all."

*

In April, 2000, it was announced that United had agreed to sign Dutch striker Ruud van Nistelrooy from PSV Eindhoven for a British record fee of £18 million. But the move was put on hold when van Nistelrooy failed a medical and he then returned to his homeland in a bid to regain fitness, only to suffer a serious knee injury which ruled him out for almost a year.

At the end of the season, Beckham's future was high on the agenda. Milan claimed they had made a second, improved offer for Beckham of £40m to take him to Italy. United's incoming chief executive Peter Kenyon denied that they had made a bid and said that in any case the player was effectively unbuyable.

Several goalkeepers tried and failed to establish themselves during the season. So it was hardly surprising when World Cup and European Championship winner Fabien Barthez joined United in July 2000.

TITLE NO. 14 - 2000-01

"It is more satisfying as I now have an insight from a coach's point of view. The satisfaction as a coach is being able to observe at close quarters how the Gaffer and Mick Phelan prepare each day and how they deal with the trials and tribulations involved in maintaining the fitness, emotional well being and mentality of a large group of players on and off the pitch."

BRIAN McCLAIR

B Y MAY 2001, Sir Alex had been at the helm for all three of United's back-to-back titles, the first manager in English football to achieve the hat-trick. Liverpool had been the last team to do it, in 1982, 1983 and 1984, but this was under the supervision of two different managers, Bob Paisley and Joe Fagan. The major change to the side was the acquisition of 29-year-old French maverick goalkeeper Fabien Barthez from Monaco for £7.8 million - making him the most expensive goalkeeper to be signed by a British club. The World Cup and European Championship winner joined United in July 2000. The eccentric but brilliant French goalkeeper helped United to win their third successive title, and while attracting praise at the end of the campaign from the manager, there was a goalkeeping crisis inside Old Trafford as, in reality, it had become virtually impossible to replace Peter Schmeichel.

United were once again far superior in the title race, and

all interest focused on by what margin they would win it. They clinched the title with plenty to spare. In fact they clinched their seventh Premier League title in nine years (only Blackburn and Arsenal had broken that remarkable sequence) after a typically resilient performance against Coventry with a 4-2 victory earlier in the afternoon of April 14, after Arsenal were beaten 3-0 by Middlesbrough at Highbury later in the day. For a long time, though, Coventry, confidence high following two successive victories and scenting yet another last gasp escape from relegation, decided the only way to tackle this difficult of away fixtures was by attacking. Nine minutes remained when, with the score locked at 2-2, Ryan Giggs finally succeeded in beating Chris Kirkland, Coventry's gifted young goalkeeper, with a wonderful header of all things. Finally, the visitors' resistance crumbled, Paul Scholes produced a spectacular shot for the fourth goal. Coventry, leading twice in the first half through John Hartson, certainly had Sir Alex worried. Confessing that he could not wait for the interval to come, Ferguson said, "Coventry posed a real threat to us in the first half. For 15 minutes, I thought this could be a really disappointing game for us. They had a go because they knew that was the best way to play against us. I thought we should have been much better in our concentration going for the ball. We were too hesitant. But we corrected that in the second half and there was no more bother, really. With 10 minutes to go I was a bit concerned, but they [his players] like to keep you waiting."

Coventry manager Gordon Strachan admitted that going away from Old Trafford, the scene of some of his own triumphs as a player, empty-handed after scoring twice was "hard to take".

Andy Goram's debut as emergency cover for United's regular goalkeepers, Fabien Barthez and Raimond van der Gouw, was anything but a roaring success. At 37, the former Scottish international was looking his age. On the hour he unaccountably, picked up an obvious back-pass from Stam. Not long after that faux pas, Ferguson sent on Van der Gouw to replace Goram. The United manager insisted he made the change because he wanted the Dutchman to clock up the six

Premiership appearances required to qualify for a championship medal but it did not square entirely with his pre-match intention of protecting Barthez and Van der Gouw from injury in advance of Wednesday Champions League quarter-final in Munich. The 30-yarder Scholes drove into the top corner four minutes from the end sent the Premiership's biggest crowd to date - 67,637 - into party mode.

But the crowd had long gone by the time Arsenal's unexpected 3-0 home defeat by Middlesbrough in the afternoon ensured that the Manchester club would end the season as champions once more. Middlesbrough, another side trying to claw their way to safety at the bottom, inflicted the first home Premiership defeat of the season on Arsenal, the only team capable of catching United. Sir Alex commented, "It's all the sweeter, because this is the hardest league in the world to win. I didn't expect the Arsenal result at all, but I've got a few friends down from Scotland, and when we heard the score at half-time [2-0 to Midlesbrough] we decided to stay and listen to the rest of the game. It's a fantastic achievement and I'm very proud of the players. This is the kind of boost we can take into the game in Munich on Wednesday and get the right result for the country. I think we can get three clubs into the semi-finals of the Champions League."

Despite United's mastery of their domestic rivals, they continued to experience difficulty in overcoming the very best European sides in the past two seasons. Searching for an explanation Sir Alex suggested that the failure of the likes of Arsenal, Liverpool, Leeds and Chelsea to stretch his team may have taken the edge off their play in the Champions League. A 3-1 aggregate defeat to the Germans took some of the shine off another straightforward league campaign.

The ease with which United won their third title in a row, is exemplified by the fact that they went 11 points clear of the pack when they beat West Ham 3-1 at Old Trafford on New Year's Day. A major factor in United's racing start to the season was the form of Teddy Sheringham, famous along with another substitute, Ole Gunnar Solskjaer, for winning the European Cup in those dramatic last few minutes against Bayern two seasons earlier. Sheringham had scored 20 goals so far and the bulk of them came before Christmas. Although Sheringham's form dipped, and his goals dried up, the value of his contribution has not been lost on the United fans. At the halfway stage in the voting for 'The Sir Matt Busby Player of the Season 2000-2001' Sheringham was leading by some distance from Ryan Giggs, David Beckham and Roy Keane.

The morning following his title triumph was the same as any other – Sir Alex was pumping iron in the gym by 7am and his staff and players followed him to work three hours later. It was business as usual and onto the next target – Bayern Munich. "He is amazing," said assistant Steve McClaren, "I like to use the gym at Carrington, but I have to go after training." Ferguson spent Saturday night at Old Trafford celebrating his latest achievements with friends and surpassed Bob Paisley's mark of six domestic titles and becoming the first manager to win three in succession.

Ferguson sets an example his players have to follow. "It's a question of character," McClaren said, "It's got to be. To win a championship you have to perform away from home and only Leeds have come anywhere near to matching us. There is a level of consistency that needs to be established and our away performances have proved we have that. Our players have a certain durability and resilience that gets them results even when they are performing below par. Our first goal, our main goal, at the start of every season is to win the Premiership and we have both the character and experience to do it."

McClaren agrees that the ease with which United secured the title in record time contributed to problems in Europe, "We would rather win the championship with five games to spare than leave it until the last day of the season," he said, "but you learn, again from experience, that standards have to be maintained throughout the season. Subconsciously, however, a little bit of complacency can set in and by the time you realise, it can be very difficult to step out and step up because you haven't prepared properly."

Encouraged by victories over Charlton and Coventry, Ferguson believed all would be well when they met Bayern in the second leg quarter finals, but, of course, it didn't turn out that way.

Looking ahead Sir Alex predicted the following season's Premiership title race would be much closer. "Our aim is to win the title four times in a row," he said, "that's the challenge for us but I expect Arsenal, Liverpool and Leeds to pose more of a threat. There is so much potential for a terrific championship next season."

Explaining United's dominance, Ferguson pointed to the arrival of Barthez, "He has been a major influence," Ferguson said, "we have the best defensive record in the League, and although when Fabien joined us he had already won so much, he has not lost his appetite."

Another change to the line-up was Teddy Sheringham winning his first team place back after two seasons of mainly substitute appearances. By the end of the season, the 35-year-old Sheringham was United's leading scorer in all competitions and had been presented with both the PFA Player of the Year Award and the Football Writers' Player of the Year Award. Sheringham might have been top scorer as United completed their hat trick of titles in, but then came the arrival of Ruud van Nistelrooy and the signing of the Dutch centre-forward for a record fee at the end of the season brought in a new era, yet another team Sir Alex was building for yet more glory and trophies, but it ushered out Dwight Yorke.

Despite the devastating effect it had on him, Dwight gives the manager credit, as he explains, "That is why he is such a great manager, he is never satisfied, three straight title wins but not satisfied and that says it all about him, he is continually improving, and that's why he brought in Ruud, who is a different type of a player than myself, a pure finisher. The knack of management is to know when to improve the team and at this time Andy Cole was battling hard to stay at the club and it didn't quite happen for him and while it is easy for me to say that the manager shouldn't have got rid of us, you can now see that he was looking to the future of the club, he was looking further down the line. As a player you are thinking "at the moment...", you don't think about how the manager might be thinking ahead about how best to reinvigorate the team, how to improve it. Let's face it, he got it right. Of course I would rather my time at United had not come to an end."

*

Brian McClair returned to Old Trafford in 2001 for the start of a successful career in United's backroom staff where he has discovered the secrets of Sir Alex's title success. After coaching spells with Motherwell and Blackburn, McClair was back with United in a new role. So how different was it winning titles as part of the behind the scenes set up then as a player? "It is more satisfying as I now have an insight from a coach's point of view. The satisfaction as a coach is being able to observe at close quarters how the Gaffer and Mick Phelan prepare each day and how they deal with the trials and tribulations involved in maintaining the fitness, emotional well being and mentality of a large group of players on and off the pitch.

So is Alex the greatest manager of all time? "I think that it is disrespectful to compare or contrast mangers over the history of our beautiful game. The Gaffer, I'm sure, will be delighted to be mentioned in the same breath as his illustrious predecessors."

'Choccy' McClair wrote his name in the history books when he became the first United player since George Best to score 20 League goals for the club. But Brian doesn't believe that the lack of a genuine goalscorer was the main reason for United's lack of titles, "There is a need for all the team to contribute to goals scored and conceded." Despite McClair's 20 goals, the Liverpool of Barnes, Beardsley and Aldridge finished nine points ahead of United in Brian's first season at the club and with a vastly superior goal difference, so did it seem as Liverpool could never be caught? "Finishing second flattered us as we were never in contention; we had a great finish to that season. However there was a feeling that the Gaffer was looking to overhaul the squad. Later on, we were starting to look like a group who could win the League and losing out to Leeds was very disappointing but we were determined to use this experience to our advantage the following year. We were also written off in the media as having blown our best opportunity and that we would not recover from this experience, particularly by Jocky Hansen on Match of the Day!"

The striker turned midfield player following Cantona's arrival. One of the greatest goals from the mid-1990s – Eric's audacious chip against Sunderland at Old Trafford – was created by McClair, so how satisfying was it to create than score? "I always played midfield until I was 19, so it was easy to move there. I was the master of the six inch pass, there was that Eric goal and I passed to Beckham when he scored from half way at Selhurst Park!" As for the real Cantona, McClair says, "Eric is a brilliant person, joined in the banter and always bought his round albeit with a platinum credit card!"

Finally, the League title arrived in 1993 and Brian was also part of the the club's first Double in 1994 when, as a substitute, he scored the last goal in the FA Cup Final win over Chelsea of which he says, "I have been fortunate in my career to have many many highlights, but who has not dreamt of scoring a goal in the FA cup at Wembley?" The winning goal in the 1990 FA Cup Final was scored by left-back Lee Martin but in the three previous rounds against Oldham (semi-final replay), Sheffield United and Newcastle, McClair was on the scoresheet. In the European Cup Winners' Cup the following season, McClair scored against every team that United faced until the final, when Hughes netted a brilliant brace against Barcelona. However, 'Choccy' was the only man on target when United won the European Super Cup against Red Star Belgrade in 1991 and the League Cup at Nottingham Forest's expense in 1992. With previous club Celtic, he had won the Scottish Cup in 1985 and the Championship in 1986. He was Scotland's Player of the Year in 1987, before he joined United for a fee of £850,000. Prior to leaving United in

1998, he won another Double in 1996 and another title in 1997, albeit with a decreasing number of appearances.

But as for naming his all time best or favourite United players Brian preaches the typical coach's line claiming "I don't do favourites!"

*

The most important issue inside Old Trafford following his third successive title success was the future of a manager who had decided to pre-book his retirement. It proved to be a monumental mistake, as it created internal rifts and indecision.

Ferguson's scheduled departure at the end of the following season was always going to be a testing time for England's outstanding club of the past decade but another Champions League failure brought the problem forward by 12 months. The £20 million drop in the value of United's shares following the Champions Cup quarter-final elimination by Bayern Munich was a stark reminder of just how important European success is to the club's financial well-being. United were already Premier League champions for the seventh time in nine seasons when they went to Munich.

Eight months away from his 60th birthday, Sir Alex retained the fierce competitiveness that has helped make him the most successful manager in the history of English football. United had been competing at the very highest level of European football for so long – seven seasons out of eight since 1993-94. In a match United had to win, some questioned why, given the suspended Beckham's enforced absence, Luke Chadwick was not played as his replacement from the start. Concerned about the England Under-21 international's lack of experience at this level, no doubt, was the answer. It meant playing Scholes out of position on the right, where he has always looked uncomfortable.

In the wake of a 3-1 aggregate defeat Roy Keane suggested his club needed to "be looking to buy the best", probably "two or three players for £50 million". Giggs concurred with his captain's assessment, stressing that "we've got to rebuild for next year", although he could see no cause for a clear-out. New arrivals were inevitable, with Ruud van Nistelroy continuing his recovery at PSV Eindhoven.

Beckham's absence through suspension in the Olympic Stadium gave the champions a glimpse of life without him, particularly at set-pieces: corners from Giggs not clearing the first man and unspectacular free-kicks from Jaap Stam.

Yet it was the controversy surrounding Sir Alex's that was a constant source of instability. In December 2000, Sir Alex was sure that "I will be staying on at the club in a capacity". Contrary to the club's stated hopes, he wanted no input in choosing his successor. "I could do without the burden. You don't want a situation where `it's Alex's boy'. It's got to be United's choice." Steve McClaren, the then number two, was a genuine contender. "Yes. Definitely. He's young at the moment. In a year and a half's time, the club will know more about him but he's done very well," Sir Alex said at the time. Martin O'Neill was the other front-runner. "I don't know which other candidates come into the frame. There are all sorts of rumours. Someone said Arsene Wenger has already been approached. That's a new one to me. There are few names being bandied about from abroad." These included Louis Van Gaal, Marcelo Lippi and Fabio Capello. Sir Alex added at the time, "No matter who gets it, they will get my support – because I am a United man. They will need support because it's not an easy job."

The problems of the succession had echoes of Sir Matt Busby's complicated introduction of his successor, Wilf McGuinness back in 1969. "I don't think I will cast a shadow. Everyone is going on about Sir Matt but I'm sure Sir Matt never set out to cast a shadow. He loved the club. When you love the club you care for it. The important thing is to allow the next manager space for his own ideas."

Ferguson dismissed the theory that United need him to remain in the building simply to prevent The Team That Fergie Built from breaking up. "This is a good family club with a good environment; the players are cared for, they can have anything they want here." He liked the balance he had developed at United, "It's just people's beliefs. Maybe Arsene Wenger is more comfortable with French players. Maybe he doesn't rate English players, I don't know. I am a bit surprised by what has happened at Chelsea. The biggest surprise was changing their management. I rated Gianluca Vialli. I respected him and thought he was doing a great job. But Chelsea seem a peculiar club in that players can influence the manager." Is that the way football is going? "I hope not. It depends on the directors and chairmen."

Sir Alex planned that his managerial farewell would be at the 2002 Champions League final – at his beloved Hampden Park. "We all have dreams and it would be lovely to do that. It only holds 52,000 and I would need all 52,000 tickets!" Alex had been at Hampden 40 years earlier, among a privileged 135,000 to witness Real Madrid destroy Eintracht Frankfurt 7–3 to secure a fifth successive European Cup. "Di Stefano was angry at not being mentioned in the [recent FIFA] award for greatest player of the 20th century because he was an incredible influence on Real Madrid. He should have been in the frame for that award – him and Pele. Maradona has also to come into it through winning the World Cup in 1986. He was the star of the team whereas Pele was among a lot of great players. But then Pele, at 17, scored two goals in a World Cup final, scored 1,300 goals in Brazilian football. Even in a really bad league, that would have been a hell of an achievement, but in Brazil...!

"The description `world–class' can only be justified if a player has had success in World Cups. I think Alf Ramsey was probably right when he said he had three world–class players in his team – Bobby Moore, Bobby Charlton and Nobby Stiles. George Best did not have the right platform internationally. If Best had been a Brazilian, he would probably have been sitting on that podium in Rome [alongside Maradona and Pele who shared the award]. Hopefully Giggs does have the chance to play on a world stage. His stage is the European Champions Cup. That is his opportunity to let people know how good a player he is."

In May 2001, there were fears that Sir Alex was on the

verge of walking away from United. The Old Trafford manager confirmed his plans to quit at the end of the next season but there had been discussions described in the media at the time as "acrimonious" concerning his role beyond his tenure as manager. The split between the United board and Ferguson forced his assistant, Steve McClaren to consider his future. A disillusioned Ferguson said, "When my contract finishes next season I will be leaving Old Trafford for good. It is a disappointing situation, to put it mildly. A few months ago, I said I expected a statement from the club within weeks about my future role when I finished as manager. That is what I believed would happen at the time. That situation was not forthcoming, however, and all talks on that subject are now dead. It's over. What the club was proposing was not what I was led to believe, but life goes on and I am not going to let it bother me. I have had a fantastic time at Old Trafford over the last 14 years and I am so grateful for the relationship I have enjoyed with my players and the supporters. I have spoken to Peter Kenyon this morning and he has given me assurances that money will be available for transfers this summer, so I have to continue on that basis." Reports in Spain suggested Barcelona would tempt Ferguson to the Nou Camp while Aberdeen directors were keen to lure him back to Pittodrie in some capacity.

Ferguson, it seems, wanted more than his employers were prepared to grant him. Negotiations never went smoothly, with United unable to understand why Ferguson needed his son, Jason, to conduct the talks on his behalf. Kenyon was nevertheless desperate to keep Ferguson at United. It was suggested that Ferguson's desire to join the plc board was opposed by certain directors, while there was also a dispute concerning his salary. Ferguson had said he wanted an ambassadorial role that would allow him to pursue his other interests, in particular horse racing.

While Ferguson was with his side for the final game of the season at Tottenham concern about his future hit the headlines. Ferguson had revealed the previous December, "My time as manager will definitely finish in a year and a half, but we have talked about me staying on in another capacity. That is something

I want because I love this club, and over the next few weeks it should be sorted out."

Roy Keane suggested United's decade of domination could be "coming to an end", having also caused unrest in the dressing room by questioning the commitment of his fellow players.

*

Two games into the 2001-02 season, United fans were shocked when Dutch central defender Jaap Stam was suddenly sold to Lazio in a £16 million deal. Stam's departure coincided with claims in his autobiography 'Head to Head' that he had been illegally spoken to about a move to United by Sir Alex, before his previous club PSV Eindhoven had been informed. The club's supporters were even more shocked when Sir Alex replaced Stam with Inter Milan's 36-year-old central defender Laurent Blanc.

During November and early December in 2001, United endured their worst league form in over a decade - six defeats in seven Premiership fixtures, three defeats at either side of a win. On 8 December, 2001, United were ninth in the Premiership - 11 points behind leaders Liverpool who had a game in hand. Sir Alex had already written off his side's chances of claiming a unique fourth successive Premiership title. Then came a dramatic turn-around in form. Between mid-December and late January, nine successive wins saw United climb to the top of the Premiership and put their title challenge back on track. In the end, United finished third in the Premiership, their first finish outside the top two since they finished sixth in 1990-91 First Division.

Sir Alex's dream of a Glasgow finale also faded with an away goals defeat to Bayer Leverkusen in the Champions League Semi Finals while they were knocked out of the FA Cup in the fourth round by Middlesbrough and in the third round of the League Cup by Arsenal. This meant that United had failed to finish winners or runners-up of a major competition for the first time since the 1988-89 season. United's misery was compounded as Arsenal clinched the Premiership title at Old Trafford with a 1-0 win in the penultimate game of the season.

The 2001-02 season was to have been Sir Alex's last as United manager, and the looming date of his retirement was cited by many as a reason for the team's loss of form. Ferguson himself admitted that the decision to pre-announce his retirement had resulted in a negative effect on the players and on his ability to impose discipline.

But in February 2002 he had agreed to stay in charge for at least another three years. The club insisted the U-turn was instigated by the manager. According to the club, there had been no pleading by the board with Ferguson to stay on he had simply had a change of heart. The timing suited United because their leading choices to succeed Ferguson – Celtic's Martin O'Neill, Bayern's Ottmar Hitzfeld and England's Sven-Goran Eriksson, were not available. Confirming that they were "approached by Sir Alex Ferguson on Sir Alex remaining as manager of the club beyond this season", United could hardly contain their glee. It was made clear to Ferguson that if he ever had second thoughts on retiring, it would be good to talk. Yet, Ferguson was already working on a book commissioned by publishers to chronicle his "final season". So why stay on?

David Beckham's father, Ted, one of the shrewder observers of life at Old Trafford, probably came closest to the truth on the reason for Ferguson's remarkable U-turn when he said, "I just couldn't see him sitting around with his pipe and slippers after all he's put into the game." The way he celebrated United's famous come from behind FA Cup victory at Villa Park was a vast difference to earlier in the season, when Ferguson looked as tired as his team. He was also impressed and influenced by the way Bobby Robson continued to thrive at the age of 68, pushing the champions hard with his vibrant Newcastle United side. Ferguson came to the conclusion that 60 was too young to retire. It was reported that Sir Alex's salary would rise from £1.67 million to £2 million a season the previous summer so his new deal would surpass Arsene Wenger's reported £2.5 million-a-year.

Paddy Crerand, a European Cup-winner with United in

1968, captured the mood when he said: "Every Manchester United supporter will thank God. They will be absolutely delighted. I'm sure the players will be delighted too and all the younger generation of players look up to Sir Alex as a father figure."

Around the New Year, after a thorough medical had showed him to be fighting fit, he realised that he had made a mistake. Close friends and family had urged him to reconsider for months. Ferguson "learned to enjoy the job again" according to one insider. He change course just 13 weeks before he was scheduled to walk away.

Sir Alex has since said that he will not make the same mistake again and when the time does come to call time on his illustrious career in football he will not prolong the agony for the club, "There obviously will be a point when I do quit and when that is I absolutely have no idea because I tried that, and it was an absolute disaster. [I was in] Agony, absolute agony [at the thought of retiring]. My wife made me change my mind and she was dead right. I think she thought she would soon be fed up with me around the house."

TITLE NO. 15 - 2002-03

"He continues to win year after year. He continues to change the team around. When people think the team's perfect he brings players in and United just carry on. It's not all about spending loads of money. It's about having the right people at the club and in the team and United always have that."

DAVID BECKHAM

SIR ALEX'S MAJOR SIGNING in the summer of 2002 was the then 24-year-old Rio Ferdinand, one of England's best performers at the World Cup Finals in Japan and Korea. The £30m acquisition from Leeds added the steel that had been missing from United's defence since the departure of Jaap Stam to Lazio.

United won their eighth Premiership title in 11 seasons, yet just over two months before the end of the season they had lost to Liverpool in the League Cup Final and slipped eight points behind leaders Arsenal on the same day. But an improvement in form for United, and a decline for Arsenal, saw the Premiership trophy gradually slip out of the Londoners' grasp and push it back in the direction of Old Trafford.

On 4 May, 2003, United's title success was confirmed when Arsenal lost 3-2 at home to Leeds United - a result which ended the Gunners' title hopes and secured Leeds's survival. It was to be Arsenal's last Premiership defeat for 49 games - a run which was ended in October 2004 by United, a run which included Arsenal completing the entire 2003-04 season as unbeaten Premiership champions.

That summer David Beckham joined Real Madrid after the two most glamorous clubs in the world agreed a fee of around £30 million for the England captain. Under the terms of the deal agreement, 7.5 million euros of the total fee would be paid by Real upon completion of the sale and 17.5 million euros over the following four years in equal installments. The remaining 10 million euros was conditional upon Real Madrid's performances in the Champions League. Beckham would earn six million euros a year plus bonuses at the nine-times European champions. The midfielder, who had travelled to Japan as part of a promotional tour of Asia for his sponsors, issued a statement through his agents SFX saying he was delighted to move to Spain. "I recognize that this is an amazing opportunity for me at this stage in my career and a unique and exciting experience for my family," he said. "I know that I will always regret it later in life if I had turned down the chance to play at another great club like Real Madrid. I will always hold precious memories of my time at Manchester United and Old Trafford as well as the players, who I regard as part of my family, and the brilliant fans." Madrid sporting director Jorge Valdano added, "We are delighted with the arrival of David Beckham. It is a signing that will help us become more competitive."

Italian clubs Inter and AC Milan had showed an initial interest in Beckham but a week earlier United announced they had agreed a conditional deal to sell him to Barcelona. Beckham's agents issued a statement saying he was "surprised and disappointed" at United's announcement and within days Barcelona's greatest rivals, Real, emerged as favourites for his signature. In the previous three years Real had held a virtual monopoly on buying the world's best players. Zinedine Zidane, Luis Figo and Ronaldo, all winners of the World Player of the Year award, had arrived at the Bernabeu for a combined transfer total of more than $160 million, with Beckham taking the outlay to more than $200 million. The club won the Champions League in 2000 and 2002 after selling their training ground to wipe out a $240 million debt. But even the most star-studded team in the sport's history had not been good enough this season as they were knocked out by Juventus in the semi-finals after beating United in the quarters.

While Beckham's immense talent, particularly in delivering deadly crosses and finding the net with fizzing free kicks, would be a boon to Madrid, the Spanish club would also be take advantage of the commercial opportunities afforded by one of the most marketable men in the world.

Beckham was hugely popular at United, a club he joined as a schoolboy, but his last few seasons at the club his relationship with Sir Alex had become strained. Beckham, married to pop star Victoria Adams and with two young children, led a high-profile celebrity lifestyle that was not always been appreciated by his manager. The Scot kept Beckham on the bench for several high-profile matches toward the end of the season, sparking the initial speculation that he would be moving overseas.

The strain really began to tell after United were knocked out of the FA Cup by Arsenal. A furious Ferguson kicked a boot in the changing room which cut Beckham over the eye. Sir Alex refused to apologise for Beckham's eyebrow injury. The United boss laughed off the incident, which he again described as "a freak". He jokingly added, "If I'd tried it 100 times or a million times, it wouldn't happen again. If it did, I would carry on playing." He said the England captain had not received stitches to his left eyebrow, but just a graze, which was dealt with by the team doctor.

At one of his regular press conferences, Sir Alex said that whatever happens in a dressing room "remains sacrosanct" but added, "there's no way I could betray the trust of the players. It is 100% loyalty. It can never be anything less than that." Sir Alex said everyone must now "move on" and then left the press conference - called in connection with a Champions League match against Juventus - refusing to answer further questions.

Earlier United fans urged Sir Alex to apologise publicly over the boot incident. Many thought it was the best remedy to heal the rift between manager and player which was vividly illustrated by Beckham's willingness to show off the wound caused by Sir Alex kicking the boot at him in a post-match tantrum. The England captain strolled defiantly along Manchester's most prestigious shopping street, knowing he was being photographed.

Beckham's dad, Ted, said his son would put the flying boot incident behind him and concentrate on the European tie with Juventus, commenting, "I'm not going to add fuel to the fire." Ex-United boss Tommy Docherty called Sir Alex a bully and said he should be disciplined; "I think it is an act of total frustration. Fergie being Fergie he went berserk. He is a law unto himself. He is a bully. There is a set of rules for him and one for all others. There is no way he did it deliberately, but I don't think he should get away with it." But Beckham and his wife Victoria were reported to be furious. His agent at the time, Caroline McAteer, said he intends to remain quiet about the whole affair. Bookmakers William Hill offered odds of 4/7 that Beckham would cease to be a United player before Fergie ceases to be the club's manager. They offered 5/4 that Ferguson would go first.

The Prime Minister brought laughter at a televised press conference at Downing Street when he joked about the other story dominating the news. Tony Blair, facing tough questioning from reporters over Iraq, joked, "I have got a stack of football boots under here you know!"

Beckham "went for" Sir Alex when his manager kicked a boot which hit his face but was restrained by team-mates as he lost control after being hit by the boot, according to his autobiography, My Side.

Ferguson's frustration following United's defeat to Arsenal was obvious – he allegedly blamed Beckham for one of the goals, prompting the dressing-room altercation. "I felt like I was being bullied in public, and being backed into a corner for no reason other than spite," Beckham said. Of his reaction when he was hit by the boot, he said, "I went for the gaffer. I don't know if I have ever lost control like that in my life before." His team-mates Ryan Giggs, Gary Neville and Ruud van Nistelrooy restrained the England captain, who likened the scene to a gangster movie. Ferguson apologised shortly afterwards. The team went on to overhaul Arsenal and win the Premiership, but Beckham was sold to Real Madrid.

Excerpts from Beckham's book revealed how the relationship between the pair had soured over the previous two years. Beckham said it started to deteriorate after his manager criticised him for visiting the Queen. Beckham had sustained an injury the previous season and went to Buckingham Palace the following week with the rest of England's World Cup squad. "I had a broken rib," he said, "I didn't have any choice but to rest it. The whole England squad was invited to Buckingham Palace, which was something I couldn't miss out on. I felt unbelievably proud, being introduced to Her Majesty as England captain." When he returned to training at United, he said he "began to feel a chill in the atmosphere between me and Alex Ferguson. He reckoned I'd have been fit sooner if I hadn't waited those extra couple of days before going away."

Despite these tensions, Beckham played a full part in United's title victory, helping the club win 8 of their last 9 fixtures to win the title by 5 points from an Arsenal side who had started the season in rampant form. Beckham's final flourish was to score in his last two games in a United shirt .

Yet United's failure to repeat their Champions League success of 1999 led Ferguson to re-evaluate his squad. He decided that to bring in new blood - Brazilian playmaker Ronaldinho was top of his shopping list and he would raise funds via the sale of the club's most valuable commodity. London-born Beckham had been at United since signing as a schoolboy and had two years remaining on a contract he signed a year earlier. Peter Kenyon, chief executive of United, said at the time, "While we are sad to see David go after so many great years at Old Trafford, we believe this is a good deal for the club, and we now look forward to building on the success of last season's championship title."

He was the highest-profile English player to have moved overseas since Paul Gascoigne left Tottenham Hotspur for Italian club Lazio in 1992. Very few British players had made a success of such a move. Former Liverpool midfielder Steve McManaman helped Real to two Champions League titles but remained a regular on the substitutes' bench. Other British players including Gary Lineker, Mark Hughes (both Barcelona), Ian Rush (Juventus) and Paul Ince (Inter Milan) failed to deliver their best form in new surroundings.

Beckham's exploits at Real are well documented, his run in with Fabio Capello, and his decision to make a shock exit to LA Galaxy, and then even attempting a Premier League short term comeback with Spurs. Now back in LA and warming up for the new season, he remarked that he didn't believe City could ever take United's place as English football's premier club. He observed, "The money that has been pumped in has been incredible. Players have been bought and that does a lot for the club and for the team. But United have that history and it's not all about paying fortunes for players. It's important the players get along with each other – that makes team spirit. As much as they have got the money to bring players in, sometimes that doesn't work. If they continue they will be a threat but there are no guarantees. I don't know. I haven't been around their team and their squad and I wouldn't want to be around Man City. But if they continue to bring players in, then who knows? You saw it with Chelsea when Roman [Abramovitch] arrived. They won two leagues and they won them on the trot. It works sometimes but hopefully it won't work at City."

Asked about Tevez, Beckham said he was convinced the City board will spend regardless of what happens with the striker. "Tevez was a really strong player for them last season, so if they lose him it will be disappointing. But they've got a lot behind them, so they can afford to bring world-class players in." When Beckham starred for United shirt (1993-2003), games with City were straightforward, "Every time I played against them it was during a spell when we were winning everything. They were the games the fans looked forward to and wanted us to win, so every time we came up against them we were winning. It was good to be a United player at that time."

His relationship with Sir Alex soured but he has long since forgiven him and for Beckham "there is no better manager". He added, "He continues to win year after year. He continues to change the team around. When people think the team's perfect he brings players in and United just carry on. It's not all about spending loads of money. It's about having the right people at the club and in the team, and United always have that. I can't see Sir Alex stopping. He is a legend and I have so much respect. He was a father figure to me. He works hard at what he does. He is the best at what he does. He is No1. He is the best manager in football."

So at 36 what about a return to the Premier League to play against United? "I wouldn't like to. I have played for the biggest club in England and I wouldn't like to play against them. I still feel good and fresh but I can't see it happening. The Tottenham thing didn't happen and it didn't happen for a reason. At the end of the day I only want to be known as a Manchester United player and that's the way it will stay."

Referring to the match as "just a small game", Beckham said he was looking forward more to the All Stars game against United, "but City coming here will be great for the fans. They will see some great players. There is no extra motivation because it's City. It's not special to me because I am a United fan. They have some great players but they are never gonna be United."

*

New signing Rio Ferdinand helped United to recapture their Premiership title but the calendar year ended on a low note for the defender – he was punished by the FA for failing to attend a mandatory drugs test at Carrington and was suspended for eight months. In the period without Rio, the Reds lost their title – to Arsenal again – but won the FA Cup for a record eleventh time, beating Millwall 3-0 in the 2004 final at Cardiff's Millennium

Stadium. United finished third in the Premiership and suffered Champions League elimination at the hands of eventual winners FC Porto, and a League Cup defeat by Aston Villa. This was partly caused by the absence of Ferdinand but also new signings like Eric Djemba-Djemba and Kleberson were disappointing, but there was at least one productive signing – 19-year-old Portuguese winger Cristiano Ronaldo, who had been signed from Sporting Lisbon for £12.24 million. Having failed to land their primary transfer target – Brazilian star Ronaldinho, who turned his back on a move to United and instead joined Barcelona, the Portuguese proved to be more than adequate compensation.

Managing director Peter Kenyon was blamed by many for failing to secure Ronaldinho's signing, after several months of negotiations and Kenyon later departed United to join rivals Chelsea. Following a disastrous performance against Real Madrid, during which he managed to save one shot over two legs, Fabien Barthez spent the 2003-04 season on loan at Marseille before being sold permanently and his place in the United goal was filled by American goalkeeper Tim Howard. Despite a reasonable record, Howard was blamed for United's Champions League exit – his weak clearance from a free-kick gifting the Portuguese a late winner.

At the beginning of the 2004-05 season, United paid an initial fee of £20 million for 19-year-old Everton and England striker Wayne Rooney, whose performances led to him being voted PFA Young Player of the Year at the end of the season. Argentine defender Gabriel Heinze also proved to be a successful new signing, while Cristiano Ronaldo continued where he had left off the previous season by putting in more match-winning performances. United were never favourites to win the Premiership title; again, their failure could be put down to a player's absence – high-scoring striker Ruud van Nistelrooy was unavailable for almost half of the season due to injury and his deputy Alan Smith suffered from a long dip in form. Ferguson guided the club to a third-place finish for the third time in four seasons; in the FA Cup they lost on penalties to Arsenal after a completely dominant United failed to break the Gunners' tight defence down in the FA Cup final after a goalless draw. Ferguson compared the setback to losing the League title to Leeds in 1991/92 and hoped the experience would galvanize his squad into a successful 2005/06 campaign. Chelsea, invigorated by the money of Roman Abramovitch and the management of Jose Mourinho had taken the Premiership and Carling Cup and it was the Gunners who triumphed on penalties despite a dominant display from United – for whom Rooney and Ronaldo were outstanding.

The following season brought maiden silverware for the pair as the Reds beat Wigan Athletic in the Carling Cup Final in an otherwise disappointing season. Ferguson's preparations for the season had been disrupted by off-field drama at United. Some years before Ferguson had been involved in a high-profile dispute with major United shareholder John Magnier, over the ownership of a racehorse. When Magnier and business partner JP McManus agreed to sell their shares to American business tycoon Malcolm Glazer, it cleared the way for Glazer to acquire full control of the club. This sparked violent protests from United fans and disrupted Ferguson's plans to strengthen the team in the transfer market. In spite of this, United looked to solve their goalkeeping and midfield problems. They signed the Dutch keeper Edwin van der Sar from Fulham and Korean star Park Ji-Sung from PSV.

United made a poor start, Ferguson's 32nd consecutive season in football management and his 20th at United. Sidelined due to injuries were many senior players like Gary Neville, Gabriel Heinze and their captain Roy Keane. In an MUTV interview following a 4–1 humiliation at Middlesbrough, Keane was very critical about some of his fellow players. The interview was not aired subsequently but the press reported his thoughts on the performances of Rio Ferdinand, Darren Fletcher, John O'Shea and Alan Smith. Despite this, United bounced back with a thrilling 1–0 victory over Premiership champions Chelsea. The game was famous for a goal from the under-fire Darren Fletcher and a stunning holding role played by Alan Smith, who was named the Man of the Match.

On 18 November, Roy Keane left the club, his contract ended by mutual consent. He returned for a testimonial at the end of the season, but infamously prevented Ferguson from delivering a tribute to the crowd. The two did shake hands, however, and Ferguson described Keane as the best player he had ever managed at Manchester United.

As if to compound a desperate season, for the first time in over a decade United failed to qualify for the knock-out phase of the UEFA Champions' League. United lost to Benfica 2-1 in their final group stage match and bowed out. With just one win in the entire group matches, United also failed to qualify for the UEFA Cup. The signings during January 2006 of Serbian defender Nemanja Vidic and French full-back Patrice Evra smacked to many of desperation. Evra's fraught debut in the 4-1 Manchester derby at Eastlands did not bode well, while an early Vidic outing saw United go down 4-3 at Ewood Park.

Upfront meanwhile United continued to struggle. Ruud van Nistelrooy, for the past four seasons the focus of United's attacks, seemed to be out of sync with the new tearaways Ronaldo and Rooney, two of the hottest properties in European football. Sir Alex, sensing that the Dutchman was slowing United's new found counter-attacking style, began to favour the fragile but very fast Louis Saha and stuck with this partnership in the League Cup final, the Dutchman watching from the sidelines as the team triumphed 4-0 without him. It was the beginning of the end for Ruud who played only 4 more games for the club before he was sold to Real Madrid for 24m Euros.

After the League Cup victory, United managed to close the gap on leaders Chelsea to seven points at one point. Talks of an amazing comeback were building but these hopes faded following a 0-0 draw at home against Sunderland. On 29 April, United faced Chelsea at Stamford Bridge in what turned out to be the title decider for Chelsea, as the reigning champions comfortably won 3-0 and retained their title. There was to be more bad news for Manchester United with star player Wayne

Rooney breaking a metatarsal for the second time in two years after falling awkwardly from a benign tackle by Paulo Ferreira. It not only ended Rooney's league season but put his involvement in the 2006 World Cup in doubt; however Rooney returned in England's second game against Trinidad and Tobago. Nevertheless, after their highest league finish in four years and closing the gap on Chelsea, United's hopes for the 2006/07 season were raised. Ferguson hoped to end his illustrious managerial career on a high, by halting the dominance of financially-powerful Chelsea and delivering another championship trophy to Old Trafford.

TITLE NO. 16 - 2006-07

*'I am very happy at the club and I want to win trophies and hopefully
we will do that this season.'*

CRISTIANO RONALDO

CRISTIANO RONALDO, who had joined United as an
18-year-old in 2003, was Player of the Year and Young
Player of the Year as he inspired United to take the title
from Jose Mounriho's Chelsea. The then 22-year-old Portuguese
winger signed a new five year contract in April ending speculation
over his future after being linked with a move to Spanish giants
Real Madrid and Barcelona.

"I am delighted. I spoke with Sir Alex Ferguson about
my future and everyone knew that I wanted to stay. I am very
happy at the club and I want to win trophies and hopefully we
will do that this season." Sir Alex added: "It is fantastic news, it
emphasises the point that Cristiano is happy here and that he is
at the right club. He has a great relationship with the team, staff
and the fans and he will go on to be one of Manchester United's
great players." Ronaldo was in scintillating form for United who
were still in line for the treble of the Champions League, the
Premiership and the FA Cup when he signed the new lucrative
deal.

Ronaldo had joined United from Sporting Lisbon for £12m
in August 2003, following an outstanding performance in a

friendly against the Reds during which he turned full-back John O'Shea inside out. Yet the Portuguese winger's first few seasons at the club were frustrating for many. His debut against Bolton at the start of the 2003-04 season had persuaded many that here was a major talent but inconsistency and petulance had marked many performances which included his dismissal in the Manchester derby in early 2006. Nevertheless there were glimpses of a world class player – his starring role in United's 4-2 destruction of Arsenal in February 2005 being a case in point.

Yet his blossoming partnership with Wayne Rooney was put in jeopardy at the 2006 World Cup following England's clash with Portugal in the quarter-finals. Rooney was dismissed and Ronaldo was pictured winking at the camera causing uproar in the English media. As a consequence, he was strongly linked with a move but Ronaldo returned to England to lead United's charge on the treble and took his goals tally to 20 with a double in the 7-0 rout of AS Roma. Many pundits believed he was by this stage the best player on the planet, with team-mate Patrice Evra even suggesting he had the ability to make the same impact as Pele and Maradona. Sir Alex found it hard to disagree, "At 22, he has the same skill factor as Maradona and Pele. He is one of the best signings I have ever made. The measurement of his improvement this year is astronomical. In terms of top-flight football, where do you find a winger who has scored 20 goals. It is incredible. Without question, Cristiano is getting to the level of best player in the world. Thereafter, it is up to others to decide whether he is as good as Maradona and Pele. That is the challenge in front of him now."

Ronaldo began the campaign under a cloud after the adverse publicity he received following his part in England's World Cup demise. But Ferguson said he always felt Ronaldo would cope with the flak that came his way. "We had dinner with him in Portugal and stressed this had happened before to David Beckham," revealed Ferguson. "It is a seven-day wonder really. There is nothing wrong with booing. We get booed at most places. But he had the nerve to handle it. He still gets a bit of it but that is only because he is a great player."

Sir Alex was sure Ronaldo made a wise decision to stay. "There was no reason for him to think about leaving, other than the fact people perceive Real Madrid as a club for galacticos, or whatever they call them. They have this notion about themselves and Barcelona are a fantastic club, too, but I can't say they are miles in front of Manchester United. Most people recognise we are one of the biggest clubs in the world and we believe Cristiano is in the right place."

However, Real were out to get their man, and when they want someone, they usually get them in the end. A month before Ronaldo committed to a new contract Real made public their desire to lure Ronaldo. Real president Ramon Calderon told a Spanish TV station, "We really like him but he belongs to Manchester United and they have to decide to sell him first. If that is the case then we'll be first in the queue." Calderon, who also planned to prise Brazilian midfielder Kaka away from AC Milan, insisted Real would not pay a £54m (80m euros) price tag reputedly placed on Ronaldo. "I don't think any player, even someone with Cristiano Ronaldo's quality, is worth that money, but we are definitely interested if Manchester United want to sell him," he reiterated. "I would love to see both Kaka and Cristiano Ronaldo play for Real Madrid next season but it won't be easy. Any big club would have this sort of objective and Real Madrid is a big club." Ronaldo responded, "It is a good sign to know I have so many clubs interested in me, such as Real Madrid. It means that I am valued. But I am very happy where I am and I hope to stay at Manchester United for many years. I have a good contract, in financial terms, but what really matters to me is to show my best form."

For Sir Alex and his players, the main aim remained Premiership glory, which duly arrived as United notched a 16th League title, finishing six points clear of former incumbents Chelsea. While the whole squad performed admirably to snatch the title back from Stamford Bridge, the man who took most of the plaudits was Ronaldo, who collected 13 personal honours during the campaign – including the PFA Player and Young Player of the Year award.

The previous summer Michael Carrick had been signed as a replacement for Roy Keane for £14 million, although the figure rose to £18.6 million depending on appearances and results. United started the season well, and for the first time ever won their first four Premiership games. They set the early pace in the Premiership and never relinquished top spot from the tenth match of the 38-game season.

The January 2006 signings had a huge impact on United's performances; Patrice Evra and Nemanja Vidic came in to form a solid back line along with already existing players Ferdinand and skipper Gary Neville. Vidic proved himself the natural successor to Bruce as a goal-scoring centre back, contributing four goals in the season. The signing of Carrick, which was questioned and criticised by a large portion of the media, brought stability and further creativity in the United midfield, forming an effective partnership with the evergreen Paul Scholes. Park Ji-Sung and Kieran Richardson both underlined their value to the first team squad by adding significant pace and incisiveness in attack with Rooney and Cristiano Ronaldo.

Ferguson celebrated his 20th anniversary in charge of United on 6 November, 2006, with tributes from his players, past and present, as well as his old foe, Arsène Wenger and former captain Roy Keane. The party was spoiled the following day when United endured a single-goal defeat at the hands of Southend in the fourth round of the Carling Cup. However, on 1st December it was announced that United had signed 35-year-old Henrik Larsson, a player that Ferguson had admired for many years, and attempted to capture previously. On 23rd December 2006, Cristiano Ronaldo scored the club's 2000th goal under Sir Alex's reign.

By late April, United were three points ahead of Chelsea at the top of the Premiership. Both sides were playing at the same time but at half time United were 2-0 down to Everton at Goodison Park while Chelsea led 2-1 at Stamford Bridge; it looked as though Chelsea were on the verge of catching United. However, a sensational turnaround of events saw United launch another trademark comeback to win 4-2, with Chelsea being pegged back to 2-2 thus handing United a five point lead with three games to go. The points on the table meant that if the Red Devils could win away in their derby against Manchester City and Chelsea failed to beat Arsenal the following Sunday at the Emirates, then Sir Alex's men would clinch the title.

United were a goal up via a Cristiano Ronaldo penalty when late drama saw Manchester City awarded a penalty of their own courtesy of a much-debated 'challenge' by Wes Brown on Michael Ball (replays showed Brown had pulled out of the tackle, only for Ball to launch himself into Brown) in the 80th minute. However, Edwin van der Sar came to United's rescue and saved Darius Vassell's penalty to give the Red Devils victory and put United within touching distance of their 16th League title. The next day, Chelsea drew with Arsenal and handed United their ninth Premiership title.

Two weeks later however, Sir Alex missed out on a sixth FA Cup when Chelsea pipped his side 1-0 in extra time in another exceptionally bad match featuring the top two teams in the League, at the new Wembley Stadium.

TITLE NO. 17 - 2007-08

"Manchester United are all about being a team and helping each other, it takes a team to win titles not individuals!"

PAUL SCHOLES

THIS WAS MANCHESTER UNITED'S second most successful season ever as they retained their Premiership title and landed the Champions League. To an already successful side, Sir Alex added four players before the start of the season: Anderson, Owen Hargreaves, Nani and Carlos Tevez. The controversial and in some quarters unpopular owners, the Glazers, continued to back their manager in the transfer market, recouping some of the money through fairly steep rises in ticket prices.

But for all the changes Sir Alex initiated, whether wholesale or gradual, there were constants, Ryan Giggs was one, another was Paul Scholes. In an exclusive interview for '20|13', Paul Scholes, uncovers the secret of United phenomenal success, is that it is about the team ethic developed by Sir Alex Ferguson and not about the star system of big name individuals, even though United have had more than most spectacular individuals. In the interview for '20|13' Scholes was asked about the players who played the key roles in the pursuit of trophies and he explains, "Manchester United are all about being a team and helping each other, it takes a team to win titles not individuals!

It is an unbelievable achievement by the manager and I'm sure he will want to stretch the lead on Liverpool even further. My favourite moments....well, they are every trophy we've won, especially the first one and also the last one to surpass Liverpool's total of 18. My favourite Manchester United players are Bryan Robson, Ryan Giggs, Roy Keane, Nicky Butt, Gary and Phil Neville and David Beckham!"

Sir Alex, though, has no doubt the value of Scholes over the years, "He was such a great, consistent player for us. I don't think we will find another Paul Scholes. He was a player of a lifetime. In his 20 years at the club, it is hard to pick out a bad game, but hopefully we can replace him. Maybe we will find a different type of player. Manchester United do that. Time and time again we have faced this problem. But eventually something turns up, either through our youth system or we will identify someone. Scholesy was starting to feel his legs last season and it made it difficult to play him in really big games. I think he made the right decision. We would have liked him to carry on and play 25 games next season but he didn't want that. He's so proud that he wanted to play every game and he couldn't. Wayne could play centre midfield but not the way that Scholesy played it. They are too different. The way that Wayne would play as opposed to Scholesy is that he would be more dynamic and all over the place, using his energy to run everywhere, challenge and hit those crossfield passes that he's terrific at. But Scholes was more calculated and he always had that control about him, controlling the speed and pace of a game, which is pretty difficult to do. He was an absolute one-off. You will never replace Scholes."

Approaching a 25th full season as United manager and his 70th birthday, Sir Alex remains as determined as ever. "We've lost five experienced players who gave the club great service: Wes Brown, John O'Shea, Edwin van der Sar, Paul Scholes and Gary Neville. At the time you look at it and think it's a big slice out of the cake but we have replaced them by bringing back Danny Welbeck (from Sunderland) and Tom Cleverley (from Wigan) and adding Ashley Young, Phil Jones and David De Gea which we think fills the gap. We've actually got 11 players aged 22 and under with us, so it could be an emerging team again. There are also some experienced players who are maturing and will carry the responsibility. Nemanja Vidic, Patrice Evra and Rio Ferdinand have responsible roles. So do Ryan Giggs, even though he is 37, Michael Carrick and Michael Owen. These are experienced players, and the young players will be desperate to get in their positions so I think it's a healthy situation we're in.'

Sir Alex main concern is in replacing Edwin van der Sar, "The only area is the goalkeeping position. De Gea is 20 years of age. He's young and he's played in the Spanish League for a couple of years but it's not the English League. I think he will need time to settle. The potential is enormous, it's absolutely unbelievable and he'll improve himself. I've got the boy Anders Lindegaard, too. They may both challenge for it but in time De Gea will be in position (to take the No 1 shirt), there's no doubt about that."

After a first-team career spanning 17 years and 676 appearances, Paul Scholes is taking up a coaching position at Old Trafford from next season. At the time of his announcement he said, "I am not a man of many words but I can honestly say that playing football is all I have ever wanted to do. To have had such a long and successful career at Manchester United has been a real honour. To have been part of the team that helped the club reach a record 19th title is a great privilege. This was not a decision I have taken lightly but I feel now is the right time for me to stop playing. I would like to thank the fans for their tremendous support throughout my career, I would also like to thank all the coaches and players that I have worked with over the years. But most of all I would like to thank Sir Alex [Ferguson] for being such a great manager. From the day I joined the club his door has always been open and I know this team will go on to win many more trophies under his leadership."

A member of the famed class of '92, who won the FA Youth Cup, Scholes made his debut in 1994 and his last game was the Champions League final defeat to Barcelona. He won 10 Premier League titles and, after missing the 1999 Champions League final through suspension, was part of the team that beat Chelsea in the Moscow final of 2008. "What more can I say about Paul Scholes that I haven't said before?" Ferguson added, "We are going to miss a truly unbelievable player. Paul has always been fully committed to this club and I am delighted he will be joining the coaching staff. Paul has always been inspirational to players of all ages and we know that will continue."

Wayne Rooney added that Scholes is "the best player" he has ever played with. "He will be missed greatly," said the striker, "I tried to ask him what he was doing but you don't get much out of him. I didn't think it would come this quickly. Everyone will be sad to see him stop. He is a great player." "It is a very sad day for Manchester United fans around the world," David Gill, the United chief executive, said, "Paul has established himself as one of the greatest players to ever wear the United shirt. It is very important that the club keeps the association with these great players and we are delighted that Paul will join the coaching staff."

The 2007-8 Premiership season began slowly with United scoring no more than a goal in any of their first six matches. Eventually they got into their stride and the goals flowed, mainly from the magical feet of Cristiano Ronaldo, while Wayne Rooney and Carlos Tevez also scored freely. It was Newcastle United that conceded most goals to United, losing 6-0 and 5-1. Ronaldo was the League's leading scorer with 31 goals. While it seemed improbable that the winger could top his heroics of the previous season, he did just that. Ronaldo played a major part - scoring 42 goals in total - as United saw off the challenge of Chelsea to notch the Double.

The Premiership was more closely fought than for many seasons. United recovered from a slow start to head the table for almost the entire campaign while Chelsea suffered the setback of losing their talismanic manager Jose Mourinho in September. In the next home game, ironically against Chelsea under new manager Avram Grant, United inflicted more misery on the Londoners with a 2-0 victory. From then on United's form rocketed with a series of outstanding performances inspired by the exploits of United's winger turned goalscorer.

Nevertheless, as Sir Alex has often observed, United rarely do things easily and by late April they were in danger of throwing the League away. A resurgent Chelsea had pegged them back. That game came between the two legs of United's Champions League semi-final against Barcelona. The first leg had seen United scrap for a 0-0 draw and with Tuesday's tie in mind, the United's manager left out Cristiano Ronaldo, Carlos Tevez, Patrice Evra and Owen Hargreaves from the potential championship decider. Chelsea were also in the middle of a Champions League semi-final (against Liverpool).

The game was captivating from the outset. After eight minutes, Nemanja Vidic fell victim to a knee to his chin; Drogba's intervention accidental. As the first half entered stoppage time, Drogba was allowed room to pivot on the edge of the area and cross. Arriving from the far post, an unchecked Ballack continued diagonally onwards and headed the delivery flush across the keeper to give the home side the lead/

Ferguson benefited from an extraordinary lapse of concentration from Chelsea's best defender. From a free-kick at the halfway line Paulo Ferreira touched square to Carvalho. Without looking, he clipped the ball back towards Petr Cech, had it intercepted by Rooney, and watched impotently as the striker accelerated on and finished off the inside of an upright to equalise. Belatedly, Ronaldo entered the field, soon to be faced by Anelka as Chelsea switched formation to 4-4-2, wingers playing so far up it was frequently a 4-2-4. Essien, now at right-back, attacked his wing and centred well. Carrick attempted to block and caught the ball with a tucked-in left arm - enough for the linesman to flag for a spot-kick. Where Ballack and Drogba had argued over the taking of free-kicks, there was no disputing that this was the German's. He waited for van der Sar to flex his knees and dispatched the ball to the opposite corner. Remarkably, it was the first penalty United had conceded in the Premier League. The points were Chelsea's and the title would now be decided in the final two games of the season.

In the meantime United managed to scrape past Barcelona with a pulsating 1-0 victory over Barcelona at Old Trafford, the only goal coming courtesy of Paul Scholes' 30 yard wonderstrike. Chelsea also made it to the final in Moscow with a similarly fraught 3-2 victory over Liverpool. United followed their Champions League success with a 4-1 win against West Ham which meant that the title would be decided on the last day. United went on to beat Wigan Athletic 2-0 while Chelsea could only draw 1-1 with Bolton. Despite a late charge from Chelsea, a final-day victory at Wigan, in which Ryan Giggs scored the clinching goal on the day he equalled United's all-time appearances record, secured a 17th League title for United, their tenth Premiership title in sixteen seasons.

In the FA Cup, United drew Premiership teams in every round. One of the easier matches should have been at home to Portsmouth in the quarter-finals, yet despite dominating the game, a late penalty won it for Portsmouth, who then went on to win the competition.

Ronaldo won the Football Writers Association Footballer of the Year, to become only the second player - after Thierry Henry in 2004 - to retain the title. Blackpool winger Stanley Matthews won the first Footballer of the Year award in 1948. It follows the then 23-year-old's PFA Player of the Year award, which he also claimed the previous season. Liverpool striker Fernando Torres and Portsmouth keeper David James finished second and third respectively. Ronaldo's awards consolidated his position as the most highly-rated player in the English game. "To score 38 goals in a season - so far - is an astonishing feat for a winger," said FWA chairman Paul Hetherington, "he did not exactly get 100% of the vote, but from the moment voting started he moved to the front and stayed there. Given his age, he has the potential and ability to dominate this award for years in an unprecedented way."

And so to the Champions League final in Moscow in the rain. It was the first all-English European Cup Final and proved every bit as tight as the title race. Ronaldo scored first during a period in which United were dominant – soon after Tevez and Carrick missed clear chances to add to the score. Approaching half-time a fortunate deflection fell into the path of Frank Lampard who equalised and the second half saw Chelsea dominate, hitting the woodwork on several occasions.

The game went to extra time, both teams had clear chances as the rain scudded in off the Steppes. Then, with minutes to go, the game boiled over as Carlos Tevez and Didier Drogba became embroiled at a disputed throw-in. The Chelsea striker was seen to have been the aggressor and was dismissed, a red card that would soon have deep implications...

On to penalties. All the early penalty-takers scored, except Ronaldo – as he approached he looked far from confident and Cech parried away a feeble effort. Was this to be an unfitting end to a sensational, record-breaking season? Chelsea continued to slot their spot kicks and it fell to the last penalty taker to step forward. Under normal circumstances the taker would have been Drogba but as he had been sent off Chelsea captain John Terry adjusted his armband and took responsibility.

As the rain worsened Terry stepped forward, placed the ball, ran up and, at the vital moment of impact, lost his footing, sending van der Sar the wrong way but the ball against the post. From then on Chelsea seemed to wear the look of a defeated side. Nani, Anderson and Giggs all scored for United while Kalou slotted for Chelsea. Anelka's kick was saved by Edwin van der Sar and United had won Europe's premier tournament for a third time.

The team was led up to receive the Champions League trophy by Bobby Charlton. It was fifty years since the team he played for in his youth was destroyed in Munich attempting to win the European Cup. The fiftieth anniversary of the Munich air disaster had been marked in Manchester in February. A new 'Munich Tunnel' was opened at Old Trafford. The game in February against Manchester City was preceded by a one minute silence. Both teams played in 50's style kit. Perhaps overawed by the occasion, United lost 2-1.

For the legend who claims "records mean nothing" Ryan Giggs scored the penalty that won the Champions League and broke the club's appearance record on one of the greatest nights of a staggering career. When the Welsh winger appeared as an 87th minute substitute against Chelsea in Moscow, Giggs broke arguably the toughest record of them all, surpassing Sir Bobby's 758-game feat to become United's all-time record appearance holder.

With the penalty shoot-out entering sudden death, Giggs stepped up to score the decisive spot kick, completing an unprecedented personal 10 championship titles, a Professional Footballers' Association team of the century place, scorer of one of the greatest-ever FA Cup goals, joint record for FA Cup trophy wins and the only player to score in every Premier and Champions League campaign and, perhaps his greatest ever accolade - the first British footballer to be featured in The Simpsons!

Giggs, AC Milan icon Paolo Maldini and Real Madrid legend Raul are the greatest one-club men of their generation. Giggs was now the owner of a 20th major medal spanning his 18 years as a professional. "That's why if you asked any player or pundit in the world which left-winger is in their ultimate dream team, they'd say Ryan Giggs," said his first Manchester United captain Bryan Robson.

TITLE NO. 18 - 2008-09

'It's a fantastic achievement to win 18 but I think it would be even better to go one better than Liverpool and win 19,' said Sir Alex. 'That has to be our goal now.'

SIR ALEX FERGUSON

HOW DO YOU emulate a season in which you have won the Champions League and Premier League titles? Well, Sir Alex's men did their very best and only defeat at the very last hurdle, against Barcelona in the Champions League Final, prevented United from a historic trophy haul.

Despite ultimate disappointment in Europe, United dominated almost every other competition. In December, United flew to Japan to compete in the FIFA Club World Cup and a solitary Wayne Rooney goal against Ecuador's Liga de Quito in the final was enough to crown United world champions. But what sort of effect would a gruelling mid-season trip to the Far East have on the Reds' domestic aspirations? As it turned out, it only made United stronger: Sir Alex's men reeled in Liverpool, seven points clear when United returned from Japan, before going on to win a record-equalling 18th League title and equalling Liveprool's haul of titles.

Before Gary Neville lifted the League trophy, United had tasted success against Tottenhan in the Carling Cup, goalkeeper Ben Foster was the penalty shootout hero after scores remained level after 120 minutes. Foster wasn't the only youngster who impressed that day, or indeed over the course of the season, as Federico Macheda burst onto the scene with a stunning debut goal, an injury-time winner, against Aston Villa, while Danny Welbeck and Darron Gibson announced their arrivals with spectacular strikes.

Ahead of the penultimate game of the season, as United just needed to avoid defeat against the Gunners to clinch the title in front of their home fans for the first time in a decade, Sir Alex warned Liverpool that United would go on to break their record of 18 League titles – and hinted he may stay around to oversee it. Asked about the prospect of equalling Liverpool, Sir Alex said, "That's a fan thing. To me, I'm not looking at equalling anyone. I just want ourselves to be the best. This team has got a bit to go yet, it can go on to win many more titles and that's exciting for me. The prospect of winning more titles with this team resonates with me far more than equalling somebody. This team is young enough to win more titles. I'm sure they can do it. We have a lot of young players in the squad now and that's the healthy part. We obviously still have the dinosaurs like Giggs, Scholes and Neville. We hope they can last another two years because the younger players will really benefit from that. The likes of Danny Welbeck, Federico Macheda, Darron Gibson, Jonny Evans and Rafa da Silva – they all have the potential. The level of football that they are showing – that potential is higher and harder then when Ryan, Paul and Gary came into the team."

Ferguson added: "No doubt the League is more competitive these days and that would make this achievement satisfying. Teams have been taking points off teams that they wouldn't normally take them off. That tells you the strength of the League. It's the toughest in the world and you see that with the impact of the teams in the Champions League." United fans were encouraged to hear their manager talking about the years to come.

United outplayed Arsenal at the Champions League semi-final stage and then saw the Gunners embarrassed 4-1 at home by Chelsea. But Ferguson warned that Wenger and his team were out to recover some pride on a ground where they themselves clinched the League in 2002. But the United boss – still without the injured Rio Ferdinand – added: "We've had some good tests in the past few weeks in terms of the resilience of the team. We were 2-1 down to Villa, 2-0 down to Spurs, 1-0 down on Wednesday at Wigan, which was probably the biggest test considering there were only three games left and it was the last opportunity for us to throw it away. But we've overcome that by showing our resilience, strength and patience."

As it turned out, club captain Gary Neville lifted the Premier League trophy as United equalled Liverpool's record by securing the title with a 0-0 draw with Arsenal. United needed only the point to clinch the title, and the result put the club out of reach of second-place Liverpool, who were seven points behind with two games to play. Arsenal ensured United did not earn their prize without a fight. Robin van Persie and Cesc Fabregas both wasted opportunities to drag the title race into its final week and leave United with more work to do at Hull City on the last day of the season as nerves jangled in the closing stages. But United's defence, so often the bedrock of their success this season, delivered another clean sheet when Ferguson needed it most and Old Trafford erupted in ecstasy at the final whistle as an 11th Premier League success was confirmed.

Arshavin was restored to Arsenal's side after illness, and he saw plenty of possession in a first 45 minutes that saw Wenger's side acquit themselves far better than when the pressure was on in the recent Champions League semi-final against United. Rooney missed United's best chance with a first-half header and there was an intriguing cameo when Old Trafford voiced its resounding disapproval when the popular Carlos Tevez was substituted in what would prove to be his final home appearance. Tevez's spectacular equaliser at Wigan earned him a starting place ahead of Berbatov – with Ferguson clearly unmoved by continued speculation surrounding the Argentine's future. United had struggled to create clear-cut opportunities, but Fabianski had to be alert on the hour to block Tevez, with Ronaldo firing the loose ball yards over the bar. It was the final contribution for Tevez, who was replaced by Ji-Sung Park. The decision was met with open derision as the popular striker made his way to the touchline. Tevez milked the situation, waving to all sides of the ground in apparent farewell – going a step further by acknowledging the fans after taking his place on the bench.

It set the seal on a title race that had been deceptively close. Liverpool, for once living up to pre-season hype, stormed into an eight point lead by Christmas following a 5-1 destruction of struggling Newcastle at St James' Park. But, almost as soon as they got there, their lead evaporated and many believed that their manager and star player were the chief culprits. Within days of reaching the Premiership's summit, Rafa Benitez held a bizarre press conference in which he produced a sheaf of 'facts' intended to prove that Sir Alex Ferguson and Manchester United were favoured by referees, the FA and the Premier League. Just days earlier the hitherto squeaky clean Steven Gerrard had become embroiled in an altercation in a Southport bar and been charged with assault.

Liverpool, clearly damaged by the media fallout surrounding these incidents, went on to drop points in their subsequent away match at Stoke and won only three of their next seven games as United won nine games on the bounce to move 7 points clear ahead of Liverpool's visit to Old Trafford in mid March. Yet the Merseysiders shocked even their own supporters with an amazing 4-1 win as United imploded. Fernando Torres gave Nemanja Vidic a torrid time as he pounced on an error by the Serb to equalize. United, normally so fluent at home, were caught on the counter-attack again before half-time and went on to implode as they sought parity in vain in the second half.

Buoyed by this success and victory over Real Madrid in the Champions League quarter-finals, Liverpool marched on winning eight of their last nine fixtures to pile on the pressure. United blew their lead completely the following week with another unlikely defeat at Fulham and were 2-1 down to Aston Villa with just 10 minutes remaining before Ronaldo levelled, a prelude to an incredible debut winner by Frederico Macheda.

Macheda was on hand a week later at Sunderland to apply the fortuitous touch that secured United victory in the north-east before a routine victory over Portsmouth back at Old Trafford. By half-time in the next game however, United looked sunk once more. Trailing 2-0 to a rampant Spurs, Sir Alex threw on striker after striker, with the four musketeers – Tevez, Rooney, Ronaldo and Berbatov detailed to fire a comeback. This 'devil may care' approach worked in the end but it took a controversial penalty decision by Howard Webb to turn the tide as Rooney and Ronaldo both grabbed a brace to win the match 5-2.

Having got over their now traditional late season wobble, United coasted home with wins against Middlesbrough and Manchester City before a come from behind victory at Wigan was sealed with a late Michael Carrick goal. With United content to see out a goalless draw at home to Arsenal, all that was left were the now traditional end of season celebrations at Old Trafford.

After the triumph Sir Alex immediately set his sights on reclaiming the League crown again after sealing another hat-trick of titles, "The great challenge now is to try to win it next year because that would be something special. I am already thinking about next year. You have to do it here. There is nothing else for it. You just drive on. I do take a lot of pride from equalling Liverpool. When I came down here they were the top guns. My job was to try to change that. I never thought we could get 11 titles - never in a million years."

When asked whether equalling Liverpool's record was a special moment, Ferguson added, "It'll make it more special when we are in front of them. Next year we are going for it again. It's a great side, a great squad. I could have picked two teams today. It's not easy." Ferguson admitted equalling Liverpool's record had been his almost Mission Impossible target at the start of his Old Trafford reign, "That was the target because they were the greatest side in the land," he said.

Despite a lacklustre game, the final whistle set off a massive title celebration at Old Trafford as the team were presented with trophy on the field, with the players hugging and spraying champagne at each other. Ferguson had now won 25 major trophies since his arrival at the club in 1986 and hoped to make it 26 when United faced Barcelona in the Champions League final in Rome. "It makes you want to go on for ever," the 67-year-old Scot said on the pitch. The trophy was carried onto the pitch by four soldiers who had just returned from a four-month tour of duty in Afghanistan. As the medals were presented and fireworks exploded, the rain that had lashed the pitch throughout the match cleared and Old Trafford was bathed in sunshine.

For the manager however, retirement remained a distant proposition, "I'm not contemplating it. I'll carry on. I'm going to stay as a manager and my health will tell me when to quit."

He felt his side could not be in better health as they aimed to become the first team to successfully defend Europe's premier cup. "Now we have won the League we are bouncing into the final. The players and fans are up. It is a very positive note we are striking at the moment. You get that same wonderful feeling when you win a trophy. When you see the fans celebrating at the end of the game, all the hard work and the pain is worth it." Ronaldo had come closest to winning the match for United with a wicked second-half free-kick that flew just wide of the right-hand upright. "It was the longest 90 minutes in history," joked Ferguson. "There was only one save in the match – it was a cautious match."

Giggs, the man who has shared all 11 of those titles with Ferguson, agreed. "The second half was agony to be honest. I'm sure it was for the fans as well. The one team you don't want to play is Arsenal as they keep the ball so well, and they came to spoil the party." Giggs celebrated his 11th Premier League title and immediately set his sights on a record-breaking fourth on the trot. Giggs enjoyed almost all the success United achieved under Sir Alex. United become the first club to achieve a hat-trick of titles twice, having done what Huddersfield, Arsenal and Liverpool previously achieved between 1999 and 2001. Giggs commented, "I hope we win another one next year. No-one has ever won it four times on the trot so that is another record for us to break." It would go alongside the Club World Cup, the PFA Player of the Year award and a landmark 800 appearances for United this season alone, Giggs having missed out on the Carling Cup final triumph against Tottenham. "It has been a special season for me," he said, "I would rather have league titles than personal accolades. But I was so happy to win that PFA award at my age. And being a United fan growing up, to play 800 times for the club is brilliant for me. It has been a special time for the club since the manager took over. We have been fortunate to win so much, hopefully we can carry it on. This year we have the best United team ever. But to talk of a great team, you need six or seven consecutive years of dominance. This side is good enough to do that because all our young players can improve. I was there at the beginning and it seems unbelievable that we've now won 11 Premier League titles. The first one, we always thought, was going to be the hardest. Now we've got the winning mentality and that stems from the great man himself."

Gary Neville believed the quality and depth of the squad was the key, "The thing about us this season is you can't name our best side. It has been about our squad, and everybody has contributed – whether they have played enough games to win a medal or not. We've never really had a consistent team. We've had 20 players... Kiko (Federico) Macheda himself could have won us the League and he's not even got a medal today. It was an incredible effort all year round. Today it was a brilliant performance, the lads really dug in against a good Arsenal performance." Gary was particularly delighted with his team's league triumph given the extent to which they have been challenged by Liverpool in the title race. "It's a fantastic achievement. They (Liverpool) pushed us really hard this season and they finished in championship form themselves. Liverpool have finished in title-winning form but we have not panicked, we have fought hard and had to show some guts to win it this time. Next season we know we'll have our work cut out to make sure we do it again and get past them."

Andy Cole, who played for United between 1995-2001,

making 275 appearances, scoring 121 goals observed, "This side can be the best ever – but they still have to beat Barcelona in the Champions League final to be considered above our 1999 side. If they do that, they will have created history as the first team to defend the Champions League successfully. Until then, you have to keep my '99 team as number one. A lot of our players, maybe most, could have played in this team. Gary Neville, Ryan Giggs and Paul Scholes are still there. But could Peter Schmeichel or Roy Keane get into the current side? Of course. And did you ever see a better full–back than Denis Irwin, on the right or left? The secret to our success was the team spirit, it was awesome. We had to fight every step of the way, but the spirit shone through."

Sir Bobby Charlton hailed United's new champions as the greatest team in the club's illustrious history – and the completion of a second hat-trick of Premier League titles as Sir Alex's most remarkable achievement. "Being part of Manchester United is the greatest ride in the world," said Charlton, "I am human like anyone else and I have been kicking every ball these past few games. This team are better than any we've ever had. Some of the football they play is fantastic. It is in the best Manchester United traditions. It has been hard playing three games a week at times, but we deserve to be champions."

United hauled their way back after starting the season in the bottom six and Charlton admits that it has been hard on the blood pressure. "It is the way United play – adventurous," he said, "sometimes when you are adventurous, you get caught. It drives you mad if you are involved in it. At times, you have to go to the brink. Sir Alex has followed on from Sir Matt, whose philosophy was always that you have to please the fans. He said United had to play attractive football, and Alex has continued it."

What impressed Charlton most is the way United's players have coped with an extraordinarily crowded fixture list. Flying to Japan to play three games in December in the FIFA Club World Cup led to a packed schedule on their return, made even more crowded by runs to the finals of the Champions League and Carling Cup and the semifinals of the FA Cup. "'This season we have been to the other side of the world and had to play catch-up," said Sir Bobby, "It's hard when you are playing three games a week and you have to win every game. It is such a long slog. But the players have got there in the end and three titles in a row is amazing."

Charlton believed that now Ferguson has equalled Liverpool's record of 18 League titles, he will not rest until he has passed it. "Alex is the greatest of all time," added Sir Bobby, "His ambition keeps him going. He said when he arrived at Old Trafford that he was only interested in United being champions and that is the way it has always been. We have a statue of Sir Matt at Old Trafford. There will have to be one of Sir Alex one day. In fact, they might have to put up five or six!"

The big decisions revolved around Ronaldo and Tevez; both were destined to leave, but there was still uncertainty as the celebrations began. Tevez, applauded all four stands but there was no embrace from Ferguson until the celebrations broke out on the pitch after the final whistle. "It's a good sign he was so emotional as we want him to stay, I just felt he was tired, so don't read anything into the substitution." said Ferguson. But not for another £25million he didn't. Despite the absence of chances, there was an intensity to the contest. Patrice Evra had claimed the European clash was 'men against babies' and he bore the brunt of it, taking kicks from Van Persie, Samir Nasri and Fabregas. "Win or lose, I think you should show respect," commented Arsenal manager Arsene Wenger pointedly, "the best answer is to play better on the pitch, but when you are young, it's understandable when players are sensitive about this." The willingness of Arsenal players to make a point meant that five of them ended up with yellow cards.

Tevez was cheered by United fans throughout, with continual chants of 'Argentina' and 'Fergie, sign him up!' He received the loudest cheer of the day when he received his Premier League winner's medal. The player had wept after being substituted on 67 minutes, a decision greeted by widespread boos before the 74,000 crowd at Old Trafford rose to applaud him off the pitch.

After the game Tevez said in faltering English, "It is difficult to [go] out [from] Manchester United. It is very emotional. I like Manchester United fans. It's maybe goodbye. It's very difficult." Earlier, speaking in Spanish on Argentine TV station TYC, he confirmed that he would be leaving, with Manchester City, Chelsea and Liverpool expressing early interest. Tevez said: "I know that I am not going to continue at Manchester United. I feel that they have lacked respect towards me. It's not about whether they pay £5m more or £5m less but I feel I have been badly treated. There are ways in which the club is managed that I don't understand. When you don't agree with the manager in how the club is run... I don't have faith in a lot of things that happen here. I've been here for two years and the directors have never come to speak to me. Not once have I had a meeting with them. Therefore, it's best that I leave the club so as not to clash with Alex Ferguson and the directors. Neither do I understand why I don't play in the team. I've asked Kia [Joorabchian – Tevez's agent] not to speak to me about offers during the next 10 days. I want to concentrate only on the final matches that we have to play. Afterwards, I've got a month to take a decision and choose where to go."

When asked whether he was bidding farewell, Tevez added, "Maybe goodbye. It's very difficult." The type of ownership of economic rights which Joorabchian exercises over Tevez had been banned by the Premier League but the rule could not be applied retrospectively. Even though he was out of contract and could command a huge signing on fee, running into several million pounds, as he moved on a free transfer, he would cede that money to Joorabchian's company after signing a contract with them five years ago when he was playing in Argentina. Gordon Taylor, chairman of the players' union, the Professional Footballers' Association, condemned the arrangement of third-party ownership of player's transfer rights. "You can't have people 'owning' other people," he said, "it's incredible to talk like that in this day and age. This type of third-party ownership is wrong and is in danger of bringing the transfer system down. We should take the strongest possible action to outlaw it."

Tevez broke down in tears when he appeared to wave goodbye to United and he was given a standing ovation as Old Trafford celebrated clinching the title. Despite reassurances from Sir Alex that the club want him to stay, Tevez resigned himself to leaving after United declined to meet the £25 million fee due to the company run by Kia Joorabchian that claimed to own the Argentinian.

For his part Cristiano Ronaldo enjoyed the title celebrations but stopped short of committing his long-term future to United in his post-match interview. "It's brilliant, the atmosphere here is unbelievable, the supporters screaming, singing songs... it's amazing but the future you never know. But as I said before, I'm really, really happy here. It's a fantastic achievement, to win at home the Premier League again, it's a brilliant feeling – always brilliant. All the supporters and all the fans are brilliant. I try to do my best all the time. We win the League and now we go to win the Champions League. We have to enjoy this moment. This moment is very special. In the next two or three days we have to concentrate on the Champions League because everyone wants to win this competition."

Ronaldo's demeanour seemed to change the moment the final whistle blew on United's 2-0 defeat by Barcelona in Rome. Having started the game hot favourites, the reigning European champions dominated the opening exchanges with the Portuguese winger keen to shoot from seemingly anywhere within range of goal. However a Vidic slip-up allowed Samuel Eto'o to open the scoring and Barca never looked back. After the final whistle Ronaldo was asked the inevitable questions about his future and to English interviewers he sounded committed. It was a different story however in his native language and within days the rumours that had circulated became concrete as United reluctantly accepted a record breaking £80m bid. The Ronaldo saga had disrupted United's pre-season the previous summer and it took a personal visit from Fergie himself to persuade him to stay on. Many now believed that the deal the pair struck was for one season more and now Ronnie was on his way.

The Tevez saga took longer to sort out and there was a twist as the Argentine moved across the city to Eastlands for an estimated £47.5m fee. City had acquired new owners earlier in August 2008 following the controversial ownership of Thaksin Shinawatra. Now backed by oil rich sheikhs keen to provide a window on their spending power, City set about bidding for almost every player available – and a few who weren't... Tevez's move to Eastlands sparked a poster campaign with the infamous slogan 'Welcome to Manchester' plastered on a billboard near the city's cathedral – if nothing else his move would further spice up that rivalry.

★

Reflecting on a disappointing end to what should have been a triumphal season, the vastly experienced Rio Ferdinand believes the 19th title was something to savour as the team failed to really enjoy the 18th title success, "The time before in Rome, when we lost to Barca 2-0 in 2009, I spent my whole summer moping around even though we had won the League. I just think you have to savour moments like that. The 19th title was a big event." Ferdinand, now 32, argued that United have not had the credit they deserve for landing their 19th title. "It is ridiculous and makes me laugh. We've won the League four times out of the last five. Half of it is people wanting someone else to win. Our 19th title was fantastic but we lost the Champions League final to Barcelona. When you dust yourself down and analyse it all, we had a successful season. We should enjoy it." Ferdinand, speaking in Seattle during Manchester United's pre-season tour in July 2011, added, "At the start of the season, if someone had said we'd reach the Champions League final and win the League, we would have accepted it." Despite being delighted with last season's triumph, Ferdinand promises no one at the club will be resting on their laurels, adding, "There is a challenge every year and you have to rise to it. We are really looking forward to it."

Ferdinand knows how tough it will be to replace Paul Scholes, and he nominates Scholes as his favourite player. "I have always said it, Paul Scholes is my favourite player,' said Ferdinand, "He is one of the top two players I have ever played with and I thought he could have gone on for a couple more years. But it is his decision to stop and you have to respect that." Because of Scholes' quality, Ferdinand believes it is pointless trying to find someone of a similar stature. Instead, he believes United may have to tweak their playing style, and the man to assume Scholes' role may already be within their midst. "When people like Roy Keane and Ruud van Nistelrooy left, we didn't go like-for-like in replacements. We got different players who had a great impact. We have players in the squad already who have the potential to do that. Anderson has had a lot of injuries over the last couple of years and missed a couple of pre-seasons. Hopefully this time he will have a good pre-season and we will see the best of him."

The acrimony surrounding Tevez's switch from blue to red have continued unabated. Sir Alex's suggestion that the striker wasn't signed by Manchester United on a permanent deal because he said he was going to quit football in four years' time was been denied by the player's spokesman. Tevez was at Old Trafford for two years on loan but United chose not to take up the option to keep him and he joined City. Since then, the Argentine has gone on to become one of the best players in the Premier League, leading many to question Ferguson's wisdom over the decision to let him go. Sir Alex stoked the fires by claiming that it would not have been a worthwhile long-term investment. "Tevez told us he was only going to play for four more years," Ferguson said on the eve of the new 2011-12 season, "if we had signed him on a five-year contract knowing that he was going to quit in four, there would have been no re-sale value for us." The now 27-year-old forward responded by insisting that he will continue his career for another eight years. "'At no time did he discuss retiring with the Manchester United management and Mr Ferguson has not mentioned this at any time before,'" a spokesman for Tevez said, "'In fact Carlos feels he is capable of playing for a further eight years and though he has been in the form of his life, he feels he is only going to get better in the coming years."

Whatever the real reasons behind Tevez departure from Old Trafford, it left Sir Alex with a major rebuilding job in attack, which he attempted to resolve with the acquisition of £18m winger Antonio Valencia's from Wigan. Yet the 2009-10 season would prove to be frustrating. Wayne Rooney rose to the challenge of replacing the goals lost with Ronaldo's departure and his form carried United to the top of the table entering the final stages with familiar foes Chelsea snapping at their heels. However an injury sustained in the final minutes of a Champions League match in Munich scuppered Rooney and United's season. Within days the Reds were knocked out of Europe and ceded control of the title race as a Didier Drogba inspired Chelsea won 2-1 at Old Trafford. Forlornly United battled to the finish but with the Pensioners in rampant form they took the title by a point on the final day.

In the following close season United sought to bolster their attacking options with the acquisition of Mexican striker Javier Hernández, a 21-year-old who would be formally announced as a United player on July 1 once an application for a work permit was approved. United initially paid Chivas just over £6 million for the player, a fee that would rise with appearances. As part of the deal, United would play in a match to mark the opening of the new 45,000-seat Chivas Stadium in Guadalajara.

Nicknamed "Chicharito", or Little Sweet Pea, Hernández came from a rich line of footballers. His father, Javier Sr, who was known as "Sweet Pea", played in the 1986 World Cup finals for Mexico and his grandfather, Tomás Balcázar, represented the country in the 1954 tournament. His arrival was announced after United Champions League win over Bayern Munich but delayed until the summer. Chicharito's promising performances

Hernández was United's second signing for the coming season with Chris Smalling also due to arrive in July in a £12 million move from Fulham. Hernández had an impressive strike-rate at club level, scoring almost once every two games, four goals in four appearances and his performances at that summer's World Cup, where he was clocked as the fastest player of the tournament, showed United might have unearthed a gem. United beat off competition from Arsenal for Fulham's Chris Smalling. The centre half, who had been playing non-league football just two seasons before for Maidstone United, was another who could be said to represent value in an increasingly inflated transfer market.

TITLE NO. 19 - 2010-11

"I supposed it's the basic fact that Manchester United have had the best team over the last 20 years. I always think it's important to have stability at a club and Sir Alex has made sure the players had had that. There has been a generation of players who have stuck together, know each other's game and the manager has added players here and there who have complemented these where and when necessary."

MICHAEL OWEN

AFTER ALL THOSE GLORY YEARS with Liverpool as one of the world's greatest goalscorers, Micheal Owen finally won his first Premier League title medal with Manchester United with just 11 League appearances, 10 from the bench, enough also to warrant a one-year contract extension at the end of the season. There can be few more qualified to discuss the United–Liverpool divide than the former England.

So how important, from his personal point of view, was it to win his first League title medal? "I've been hugely honoured to have played with some of the greatest players who have played the game and at some of the biggest clubs in the world. Saying that, you are judged by not only how many goals you've scored but also by what you have won as a player and it's great to look back and to be able to include a Premier League medal to my other achievements including winning the Ballon d'Or, 89 caps for England and 40 goals for my country."

For the purposes of this book the key question is, of course, why was it so difficult to achieve winning the League title at Liverpool for so many years? "Football is cyclical," Michael explains, "Liverpool were dominant in the 80's, Manchester United were dominant in the 90s and also now, with Arsenal and Chelsea being our main rivals over the last decade. I supposed it's the basic fact that Manchester United have had the best team over the last 20 years. I always think it's important to have stability at a club and Sir Alex has made sure the players had that. There has been a generation of players who have stuck together, known each other's game and the manager has added players here and there who have complemented these where and when necessary."

"Every year you set out to win the domestic title. European Cups are the big target and the domestic cups are your bread and butter. When I was at Real Madrid, they shared the same opinion of La Liga as well." So were the 2011 team worthy winners? "It's difficult to understand how people say we weren't! We won the League by nine points and got to the final of the Champions League and the semi-final of the FA Cup. I think it's hard to argue against those statistics.

"My best memory from the season was when the final whistle went against Blackburn Rovers at Ewood Park and the realisation dawned on me that we had won the Premier League. I would say Edwin van der Sar, Nemanja Vidic, Ryan Giggs, Nani and Berbatov were they key players. It was also great to see Hernández having a great season which is promising for the future." The 31-year-old striker expressed his desire to prolong his career at Old Trafford by signing a new one-year extension to his contract adding, "to play alongside so many great players, under an exceptional manager and in front of so many passionate supporters is a real inspiration."

Owen arrived at Old Trafford in July 2009, which raised eyebrows because of his Liverpool connections. The Chester-born forward collected more than 200 goals for Liverpool, Real Madrid and Newcastle United, plus 40 goals in 89 England internationals prior to signing for Sir Alex. Owen burst to prominence at his boyhood side, Liverpool, where he scored on his first-team debut aged just 17. Owen was elevated to world fame in the 1998 World Cup in France, scoring an incredible solo goal in England's second-round tie with Argentina. He played a major part in 2001 in the Merseysiders' triple cup haul of UEFA Cup, FA Cup and League Cup, plus a hat-trick against Germany in England's famous 5-1 win in Munich. These performances earned him the Ballon d'Or and FWA Player of the Year awards. He left Liverpool after eight years following the arrival of new manager Rafael Benitez, moving to Real Madrid but he was only in La Liga for a season, Owen bagged 14 goals in 22 starts for Real before a surprise £16 million move to Newcastle.

Injuries hindered Owen at St James' Park and his four seasons brought only 65 starts, yet 30 goals. Michael's contract expired in the summer of 2009 and Sir Alex brought him to Old Trafford on a free transfer and a two-year deal to add fire power following the departures of Cristiano Ronaldo and Carlos Tevez. The striker's first official goal for the Reds came in the 5-0 away win over Wigan Athletic on 22 August 2009 but it was his second strike, on 20 September, that earned him instant notoriety and a place in Old Trafford lore. After coming on as a late substitute, he popped up in the 96th minute to collect Giggs' penetrative pass and make it 4-3 to United in a thrilling Manchester derby. Although two thirds of his appearances were as a sub, Owen's nine goals in all competitions more than justified his arrival in his first season in Manchester. He always seems to score important goals, a hat-trick away to Wolfsburg in the Champions League and the opening goal in the 2010 Carling Cup final being cases in point. Owen's injury curse came back to haunt him shortly after that, curtailing his first season at United.

"Michael has proved to be a top footballer," adds Sir Alex. "It is unfortunate that he did not get more opportunities but the form of Hernández put everyone in the shade and his partnership with Rooney proved invaluable. I am delighted Michael is staying for a further year and we will look to give him more opportunities in the new season."

United's record 19th English League title, the 12th under Sir Alex, was secured on the penultimate day of the season as the Reds came from behind to draw 1-1 at Blackburn Rovers. In a topsy-turvy, roller-coaster ride of a season, the experience of Sir Alex's squad ultimately paid dividends in the title run-in, with a May win over Chelsea at Old Trafford all but securing the precious 19th title. The biggest contribution was the team's sparkling home form – of United's 18 Old Trafford league games, the Reds won 17 and drew one and that was a point thrown away after the home side led 2-0. This meant defeats on the road were absorbed – not that there were many defeats.

Sir Alex's team didn't lose in the League until February, at Wolves, but then lost at Chelsea, Liverpool and Arsenal in quick succession to allow the pack to close. The stumbling block was their inability before Christmas to turn away draws into wins: six of the seven away games in 2010 yielded only a point. Less than consistently scintillating, United attracted inevitable criticism with many claiming that this was Fergie's worst team since the trophy less class of 2004/05. Yet, from mid-December, they were top of the League and many have argued here that United were worthy winners with a victory built on collective rather than individual ability. Outstanding contributions from the likes of Nemanja Vidic (the Barclays Player of the Season), Dimitar Berbatov (Golden Boot winner), Nani (the League's top goal-maker) and Wayne Rooney who emerged from a personal and professional crisis with a magnificent overhead kick against Manchester City to guide United home.

Rooney had almost single-handedly kept United in the title race the previous season before injury in March derailed his season. Then, following a disastrous World Cup, Rooney came close to leaving the club in October before finally renegotiating a new contract. His record of just one league goal before New Year's Day underlined a lack of confidence as off the field rumours circulated. Yet that sensational winner against City sparked something in him — almost instantly he was transformed back into United's best player, even if the spark occasionally spilled over into something more sinister. By May Rooney was keeping his cool at Ewood Park to dispatch the penalty that ultimately sealed the title – a fitting end to a run-in in which he had more than made up for the disappointing late season form of others.

The season had begun with Chelsea continuing where they had left off in 2010 and for a while United struggled to live with the Stamford Bridge outfit. However the dismissal of assistant manager Ray Wilkins heralded a disastrous autumn for the Blues while United's form improved. The seven-goal mauling of Blackburn in November, a thrilling win over Liverpool and a disciplined display against Arsenal were the stand out games but most results had been ground out, with valuable points gained at Sunderland and Aston Villa, plus a scrambling success at West Brom on New Year's Day compensating for late disappointments at Fulham, Everton and Birmingham.

As Vidic told *Inside United*, "We know that up until the win over Blackburn we hadn't performed as well as we could. But from my experience, this sort of time is when we usually come into good form. We all wanted to win the trophy. Last season was very disappointing. We just need to keep pushing hard and playing well. If we do that, we have a good chance of regaining it. The quality has improved. We saw last season how competitive the League is and it's been even more so this year. Sides such as Tottenham and Manchester City have raised their game, whilst other teams understand they have to improve if they want to stay in the League because it is so competitive. They have done that. It is a physically strong league and players have raised their game in that way too."

Gary Pallister believed United restored the foundation on which to build a title-winning run. Evans' renaissance and Smalling's emergence as a solid prospect provided Sir Alex with back-up to Ferdinand and Vidic. After the 'give-away' period of early-season when the Reds conceded a hatful of damaging late goals, Pallister thought United were ready. "Going back two years ago it was the 1-0 results that won United the 2009 title," Pallister told MEN Sport. "Those are the score-lines that break the hearts of teams chasing you. It is devastating for a rival when you see another challenger scrape out 1-0 victories. I think the Reds have got the solidity and strength in depth in the back four, particularly at the heart of the defence, to dig out those kind of results." If Rooney's new contract was a major triumph persuading Vidic to remain at Old Trafford was equally important. The Serb was brilliant throughout.

Over the course of the season, United were often forced into the type of comebacks for which they are famed. At Blackpool, the home side found themselves two goals up at half-time thanks to former Old Trafford defender Craig Cathcart and striker DJ Campbell. The Tangerines deserved to be even further ahead after a shock first-half display from the leaders. It could have been worse had referee Peter Walton not looked so leniently on Rafael's clumsy challenge on Varney in the penalty area early in the second half. Sir Alex had ordered his side back out on the pitch two minutes before the end of the half time interval, as if to stress that they needed to get the job done in the first ever Premier League meeting between these two clubs.

Gradually United forced the home side back and two goals in quick succession from Berbatov and substitute Hernández, on for a hapless Rooney who was supposed to be celebrating his 300th appearance for the club, silenced Bloomfield Road before Berbatov snatched an 88th-minute winner to put the visitors five points clear of Arsenal. Many credited the turn around to an inspired tactical re-think which saw Giggs come on. "We were deep in the mire," admitted Fergie, "we were all over the place. I wonder if the players were a bit over-confident before the game and got a rude awakening. But this club never gives in — history tells you that. Ryan Giggs made a tremendous difference and we started to penetrate. I think we were deserved winners in the end."

Edwin van der Sar, who announced he would retire at the end of the season, was another of the season's heroes. A virtual ever-present since his arrival in 2005, Edwin's performances were such that many fans now felt he was the equal of Peter

Schmeichel. As Bobby Charlton pointed out earlier in this very book, it is no longer a given that the Great Dane is the club's greatest ever between the posts.

Of his retirement the Dutchman admitted, "I cannot really identify a time when it [the decision] happened. Let's just say that it was playing on my mind from the moment Annemarie had her stroke. She has fought back from it. We decided on another year in England and thus to stay at Manchester United. But, once engaged in the season, the thought of saying goodbye started to gnaw a bit more emphatically."

United goalkeeping coach Eric Steele believes van der Sar will go down alongside Peter Schmeichel as one of the club's greats following his decisive penalty save from Nicolas Anelka in the Champions League Final shoot-out against Chelsea in May 2008, a moment van der Sar himself says he will treasure above all others from his time with United. "I have made better saves, but it was so decisive," he said. " The joy I experienced afterwards with the guys was so intense that I will never forget. To win the highest prize you as a player and as a club can get. It was great." Steele added: "It has been a mutual decision between the manager, the team and Edwin. He has been a fantastic servant. I was very lucky. I worked alongside Peter Schmeichel at Villa and I worked with Edwin for two and a half years. That penalty save in Moscow has elevated Edwin alongside Peter."

Van der Sar commented, "One minute you're out. The next, you question it again. I thought about stopping, maybe a year ago. After a defeat, I thought differently than after playing a few good games in a row. My age played no role. I am 40 years old, but I still feel fit. And then the decision came suddenly. Do not ask me how or why, but suddenly you know. That was sufficient. The time has come to devote greater attention to my family – although they have never complained. Everyone in the family has indeed always had to focus on me, but we have also had a lot in return."

Nemanja Vidic has been another inspirational figure. After ending speculation about his future by signing a contract extension, the Serb inherited the captain's armband from Gary Neville. Former centre half Gary Pallister believed his contribution was crucial, "Nemanja has been immense this season. He is certainly up there as the player of the season. The manager has given him the captain's armband, which shows the trust he has in him. A lot of things were said about Nemanja and whether he wanted to leave. That was put to bed with the new contract and now he looks really settled on the pitch." Pallister feels the captain's armband brought an extra dimension to his game, one that brings the best out of those around him. "He has been a great leader," he said, "he is so determined in everything that he does. He doesn't hold back from any challenges and is very physical. Players respond to that."

There are similarities between the bond Vidic has with Rio Ferdinand and the one Pallister shared with Steve Bruce. Dubbed 'Dolly and Daisy' by Sir Alex, Pallister and Bruce brought United the defensive stability that proved the bedrock for the first of their Premier League titles in 1993. "It is a blend," Pallister said. "Steve was like Nemanja. He would put his head into places you would cringe at. They were also both threats in the opponent's box. It is no secret that you become a better partnership the more you play together. When those two are at the heart of the defence, United are very hard to break down. Last season, and the early part of this one, they were missing a lot of the time and it caused problems. They might not have been beaten but United were giving away ridiculous goals at the end of games. If that could have been sorted out, they would have been well clear at the top of the table."

United's comebacks against Blackpool and West Ham displayed something more however, "It is down to resilience and character," Pallister adds, "those players just do not know when they are beaten. They are not as fluent as they have been but their spirit has carried them through. There have been times when they should have been beaten but they have managed to squeeze something out of nothing. I always expect them to finish top. There is a great togetherness about them and you still think there is more to come. It is going to take a good team to break them down and end this run, that's for sure."

Wayne Rooney was another hero, although this time it came after a prolonged period of concern that the talismanic striker had lost form so dramatically. In January the manager defended the player saying, "Some of our critics are making a meal out of the fact that Wayne Rooney is lagging behind in the goal stakes. He is, compared with the bucketload he scored last year, but I am not worried. It is the scoring partnership that matters and the combination between our two front men has improved beyond all recognition. Last year, Wayne benefited from Dimitar's work but this year it is Berbatov enjoying the last touch. If we finish the season with Berbatov scoring 30 and Wayne on 10 – and those are the targets I have in mind – I will be more than happy. That is what I call a successful strike partnership, reminiscent of Andy Cole and Dwight Yorke."

Following Chelsea's £70m January spending spree and Manchester City's summer bonanza, United's relatively small outlay looked unlikely to improve a team beaten into second in 2010. Ferguson defended his transfer policy telling United Review, "Billionaire owners have introduced a new world that is turning football on its head. For our part, we cannot afford to sit in an ivory tower. We have to face the challenge. It is a healthy competition and it goes without saying that we will not shirk it and I don't think we are doing so. Although I let the [January] transfer window shut without signing a new player, that is because we did our homework some time ago and didn't have to rush into any emergency buying. We had an interest in one player, and I thought we had a chance of bringing him in, but the other parties involved weren't ready and so we have put it away until the summer."

Ferguson was "surprised but not amazed" by spiralling transfer fees. He examined the Torres/Carroll moves. "We have bought in January in the past. We tried one bit of business but it didn't work. Identification is the first thing. The second is getting the value. It is very difficult in today's market. You can be surprised at what happened but not amazed because the Premier League is such a high-profile industry throughout the world. It is the biggest league in the world. I think the highest transfer outside the Premier League in the window was £3m. That shows you the gulf in the spending in other countries." The exploits of 20 year-old Javier Hernández served to strengthen the manager's resolve. Signed for just £6m, the Mexican was a constant goal threat. A total of 20 goals, 13 in the League, proved an astute piece of business and contrasted sharply with Torres solitary strike for Chelsea in the last three months of the campaign.

Despite Chelsea's autumn slump and United's continued good form, the title race tightened up in early spring following United's first defeat at lowly Wolves. Chelsea, emboldened by the signings of Torres and David Luiz, now hit some form and by the time the pair met at Stamford Bridge on 1st March the gap was down to just 12 points. In an incident packed game Rooney gave United the lead with a 20 yard first half pile-driver. United looked comfortable for long periods and Chelsea could have had Luiz dismissed early in the second half following a clear foul in front of referee Martin Atkinson. Less than 60 seconds later Luiz popped up at the other end to force home a corner and level matters before another controversial decision to award a penalty against Chris Smalling gave Frank Lampard the opportunity to win the game from the spot.

Sir Alex vented his fury at the final whistle, "You hope you get a strong referee in games like this. It was a major game for both clubs. You want a fair referee – or a strong referee, anyway – and we didn't get that. I don't know why he has got the game. I must say, when I saw who the referee was I did fear it. I feared the worst. It's hard to take. The Luiz foul was six yards in front of the referee, maybe eight if we give him the benefit of the doubt, no obstructions whatsoever. I don't know how he stayed on the pitch. And the penalty was very soft. In actual fact, Chris has taken the ball and the player's left his leg in. Very soft. Amazing." These comments created a media firestorm and within days the FA had charged the United boss.

Four days later United travelled to a revitalised Anfield to take on Kenny Dalglish's Liverpool. The pair had famously clashed with Ferguson after a 3-3 draw at Anfield in 1988 when the Anfield boss had told reporters "they would get more sense from his baby daughter" after hearing Ferguson complain about the referee. Since Dalglish's departure from the Anfield hotseat, United had gone on to equal Liverpool's record of 18 league championships and would overtake their big rivals if they maintained their current position at the top.

Fired up following the signings of Andy Carroll and Luis Suarez, Liverpool bossed proceedings from start to finish and ran out comfortable 3-1 winners, Dirk Kuyt contributing a hat-trick from a combined distance of 5 yards. Following an edgy 1-0 win over Bolton, United found themselves 2-0 down to struggling West Ham within 25 minutes in their next league game. Yet again a hero emerged, this time Wayne Rooney who hit a hat-trick in the last 20 minutes to secure a remarkable 4-2 victory. After the game however Rooney was lambasted following a four letter outburst at a Sky TV camera. The fixtures continued to come thick and fast – United faced Chelsea twice in a fortnight in the Champions League quarter-finals. Following a 1-0 win at Stamford Bridge, during which the home side this time felt aggrieved about a penalty not given, United beat Fulham 2-0 before winning the return leg 2-1 against the Londoners to go through to the Champions League semi-finals.

The title race tightened further as, following their FA Cup exit at the hands of City, United drew at Newcastle and lost at Arsenal before the all-important title clash with Chelsea at Old Trafford in early May. By this time United had comfortably overcome Schalke 04 to reach the Champions League Final for the third time in four years but all eyes at Old Trafford were focussed on the title and number 19.

Back in March, when Chelsea trailed United 1-0 at Stamford Bridge on March 1, the Pensioners faced the prospect of falling 18 points behind the leaders. But their second half revival gave the champions a victory which signalled the beginning of a remarkable winning run. Chelsea had picked up 25 points from their last 27, while United had managed just 13 from a possible 21 over the same period.

For his part Sir Alex urged his players not to let their season evaporate in the space of five days. "As regards the League, we must be favourites only because we are three points ahead but that can evaporate very quickly. As I said last week, the drama isn't finished." The previous Sunday's 1-0 defeat at Arsenal threw the title race wide open but Ferguson believed his players had the mental strength to recover. "It is always difficult when you have a lead from the first leg but I think the best way is to win the match, play your normal game. If you look at the experience of last year when we lost the League after a Wednesday game against Bayern, that has to have bearing on team selection. They are two massive games, both as important as ever. Sunday's match is a huge one which is why I have to pick the right team for this one."

A Chelsea win would wipe out the United lead that once stood at a massive 15 points just two months before and represent the biggest comeback in Premier League history. Set against that, United had not lost at home in the 30 games since Chelsea took charge of last season's title race with a 2-1 victory 13 months earlier. Despite seeing a 15-point lead over Chelsea cut down to just three in the space of eight weeks, Ferguson had faith in his players to clinch the club's record title. "I don't know how many points we were in front of Chelsea at any given time," he said. "But it doesn't matter. Where we are today is exactly where we are. It doesn't matter what happened last Sunday, four Sundays ago, four months ago or even four years ago, we are where we are. We have three games left, we're three points ahead, we have the same goal difference as Chelsea, we're playing at home, two home games and one away. That's where are. Nothing can change that. And we won't be going for a draw. Everyone knows that. Chelsea know that. Our fans know that. Everyone sitting in this room knows that. So there's no point in discussing draws. Anybody coming to Old Trafford must know they're going to have a hard game, and every team that comes to Old Trafford has a game-plan. That doesn't really change. What's important is how we approach the game and how we perform."

And so it transpired. United flew out of the blocks urged on by their home supporters. Within 30 seconds Ji-Sung Park put Hernández clear of David Luiz and the Mexican striker calmly slotted past Petr Cech to give United a vital lead. Twenty minutes later, concerted United pressure forced Chelsea into conceding a corner from which Nemanja Vidic powered home. Chelsea, needing a win to keep the title race alive, had the unenviable task of finding three goals in the remaining 70 minutes. Outfought in midfield and with many of their star names looking worth fractions of their transfer fees, they had to settle for one, Lampard scrambling home a late cross.

At the final whistle Old Trafford erupted as United were now virtually assured of their prized 19th title with just a single point from United's final two games against Blackburn Rovers and Blackpool required. Sir Alex vowed that his team would not make any mistakes. "We will get the point we need. There is no doubt about it." Ferguson, who theatrically bowed to the Stretford End before he left the Old Trafford pitch, was understandably delighted with his side, adding: "It's fantastic being the most successful team in the country in terms of championship victories. As soon as we got that first one in 1993 the door opened to us. It's an incredible achievement. I would not have believed this all those years ago. But we improved and improved." Asked if his team could falter in sight of the line like the racehorse Devon Loch in the 1956 Grand National, Ferguson commented, "Don't mention Devon Loch. My dad backed that horse!"

Ryan Giggs, for one, never expected the club to stand on the brink of overhauling Liverpool's record when he won his first, United's eighth, back in 1993. Giggs' has been part of all the squads that have finished top during Sir Alex's reign since making his debut under the Scot as a 17-year-old in 1990. The Welshman, who put in another inspirational display in midfield, acknowledged that the title was "not mathematically over" but was thrilled at the prospect of surpassing Liverpool. "Fifteen or

20 years ago, you'd never have thought it," said Giggs. "It's a great achievement by the team and the manager to haul back our biggest rivals over the 1970s, 80s and 90s." Giggs admitted the win over Chelsea was "a massive step forward". He added: "We've just got to finish the job off, hopefully next week. We've got to get one point from the next two games. It's a great chance for us and we'll try and get it done as soon as possible. Blackburn's a tough place to go but I'm sure we'll have loads of fans going to that one. It'll be a great atmosphere, it always is. And as always, we won't go for the draw, we'll try and win."

Giggs added to the praise being heaped on opening goalscorer Hernández, who had become the first United player to net 20 times in his debut campaign since van Nistelrooy in 2001, and the part he has played in the title charge. "Twenty goals in his first season is unbelievable," Giggs said, "you are always in with a chance when you have a goalscorer like Javier in your team. He has made a fantastic impact, on and off the pitch. His English is perfect, which has helped, and his goal just sums up his season. Sometimes those chances can come a bit early for you. You are not quite up to speed. Thirty seconds, he gets a chance, he scores. He deserves everything that has been said about him."

In heaping praise on Hernández, Giggs deflected some away from himself. He might have been slightly fortunate to edge the official man-of-the-match prize ahead of the tireless contribution of Park Ji-Sung, but at 37, Giggs brings calm to United's performances. Ferguson raised the possibility of Giggs continuing into the 2012-13 campaign, having already signed a one-year contract extension to take him into next term.

There was a note of caution in the lead up to the Ewood Park fixture as Blackburn was the ground where all hope was lost for United the previous season and the club's record there has been patchy at best. They also had the memory of Rovers being the opponents on that fateful night in 1993 when they ended that 26-year wait for championship number nine. "We will give every respect to Blackburn and Blackpool because they are local teams to us," said Ferguson. "They are great football clubs and we will make sure we don't underestimate them."

In the end Blackburn, playing above themselves as they fought to stave off relegation, could count themselves unlucky not take all three points against a lacklustre and frustrated Manchester United. Leading following a first half Brett Emerton strike, Rovers looked comfortable for the most part and it took a controversially awarded 72nd minute Wayne Rooney penalty to secure Manchester United's record-breaking 19th League title after Rovers' keeper Paul Robinson was ruled to have brought down Hernández. Rooney kept his nerve to fire home the 73rd-minute spot-kick and send United's army of supporters into a title frenzy. The point took United beyond nearest rivals Chelsea and edged the Old Trafford club ahead of Liverpool, who won the last of their 18 League titles in 1990.

The United players were joined by Ferguson on the pitch for the post-match celebrations. "It was a fantastic performance by the lads and the supporters and for everybody connected with the club it's a great day today," Fergie said, "it wasn't an easy game, we went 1-0 down having given them a bad goal but we kept on and we don't give in. It looked like it was not going to be our day, we've always had it difficult here. It is a local derby and they are fighting for their lives, looking for that point, but we kept going and that's a good quality. In terms of achievement, it's a great day. The atmosphere today was incredible. The supporters got behind us. We gave away a bad goal but they kept on.

"In the Eighties it was all Liverpool so it was a big challenge for us. When I came down from Scotland, getting the first title was significant and there were some great teams after that. The 1993-94 team won the first Double in the club's history and since then it has been done two or three times. Success has carried on - all the players that come here know they have to win. It's not so much passing Liverpool. That thing about knocking Liverpool off their perch, I don't think I actually said it, but it's more important that United are the best team in the country in terms of winning titles. Same with the FA Cup. We have won it more times than everyone and now we've won the Premier League more times than anyone. I can hardly believe it is 12 Premier League titles. I had a great time at Aberdeen, but it was time to move on and I couldn't have picked a better club – the ideal club for me."

Ferguson believed the title was won at Old Trafford where United's form has been imperious, covering up their awful away form. "When we look back, the area in which we are most disappointed in is our away form, where we've had nine draws. The focus will be our away form, but the home form was fantastic," he said, "but we dropped points to Blackburn, West Brom, Bolton, Birmingham, Aston Villa, Sunderland and Newcastle. That is an indication of how tough the League is."

Patrice Evra suggested United are a more complete team without Cristiano Ronaldo, despite the Real Madrid man's blistering recent form for his new club, "When Cristiano Ronaldo was here he did a great job but the team was playing for him and maybe people forget that," Evra said. "But since Carlito [Tevez] and Ronny have gone, United look more like a team. I don't say that we're better without Ronny but, sure, we look more like a team. That's an achievement as well. If you were asked to pick one player this season, I don't think anyone stands out. That's why the credit for winning the title this season goes to the Man United spirit."

United celebrated their record-breaking title triumph in style with a victory parade in Manchester, on an open-top bus around the city. Old Trafford chief executive David Gill revealed the club was inundated with pleas from fans for a parade and he felt it was a perfect way to honour the season's achievements. "Breaking the record of League title wins is a big day in the club's illustrious history," he said, "we have received many letters and e-mails from fans encouraging us to hold a public celebration of that achievement and we believe this is a fitting way to mark it."

United fans ensured maximum enjoyment of the club's record-breaking title by taking their cause to Anfield on the following Sunday, unveiling a banner inside the ground before the Reds' game against Spurs. The club's supporters went to great lengths to ensure those at Anfield were fully aware of that fact. As

Liverpool fans began their customary chorus of 'You'll Never Walk Alone', United fans, organised by the Red Issue fanzine, unveiled a banner emblazoned with the words "MUFC 19 TIMES" in the Anfield Road End of the ground. Those responsible had a getaway car waiting outside the ground, plus fellow conspirators in an adjoining stand in order to get photographic evidence. The banner-baiting between the clubs has a long history, with Liverpool fans' now famous "Come Back When You Have Won 18" banner kicking things off in 1994. United fans responded to that after clinching their 18th title in 2008-09 and have now added another chapter to the ongoing rivalry.

Sir Alex could not resist having a dig at the Merseyside club at United's annual players' awards ceremony at Old Trafford. "I wish I had taken that banner to Liverpool on Sunday," he said, "I bet there were 76,000 fans wishing they had thought of that." Unsurprisingly Ferguson outlined plans for title No20; "We have some ideas in mind," he said. "Hopefully we can get them put in place. I am looking at maybe three signings which would boost our overall quality in our team."

Nani was named Players' Player of the Year, while Hernández took the Fans' Player of the Year title. Rio Ferdinand believes Wayne Rooney's decision to stay at Old Trafford was the turning point. With United's season threatening to unravel early in the campaign, the England striker had handed in a transfer request citing the club's lack of ambition as the reason behind his desire to leave. Sir Alex talked him round and England centre-back Ferdinand also had a word with his team-mate before Rooney signed a lucrative new five-year contract on October 22. "Rooney staying was a big part of what we achieved this season. There was a sense of relief from the players, the fans, everybody. Wayne is one of the best three players in the world, so to have him on our team-sheet is a bonus. I spoke to him that week when he was thinking of going. You do it with a Manchester United hat on and explain what you think is best for the club and how you want him to stay. If he had left it would have been a very big hole to fill. I'm not saying it was impossible to fill because the manager always comes up with something and you trust in his judgment. But, more than anything, Wayne staying sent a signal out to every one of our rivals in the Premier League that the glimmer of hope they had of us falling away had gone."

Ferdinand believes that Javier Hernández should have received individual accolades for his contribution this season. "If you were voting today, I'm sure Chicharito would be Footballer of the Year, he's scored so many important goals. Whenever he's been on the pitch, he's produced something. Gareth Bale [PFA Player of the Year] and Scott Parker [FWA Footballer of the Year] both had good seasons, but for me Chicharito has been the main man."

David Beckham insisted United's League-winning side of 2011 is one of the club's best of all time. "They are up there with the best United sides of all time; the proof is in the trophies they have won," Beckham told BBC Radio 5 live, "people have criticised the team but you can't ask for more than that."

United signed off their domestic campaign with a 4-2 victory against relegated Blackpool, preserving a season-long unbeaten record at Old Trafford. Ferguson dismissed critics who claimed his team are not as talented as their league-winning predecessors as "talking nonsense", lauding his current team's indefatigable spirit as they finished nine points ahead of nearest rivals Chelsea.

Unfortunately United's final match of the season, against Barcelona, proved to be a step too far. Outclassed and outpassed by the Catalans, United succumbed 3-1 at Wembley with many wags claiming that the many red banners featuring '19' were for the number of touches Barcelona allowed United on the night.

Yet, unlike in 2009, there was an acceptance that United had lost to one of the all-time great teams, perhaps the greatest of all time – as a result defeat did not take too much gloss off the incredible achievement of the previous fortnight.

NOT NINETEEN FOREVER...

REFLECTIONS ON UNITED OVERHAULING LIVERPOOL'S RECORD OF 18 LEAGUE TITLES IN 2011

"Sir Alex is on par with sportsmen like Tiger Woods,
someone who stands alone within their sport."

PETER BEARDSLEY

WHEN ALAN HANSEN captained Liverpool to their last championship, in 1990, the tally read 18-7 in Liverpool's favour, and Peter Beardsley scored a hat trick on September 16, in what turned out to be his final season in a Liverpool jersey. Beardsley's hat-trick was part of Liverpool's 4-0 drubbing of United.

What happened next is something that Beardsley, who played four years at Anfield and made one appearance for Manchester United, finds hard to evaluate, as the score has been somehow reversed to 19-18 titles in United favour.

When the then reigning champions demolished the FA Cup holders, Beardsley's strikes on 11, 32, and 81 minutes were supplemented by a John Barnes effort just before the interval. Beardsley is on record as saying, "What I remember from the day was the end of the game when I went over to try and get the match ball and United's keeper Les Sealey – who is no longer with us God rest his soul – kicked the ball into the Kop in anger so I couldn't get it. Fortunately for myself a Liverpool fan returned it to me the next day."

Beardsley, who had made a single appearance for United in a League Cup tie against Bournemouth earlier in his career, believes the turning point for both clubs' remarkable change in fortunes is down to two men, Kenny Dalglish and Sir Alex Ferguson.

Beardsley is one of more than 20 legends with connections to Old Trafford to give their verdicts on United's record 19 League titles and few are better qualified to assess the United-Liverpool divide. It was one of Manchester United's biggest mistakes, and the good fortune of Newcastle United and Liverpool, that Beardsley was allowed to leave Old Trafford after making that one senior appearance. The Red Devils let a Geordie gem slip through their fingers, one who would eventually shine on the ultimate stage with England.

Gary Lineker, who scored 48 goals for his country, rated Beardsley his best strike partner. His partnership with Lineker was forged at the 1986 World Cup in Mexico, where he scored against Paraguay. Beardsley moved to Liverpool in 1987 for a then-British record £1.9m and, in his first season, won the first of two League titles. A surprise defeat by Wimbledon denied Liverpool the double. They suffered the same fate a year later in the club's most traumatic season. The Hillsborough disaster forced the FA Cup Semi-Final with Nottingham Forest to be abandoned. Liverpool beat Merseyside rivals Everton in a fitting final tribute but Arsenal pipped them to the title with a last-gasp goal. Beardsley was a title winner again in 1990, and went on to reach the semi-finals of the World Cup with England in Italia '90 under Sir Bobby Robson.

Beardsley told me, "It keeps on cropping up from time to time that I was in Liverpool's last championship wining team, I realise the statisticians come up with it, so there is no escaping it. But at the time, when we won the title in 1990, I was convinced that Liverpool would go on to win many, many more titles and never be overtaken."

What does Beardsley think about what has now occurred?

"I am gobsmacked!" He went on, "Hopefully the situation will now change under Kenny. Now that he has returned to Liverpool, he is the perfect man right now to do something about the 19-18 titles. But the thought of what happened since 1990 is quite amazing, hard to take in, almost impossible to believe, and really it is down to the fact that Kenny left, and that Sir Alex has been in control of Manchester United's destiny.

"Sir Alex is a genius. Sheer genius. What that man has done for Manchester United is scary. What he has achieved at Manchester United will never happen again in the modern game, the number of titles, the number of trophies, the number of teams he has built, it just won't happen again. Everyone tells you about records, that records are there to be broken but no one will ever win as many Premier League titles as this man. No way will it happened again."

There was a deep intake of breath as Beardsley tried to come to terms with the way Liverpool have been knocked off their perch, "Kenny was a massive part", Beardsley considered, "Kenny walking out of Liverpool was by far the biggest single thing to turn everything around, otherwise it is hard to put your finger on it. Kenny was a genius in those days, in the same way that Ferguson is a genius now. Kenny was a genius throughout his life, I enjoyed watching him as a kid and loved playing in the same team.

"It is a myth that I had anything to do with him walking out, although it was suggested that I did. I was accused of moaning that I wasn't in the side, and any player who isn't picked will tell you he isn't happy. But I have had plenty of conversations with Kenny since, and I have asked him about his resignation and he has assured me that I had nothing to do with his decision. Kenny must have been the first manager to use rotation and myself and Ray Houghton were victims of it for the four years I was at Anfield.

"I feel that there has never been a bigger legend at Liverpool than Kenny, Steven Gerrard is a local boy, as is Jamie Carragher, but there will never be another Kenny Dalglish and that is why his exit had such a devastating effect and why it was probably the main reason for Liverpool's decline by comparison to United and there can be no better than Ferguson for what he has achieved since then. No ifs and buts in my book, had Dalglish stayed it would have been a different story. Equally, without a shadow of a doubt, Ferguson is responsible for United's success, and to think the club might have sacked him, how ridiculous does that sound now? Frightening. Sir Alex is on par with sportsmen like Tiger Woods, someone who stands alone within their sport.

"I hope for the sake of the excitement of the game, that somebody can come near to Sir Alex's achievements, but I cannot see one manager winning more than three Premier League titles, maybe five, but no more, not possible."

To support Beardsley's argument Sir Alex is officially the greatest British manager of all time. In fact, during his Old Trafford tenure, he's won as many major trophies (36) as the esteemed Bob Paisley (18), Brian Clough (10) and Bill Shankly (8) did over the course of their combined managerial careers. Sir Alex was naturally proud and thrilled to have landed title No 19. "It's special. This is a particularly special one because it means we've won the title more than anyone in the country. It's history and great for the tradition of this club so I'm really pleased about that."

United finished nine points clear with the boss conceding: "The players have been great, there's a great work ethic in the team. I think they deserved it because there were a lot of great performances. I'm dismissing all that nonsense that it's not a great Manchester United team. It's a great feat winning this league. I think our target was to do our best. Yes, we've had some disappointing games away from home but the home form has been fantastic. Another four goals today, seven against Blackburn, five against Birmingham and we've beaten Chelsea, Liverpool, Arsenal and Tottenham all here. They're top teams so it's pretty good that."

Enjoying every moment of the celebrations, he added, "It's fantastic and wonderful because it involves all the supporters. They feel part of it and have really enjoyed today. It's great to see the players with their families and kids. I think nowadays it has to be a squad game. You look at Patrice Evra and he's played the most games, 46 out of 61 games, and that tells you the spread of players we've used. It's done because we've got a good squad. I think I could pick four or five teams for next week and they wouldn't let us down."

Sir Alex admitted he didn't really think overtaking Liverpool – who had 18 titles to United's seven when he took charge in 1986 – was achievable. In a moment of raw honesty with the 19th title in sight, Sir Alex confessed, "No, I certainly didn't envisage it at that time. The aim was to match Liverpool and be successful ourselves. That was the target. That's why I came here – to win the title. Once we won it, the club took off. I couldn't envisage being here so long. It's an exceptional period of time that I've been here and you don't tend to think about the number of titles we've won. Getting the first was the target."

When Sir Alex's remarkable journey began at Old Trafford, he was plain old Alex Ferguson and it was tough going for the first four years, charged with the task of restoring the club to its former glories. After four years with no trophies to show for it, he was almost sacked. Now a knight of the realm, his stated intention of ending Liverpool's dominance and restoring United to the summit of English football was completed with title number 19 in May 2011. Knowing Sir Alex, though, he will be far from content until he has put some distance between United and Liverpool, rather than just the one title.

When United tried, and failed, to claim a fourth successive championship in 2010, Ferguson confessed that "winning this 19th league title is very much in my soul".

Turning 70 on December 31, Ferguson's thirst for glory is not quenched, yet he commented, "I don't think it means anything to me personally at all. I must say that. It's more for the club. For the history of the club, it's important. It's like with the European Cup. You see the history of Real Madrid and AC Milan. Then there's another bracket with Liverpool, Ajax and

NOT NINETEEN FOREVER

Bayern Munich, where we should be. We should definitely be in that bracket. Hopefully we can take a step forward towards that on May 28 in the Champions League final against Barcelona."

Ryan Giggs never expected the club to overhaul Liverpool's record of 18 when he won his first, United's eighth, back in 1993. Giggs has been part of all the squads that have finished top during Sir Alex's reign since making his debut under the Scot as a 17-year-old in 1990. The Welshman was thrilled at surpassing Liverpool. "Fifteen or twenty years ago, you'd never have thought it," said Giggs, "it's a great achievement by the team and the manager to haul back our biggest rivals over the 1970s, 80s and 90s."

Liverpool skipper Steven Gerrard warned United not to get used to being English football's top dogs. Anfield hero Gerrard said: "It's hurtful because we held the record for so long. You have to give credit where it's due – they've overtaken us for the time being but the good thing from our point of view is we are on our way back up and we won't give up the fight to overtake them again – don't worry about that. That is the motivation – to know your bitter rivals have just overtaken you on League titles. We can still boast about the European Cups, of course, but we need to amend the 19–18. Myself and everyone else will be doing everything in our power to do that."

Dalglish added: "They (United) might be your rivals and competitors but it doesn't mean you disrespect them. So we will always have respect for United and what they have achieved."

Last season's title race saw a remarkable points swing between United and Chelsea, from the early eight-point advantage Carlo Ancelotti's side held to the 15-point lead Ferguson's men had over their London rivals on March 1.

When the dust settled on United's 19th record title, and then failure to beat the worlds best club side Barcelona in the Champions League Final at Wembley, I searched for the best possible impartial verdict on United's contemporary championship side, with comparison with previous title winning teams. There had been much heated debate whether the 2011 vintage was indeed up to the usual standard.

Steve Coppell has a Liverpool University degree in Economics and is recognised as one of football's rare breed, an academic, as well as a player and manager. Perhaps he has the answers to why Liverpool were so dominant and then have miraculously been overtaken by United. Using that Economics degree, the answer lies in the subtle but effective change in the rules that allowed the home team to keep all their home gate cash. For Old Trafford, now read Gold Trafford.

Apart from bumping into Steve on a regular basis at my local Waitrose, in Sunningdale, I have known him for many years, mostly during his time as manager, another rare breed, a football celebrity who is from an era of loyalty and good service. He played for United from 1975 until 1983, 396 games, 72 goals after being transferred to United for £40,000 from Tranmere Rovers, while still a student at Liverpool University. He was a very astute signing by manager Tommy Docherty. He was loved by the fans for his 100% commitment to the club and his appetite to attack the opposition full back with direct wing play.

"We finished runners up once, but way behind Liverpool," Steve told me, "Liverpool were by far the dominant force in football at that time when I joined United towards the end of the Second Division storm to promotion under Tommy Docherty. We then took the First Division by storm in our first season back up. But we were not quite the finished article to win the League, and to be fair, no one looked capable of removing Liverpool from the pinnacle of the English and European game."

So how did the seemingly impossible become possible? Well according to Steve a lot if it is down to economics. "One reason that United had the upper hand was their boat came in when the rules were changed allowing clubs to keep their home gates. Prior to that, Manchester United was the difference between a lot of clubs keeping their heads above water, or sinking, financially, as half of an Old Trafford gate was virtually the difference between surviving and not. The advantage of keeping the home gate money kicked in a couple of years later after the rule change was made. It was too late to save Dave Sexton, but when Alex Ferguson took over he spent something like £13 million in his first year, which in today's values would be a minimum of £100m maybe much more and still he didn't win anything. In fact when I was Crystal Palace manager they played a game before they beat us in the FA Cup Final, Nottingham Forest at Old Trafford and Forest beat them and I was thinking 'he hasn't got long to go'. Of course I was proved wrong there! Fergie might have been staring into the distance and at the end of his tether trying to find that winning formula, but then they won the FA Cup, and the rest is history.

"But I must admit I never saw it coming, I could see United being powerful again with the added finance from their home games, with 60,000 plus crowds every time they turned out there, but I could never see the end of the Liverpool domination.

"At the time everyone talked about 'The Liverpool Way' and no one really knew what 'The Liverpool Way' actually was, it was mystic – a mystery. People waffled on endlessly about 'The Liverpool Way' trying to replicate it, trying to find out what it was, but no one really knew, probably not even those within the club. But Liverpool had an unbelievable knack of signing all the right players at the right times. Ray Kennedy was a perfect example, he'd had a long run in the Arsenal team, and had seemed to run his course, when Liverpool signed him they converted him to a target man and he was tremendous for them, became a goal machine for many, many years. Then they signed Kenny Dalglish to replace Kevin Keegan! What a master stroke!

"I am not convinced there was a transfer policy, yet everything they touched came off, notably in the Bob Paisley era with his Chief Executive Peter Robinson. From what I heard about how they operated, the chief executive had as much pull on who was signed as the manager. They also operated a very tight squad and while it worked then, it wouldn't work now as the top teams need squads of 30 odd players to cope with all the games and high level competitions. Back then they could buy a player, put him in the reserves, give him time to adapt to the Liverpool style and then bring him on. Sometimes they bought players you would think would never fit in, but they always found players who blended within the team framework, when you would think that an individual was not quite quick enough or couldn't head the ball, he found his way into the team in a position in which he would gel.

"I have always thought, even way back then, that money will out in football, so I can believe that if anyone was going to catch up with Liverpool it would be Manchester United with their enormous income generated by keeping their home receipts, with crowds of 60,000, from that perspective I always felt it was automatic that Manchester United would be catching up. But overtake Liverpool? No, I still never saw that coming. But with investment into the dressing room, they have had a lot of financial clout to build up their teams. Ferguson has a robust acquisition policy, and its very much like the myth built around the Paisley era, in picking up rough diamonds and converting them into world class performers. With United's extra revenue streams, it also insulated them against failure. Whereas Liverpool were always making the right choices, which in itself is perhaps the mystery solved, United could afford the odd mistake or two."

Only four appearances shy of the landmark of 400 games, Steve was an ever present in the side for eight years, The most important game he played for the Red Devils was against arch rivals Liverpool in 1977 as they attempted the treble, with the title already wrapped up, United spoiled the quest with their cup final victory, 2-1 to United with Stuart Pearson and Jimmy Greenhoff scoring. It wasn't Steve's best performance but he lasted the whole 90 minutes and helped see his side to the only major trophy of Docherty's regime as manager. The year before United were cruelly beaten in the final as Southampton won 1-0 with a goal inside the last ten minutes. Just two months after the cup final victory in 1977, Docherty was sacked and a transition phase was underlined by new manager Dave Sexton. Sexton tried to get Coppell to employ a different style of game. After guiding United to another FA Cup final in 1979, Sexton was unlucky to be a loser in the game popularly remembered as the 'Five Minute Final'. Ironically on that day Coppell was immense and helped create both of United's goals with ingenious play. It was again harsh on United as they clawed back a 2-0 deficit in the last 5 minutes. Following United's dramatic late comeback and with extra time looming large, the Gunners managed to snatch a winner right at the death via Alan Sunderland. Two years later Sexton was sacked despite winning his last seven games in a row in charge, but he left the club after four years trophy less, with the 1979 FA Cup final coming closest to landing him any silverware.

Coppell recalls, "Dave Sexton was removed because Manchester United Football Club and their fans demand good, imaginative, progressive football. They expect their teams to pay in a certain way. Tommy Docherty ticked all the right boxes, Ron Atkinson ticked all the right boxes, but Dave Sexton played to a system which didn't excite. Ironically, he was sacked after the team won their last seven games of the season." After Sexton departed, Steve had two years left before in 1983, he stopped playing football having also made 42 appearances, scoring seven goals for England.

His finest moment in the national side was to score the winning goal in a 1-0 victory over arch rivals Scotland at Hampden Park. He also scored for England against Scotland at Wembley in a 3-1 victory. The habit of scoring against the Tartan army continued a year later when he scored again against Scotland in a 2-0 victory at Hampden Park. He featured in the 1980 European Championship group matches, his last major tournament, as he suffered a horrific knee injury before the 1982 World Cup, which in the end, after a brief return to club and country, saw him hang up his boots in 1983.

Steve entered management straight away for the first of four stints as manager of Crystal Palace at the tender age of 28. He also managed Brentford, Brighton and Manchester City but his most impressive time as a manager came more recently as Reading boss.

In their debut season in the Premier League, Reading finished 8th, only one point off UEFA Cup football. Steve was deservedly recognised as Manager of the Year but Reading suffering from the so called 'second season syndrome' and were relegated back to the championship. Despite this Royals fans were still firmly behind Coppell to take them back. Reading lost out in the 2008–2009 season in the Championship playoff semi-final and despite a protest from the club's fans to keep Coppell at the club, he resigned straight after the game.

Viv Anderson MBE actually selects the 2011 title winning team as one of the most hard fought and so one of the best accomplishments. Anderson, Alex Ferguson's first ever signing, told me, "This year's title was arguably the hardest for United to win. Chelsea might have gone eight points clear had they won a match they failed to clinch with just a few months left of the season. There was a feeling that having caught United up, they would romp away with it, but it didn't happen. Ray Wilkins was sacked and it seemed to go downhill, then they recovered, and looked like they would still retain their title. Arsenal were thought to be in with a good chance at one stage and were being tipped to win it. United's home record was exemplary but they had to fight and scrap for everything away from home but they showed great character and resilience, coming back from two down at Blackpool and had to come from behind at West Ham when they might have had Vidic sent off. But they pulled things out, and were especially formidable at Old Trafford.

"Overall, I would think Sir Alex must have felt as if this one was one of the most rewarding, if not one of his best. Rewarding for the way they had to battle against a couple of clubs who thought they would have won it, and rewarding for being the 19th title.'

Viv was born in Clifton, Nottingham in 1956 and became a regular under Brian Clough in the Nottingham Forest side that had so much success in the 70s, including winning two European Cups. Viv became the first black player to be capped for England. He joined Arsenal in 1984 and was later signed by Ferguson, playing 64 times for United in a four-year spell. He retains his association with United as a contributor to MUTV. Viv was inducted into the English Football Hall of Fame in 2004 in recognition of his impact on the English game, for his total of 30 caps and a distinguished career with Forest, Arsenal, Manchester United and Sheffield Wednesday, Anderson was voted the best right-back of the 1970s in a poll of managers. Nicknamed 'Spider' on account of his long legs, Anderson regards his selection for England in the friendly international against Czechoslovakia at Wembley in November 1978 as, above all, a cause for professional satisfaction, receiving a 'Good Luck' telegram from the Queen.

"Winning that first cap may have been a small step for him in his career but it was a huge leap forward for black footballers in this country," Ian Wright wrote in 1997. Anderson knew how to win league titles, although he never achieved that feat at Old Trafford. He made his mark when Forest emerged as a major force after scraping promotion from the Second Division in 1976-77, and the First Division championship was won at the first attempt on the back of an undefeated run of 26 games and a defence that let in only 24 goals in the league.

George Graham brought Anderson to Highbury in 1984. In each of his three seasons at Highbury, the team's defensive record improved, a run that ended with Arsenal lifting the League Cup. Such consistent performances alerted Ferguson, who made Anderson his first signing as manager of Manchester United, in 1987. Ferguson wanted to add experience and physical presence in a side he considered too 'lightweight' to compete for honours. "His resolute professionalism at right-back and bubbly, contagious enthusiasm in the dressing-room were worth a lot more than the £250,000 we paid for Viv," Ferguson recalled. Anderson says, "In my time at United we were always conscious of the efforts to emulate Liverpool. It was tough for Ferguson at first, and we all knew that he was 90 minutes away from getting the sack against Nottingham Forest. He had inherited a lot of young players who had not turned out to match his expectations."

Martin Buchan was one of the most influential United captains and currently works at the PFA in Manchester. He is well placed to assess the significance of the 19th title. "Sir Alex said when he first arrived at Old Trafford that his ambition was to knock Liverpool off their perch, and it has been a memorable journey, although it could have been a different story if Mark Robins had not scored a vital goal at Nottingham Forest in the third round of the FA Cup in early January 1990, when United were in 15th place in the League and out of the League Cup. United went on to beat Crystal Palace in the Final after a replay, Sir Alex's first trophy, and the rest is history."

A cultured central defender on the pitch, Buchan was just as articulate and intelligent off it. He was skipper for six years during the 70s, leading United to the Second Division title in 1975 and the FA Cup in 1977 and to this day remains convinced that had Tommy Docherty stayed the team could well have gone on to win league titles of their own. He actually played against Ferguson in the Scottish First Division and knows the man well, and this knowledge of the United manager gives him a great appreciation of how Sir Alex has managed to achieve the then seemingly impossible task of surpassing Liverpool's 18 titles.

"Sir Alex has instilled a wonderful work ethic at United" he told me, "he leads by example, arriving at the training ground every day before anyone else. I know all about his attitude from my playing days, I have the bruises to prove it. I once had the temerity to tell him that he needed to sign a certain type of centre forward. 'Like who?', he asked, 'Like Alex Ferguson', I replied. He was a real handful; competitive, determined, energetic and he never let opposing defenders settle on the ball. It's hard enough chasing after forwards, much worse when they come chasing after you and putting you under pressure. It is a wonderful feat to have replaced Liverpool as the top and I am full of admiration for the way Sir Alex has achieved it.

"Everybody and his dog has been saying this year's

champions weren't a vintage United side, and I happen to think that Ferguson pulled a rabbit out of the hat by winning the league with this squad, particularly when he trusted a couple of players in unfamiliar positions and won vital games as a result. I refer to the masterstrokes of moving Antonio Valencia to right back against Chelsea and playing Ryan Giggs at left back in the 4-2 win over West Ham. Some of the star players were not on their usual top form for much of the season but the signing of Chicharito proved to be an inspired one. The return of Antonio Valencia, missing through injury six months, made a big difference in the title run in. I think Wayne Rooney, in particular, missed his service from the right wing. I was actually surprised that the winning margin of six points was so big in the end, I thought it would have been much closer.

"The one thing about Manchester United is that they never give up, you can never write them off, which is a reflection of the manager's persona. He was like that as a player and he has instilled that attitude into his club. The number of times they score late in the game illustrates this never say die attitude."

Buchan signed for Aberdeen as a schoolboy, turning professional in August 1966. His progress was swift and just before his 21st birthday he was handed the captain's armband at Pittodrie and enjoyed early success, leading the Dons to victory in the Scottish Cup Final of 1970 – the youngest player ever to do so. Soon he was attracting attention south of the border and towards the end of the 1971/72 season Liverpool, Leeds United and Manchester United were all chasing the classy young defender. On 29th February 1972 Frank O'Farrell signed Buchan for £125,000, then the club's record signing. His early days at United weren't the happiest however. The standard of the team was not quite as high as first expected and at the end of the 1973/74 season Buchan found himself experiencing the seemingly unthinkable: relegation to the Second Division.

"With the benefit of hindsight, the team needed rebuilding after winning the European Cup in 1968. Brian Kidd played in that final as a teenager, but otherwise it was quite a mature side. Frank O'Farrell brought in Ian Storey-Moore but he had a bad ankle injury and was never the player he could have been for United. Relegation gave Tommy Docherty the opportunity to get rid of the dead wood." Despite the dreaded drop, Buchan, the object of many enquiries, was determined to stay at Old Trafford and help the club back into the First Division. A year later the Reds won Division Two at a canter. "Lou Macari told me that the Second Division was a piece of cake", Buchan recalls, "it might have seemed so for the forwards who could afford to leave the occasional stray ball they didn't fancy chasing but when it came to defending we had to be on our toes at the back all the time".

Further success followed in 1977 with a 2-1 FA Cup Final victory against Liverpool at Wembley. Buchan became the only man to captain a side to both FA Cup and Scottish FA Cup success. "We almost won the league in our first season back, if we hadn't had the distraction of the FA Cup run we could well have taken the title. We took a lot of teams by surprise; we had a bright, energetic side but some of our squad were seduced by the glamour of the Cup and we finished, for me, a disappointing third. We'll never know how far the 1977 team would have gone after winning the Cup had Tommy Docherty stayed, as we could have built on the confidence of winning our first big trophy and I am sure the momentum would have given us a real chance of winning the title.

"I'm not being dismissive in suggesting that the Second Division championship didn't matter, but this was a club that had become the first English team to win the European Cup a few short years before and we were certainly on the way back to the top. Sadly, Tommy's abrupt departure meant that we have no way of knowing just how good we could have been. Despite losing one of the biggest jobs in football, the Doc didn't lose his sense of humour – before the start of the new season, I received a note from him with a Derby County letterhead. It read, 'thanks for all your help in my time at Old Trafford, just a line to wish you and the team all the best for the new season and I hope you go on and win the lot. Yours sincerely, Tommy Docherty.' My wife's name was Lena and he added a postscript – 'ps. remember to give Lena an apple a day, it keeps the Doc away!'

"Although we eventually played in three FA Cup Finals in four years, from a professional point of view we would always have preferred to win the league, to prove ourselves the best team over the course of a season, but the FA Cup was a major trophy in those days, much more highly regarded than it is nowadays.

"I have been with the PFA for eleven and a half years and I go to Old Trafford and the training ground at Carrington on a regular basis. The attention the players experience now before a routine Premier League game is greater than the build up to the FA Cup Final in my day. Every week TV crews from all over the world gather at the United training ground. The place is packed on Thursdays and Fridays with the cameras and microphones of the media and with visitors from every continent. It encapsulates how times have changed and is one aspect of a modern footballer's life that I don't envy."

Ray Wilkins, Garth Crooks and Alan Brazil are three top TV and radio broadcasters steeped in the United traditions having played for the club for a varying periods of time but who now make their livings from the media. The Three Wise Men of the airways gave their views for '19'.

Ray Wilkins is a confirmed advocate that winning the title earns you respect. He has no time for United detractors who have poured cold water on the achievement of winning the title for the 19th time. Wilkins told me, "In my view the title race does not deserve the criticism it has attracted, In fact, it has been one of the most wide open championships for years, and for that reason it has been one of the most exciting.

"Look, it might not have been the most talented Manchester United team of all time, but they did have one of the best qualities for which Manchester United teams are renowned and that is a quiet, winning mentality and this bunch had that within their side. Their dressing room was packed with winners and that is all important. Ok, so not the greatest team on the planet, but these guys can win, and that is synonymous with Manchester United. You have to be a winner to play for United, if you are not a winner with that kind of mentality, then forget it. The club breeds winners, they buy winners. No one puts his players under more pressure to perform than Sir Alex, as soon as you walk into the place you know you have to be a winner, you have to win, and the players relish that as well if they are the right type; there's no point being a shrinking violet at Old Trafford.

"I know from my own experiences there that the players respect the club and hold their traditions dear to them, they are important to them, the players appreciate the fact that they represent Manchester United as a wonderful achievement, that was how I certainly felt. I felt extremely privileged to have played for United. I left Chelsea in 1978/79, it was more of a case that Chelsea needed the money than they wanted to sell me but going to Manchester United, you quickly realise, is being involved with something very special.

"Playing against Liverpool takes you to another level altogether – it's even more special, more important, more compelling. United very rarely lost against Liverpool in my time there - the year we thought we would win the league, we lost to the likes of Coventry but beat Liverpool. We beat the majority of the big teams, but fell down against the majority of the lesser sides. It seemed, though, that we could always raise our game, the supporters were part of that, and it was awe inspiring to play in front of the supporters at Old Trafford, at a time when there was still terracing, still fans standing, and the environment was remarkable inside that stadium. The best game of my life was when we lost 2-0 in Barcelona but then beat them 3-0 at Old Trafford, now that was something very special.

"For me winning the 19th title is massive, nothing much comes bigger. I have always said that the Manchester United-Liverpool games are bigger than any derby, bigger than the

Manchester or Merseyside derbies. Two giant football institutions going head to head is by far the biggest derby in my book and especially when the clubs are as immense as Manchester United and Liverpool.'

Wilkins, who has seen plenty of title winning action at Stamford Bridge in recent years, declines to make comparisons between various title winning United teams, or indeed select his favourite title team. "No, I don't have a favourite United title team because I know what is required to win a title and any team that does so deserves the recognition that goes with it. Any team that wins the league has done so on merit and that is the key rather than the best players, or which team has the most talent.

"Make no mistake, Manchester United finished ahead of a very strong Chelsea team, and to achieve that warrants recognition that this was a great achievement to win their 19th title." Wilkins should know. Until the moment he was sacked as Carlo Ancelotti's assistant by chief executive Ron Gourlay at half-time during a reserve game at Chelsea's training headquarters at Cobham, the west London club looked destined to retain the title – it took an uncanny comeback by United to overtake them.

Garth Crooks, who played very briefly for United on loan from Spurs, and is more synonymous with the north London club, is one of the BBC's most respected analysts. Crooks informed me that he doesn't usually do such interviews, but our friendship goes way back, and for my book, he stressed, he was happy to make an exception.

In an exclusive interview he told me, "I have huge respect for both Manchester United and Tottenham Hotspur because they are two very big clubs who treat their former players with great respect and high regard. Both clubs love their traditions; they are both footballing clubs where their fans demand quality football. All credit to Sir Alex, he played Barcelona with true United traditions, he didn't attempt to stifle them the way Jose

Mourinho had tried with Real Madrid, or choke the game and try to nick the prize but instead held true to the club's traditions, and took them on.

"It was very special the way Sir Alex was so magnanimous in defeat. Yes, he can be aggressive, even brutish at times, but he understands the United traditions. It was indicative that United awarded Barcelona a guard of honour, and also stayed on the pitch after receiving their loser's medals to wait for Barcelona to hold aloft the Cup. That didn't go unnoticed. It is something that is fast disappearing as players slope off, unsportingly. But both managers have high regard for each other and Sir Alex showed them the respect they deserved. That has really impressed many who noticed it.

"Equally, I do not subscribe to this notion that this United side were not really up to winning the title. Some have said that the opposition were not as strong this year, and maybe they are right, but you can only take on what is put in front of you. It is very difficult to judge. They won the title, the table doesn't lie, they are the best team. They were also a very, very good team, and I emphasis 'team'. Rooney, Hernández and Giggs, are all great players in their own right but they are not a team of stars, more a team unit and it was much more of a team effort than any individual carrying them through, perhaps as they might have been in the past when they had real match winning acts such as Ronaldo or Beckham. There is much more equality in this team.

"Sir Alex is the man who made the difference. He is a like an extra player, more than the manager, and is an integral part of the team. He contributes an old school attitude, but he also has a new school approach, the combination makes him so effective. He is a father figure; not prepared to answer questions, threatening to ban reporters, protecting his players from anyone and anything, he will never criticise them in public, won't have them singled out in any way. They are his children; there is a father–son relationship there."

★

NOT NINETEEN FOREVER

Alan Brazil who, like Crooks, spent a short but eye-opening spell at Old Trafford, doesn't share the same view. The outspoken and controversial Talk Sport host, told me, "The real disappointment for me was United's performance at Wembley, it took the shine off the team and the club, although you have to concede that United, no matter how harsh it might sound, were beaten by the best team on earth that I have ever seen. Also, the semi-final defeat by City in the Cup. Plus, the actual 19th title came in what, for me, was not a vintage Premiership. United lost so many games, albeit away from home, while at Old Trafford they were magnificent and their home form was so good it saved them. My only conclusion is that this was not one of the great United sides."

Brazil has no doubts about United's greatest title teams, as he commented, "Those containing Roy Keane, Peter Schmeichel and David Beckham. Schmeichel was the best I've seen, and I have played with and against some of the best keepers of all time, from Shilton, Clemence and Jennings, and Schmeichel is the tops for me. Don't get me wrong van der Sar is a great keeper but you cannot compare him to Schmeichel, just as you cannot compare this team with the team that Schmeichel played in. Roy Keane had his demons, but he was the driving force. The players from the Best, Law, and Charlton team, plus the likes of Keane, Schmeichel and Bryan Robson, who would be my captain of a team in any era, make up the best United sides."

Crooks knows from personal experience that it takes a certain type of player to thrive at Old Trafford. He explained, "My time at United was short lived, but even so it was a fabulous, fantastic experience. It showed me that you require a special mentality to cope at Old Trafford, and that has proved to be the case over the years. I distinctly remember it took me a while to settle in, because it is such a massive club, but you don't have the time, you have got to hit the ground running. When I went there, I knew Bryan Robson from our under-21 days together, and they had a lot of special players such as Frank Stapleton, Arnold Murhen, class internationals. I was there for just three months, but I couldn't play in Europe or in the FA Cup, so I made five league appearances, scoring two goals. I played at Ipswich in December '83 and we won 2-0 and went top of the league, but Liverpool won the title that year. I was taken there on loan by Ron Atkinson because Norman Whiteside was injured, and Mark Hughes was a young prodigy, a great emerging talent, but not quite ready. I played in a reserve game; Hughes beat four men, and laid on a sitter for me. I told Ron how good Mark Hughes looked and that he didn't need me – 48 hours later he sent me back to Spurs!

"Even in my short time there, I came to appreciate what winning the title, and the rivalry with Liverpool meant to the club. There was a unique intensity between the two clubs. I played for United against Liverpool in a titanic match at Anfield. One of United's best ever performances came at Anfield with Scholes and Beckham in their prime, winning 2-0 and going onto to win the Treble."

Brazil never did himself justice in a United shirt and that rankles with him to this day. He explained, "My best memories of United are scoring against them. I made my debut for Ipswich at Portman Road coming off the subs bench and scored. I also scored twice when we beat them 6-0 at Portman Road. I thought I was bound for Old Trafford from Ipswich, but I went to Spurs, and by the time I got to Old Trafford I had suffered hamstring and groin injuries and in those days the physios were ex-players and there were no such thing as scans. I wasn't in the best of health and didn't do as well as I wanted to, although 12 goals in 25 appearances wasn't that bad, I suppose."

The tussle for dominance with Liverpool is built into the DNA of both clubs. United narrowly missed out on the 1991-92 title to Leeds United, finally ending their title tilt with a 2-0 defeat at Anfield in April 1992, accompanied by chants of "You lost the league on Merseyside". United have certainly made Liverpool pay since with eleven league titles and two European Cups eroding a Liverpool record which once appeared unbreakable.

Liverpool's decline mirrored United's rise and Sir Alex admits that even the high point of the 2005 Champions League triumph under Rafael Benítez contributed to the malaise that the club has endured since. "Winning the European Cup gave Rafa some leeway for a few years," Ferguson commented, "the European Cup is very important for Liverpool and that's why Rafa survived as long as he did. But the fact is they had a lot of bad results at the time."

Dalglish's return as manager only adds to the symbolism of United claiming No 19. 'King Kenny' was the last man to guide Liverpool to the title and the man responsible for giving them their once vice-like grip on that famous old perch.

TITLE NO. 20 - 2012-13

'In terms of impact he has had as big as an impact as anyone I can imagine. Cantona was an incredible impact player and I have been very, very lucky I have had some fantastic strikers right through, probably 10 great strikers at the club. I think we had an expectation. His performance for Arsenal last year was sensational and I remember Arsene saying to m 'he's a better player than you think' when we concluded the deal and I think he was right. He's in his mature years and winning the league meant the world to him.'

SIR ALEX FERGUSON ON ROBIN VAN PERSIE

TITLE NUMBER 20 was delivered by the man wearing number 20, the perfect symmetry to a season in which the Manchester clubs dominated, but the title returned to Old Trafford with the minimum of fuss. It was all too easy really - mainly due to City's failings. However, the motivation for Sir Alex and his players, had been laid in stone on the final day of the previous season.

United had suffered unbearable torture on the final day of the 2011-12 season when City landed the big domestic prize the previous season with 33 seconds to go in the season. Sergio Agüero's last gasp, last kick, knife-twisting end to the previous season stole the championship crown from United, just as they thought they had won it.

Losing the title on goal difference was a stab through the heart and he immediately vowed that it wouldn't happen again.

Sir Alex had always prided himself of producing teams who could score goals. United had become synonymous with adventurous attacking football, the 'Theatre of Dreams' where the fans chanted 'attack, attack, attack', whenever the team fell behind. Yet the 2011-12 vintage seemed short on inspiration upfront, getting by with ruthless determination following the 1-6 reverse against City which effectively settled the goal difference in the blues favour.

The solution was simple, it was burning a hole in Sir Alex's transfer budget. Go and get Robin van Persie, on his day and free from injuries one of the most deadly strikers in Europe, one already accustomed to the furious pace of English football after several years, albeit frustrating barren ones at Arsenal.

Sir Alex knew his team needed more firepower and that made him doubly determined to secure his services from reluctant sellers and rivals Arsenal. Knowing the striker wanted out of The Emirates, and also aware that City were ready to outbid him with massive personal terms, he had to convince van Persie that silverware was more important than a few more zeroes on a cheque. It proved to be far easier than expected. Van Persie was particularly influenced by chatting to fellow Dutch International Edwin van der Sar later revealing, "We talked about the options: we talked about City for five minutes, Juventus for five minutes and spent the next hour talking about United."

The next hurdle was persuading Arsene Wenger to sell knowing the player wanted to join him at a knock down price of £15 million. When that initially bid failed Sir Alex knew he had to meet Wenger's asking price of £24 million. A £60 million investment (including wages) for a 29 year old was a massive gamble. Juventus said as much as they backed off from the escalating figures. Yet the value for United went beyond the mere goals he would score regularly throughout the forthcoming season, it would send a signal to rivals Manchester City that they were about to return as serious title challengers – many have said that the title race was decided upon the signature of the Dutchman on that United contract back in August.

Immediately Sir Alex gave Van The Man Cantona status, mentioning the flying Dutchman in the same breath as the iconic Frenchman. Van Persie had endured quite a wait for his first Premier League title but the 29-year-old striker delivered in spectacular style after years of trying to land his first title with the Gunners. Sir Alex said: "He has made a fantastic contribution to our season. In terms of impact he has as big as an impact as anyone I can imagine. Cantona was an incredible impact player and I have been very, very lucky I have had some fantastic strikers right through, probably 10 great strikers at the club. I think we had an expectation. His performance for Arsenal last year was sensational and I remember Arsene saying to me 'he's a better player than you think' when we concluded the deal and I think he was right. He's mature and winning the league meant the world to him."

Rio Ferdinand made it plain how much he and his team mates had been hurt by City's fortunate title victory, as he mocked their noisy neighbours "It's always sweet when you win the title and it's nice to do it here, in the right way and in style, not on goal difference. We have won it outright and we have won it comfortably." But it was the manager and their new striker who took the vast majority of the plaudits. Sir Alex has now won an incredible 13 championships, the same number as Arsenal have managed in their entire history. "It just shows the resilience and attitude the manager has instilled in us," said Ferdinand. "A lot of teams would probably have fallen away. We played Liverpool a couple of seasons ago when they were fighting for the title, we beat them and got to the league before them and they've not been seen since. That shows the mentality and character that this club has. Robin has been a big factor. Last season, we lost on goal difference which tells you that we didn't score enough goals. We brought in a man who was top scorer last season and he looks like he is going to do that again this season. He has definitely added to what we had already."

★

The memories of the gut wrenching realisation that his 'noisy neighbours' had taken United's crown meant Sir Alex was ready to go the extra mile to land van Persie. There had been momentary premature celebrations from United on Wearside, until news filtered through of Agüero's winner with seconds of the entire season to spare. Sir Alex's instant reaction: "They know I'm not going away," wasn't an empty threat. It was a warning, that no one at the Etihad should have taken lightly.

Van Persie had indicated he would be leaving Arsenal and all the early smart money was on the striker following an increasingly disturbing recent trend for Gunners fans of Arsenal luminaries Gael Clichy, Emmanuel Adebayor, Kolo Toure and Samir Nasri to Manchester City. Arsenal grew weaker as City became stronger. Not only that but others such as captain Cesc Fagregas and Alex Song had departed for Barcelona. Many Gooners felt it was time to make with van Persie. To a degree Wenger agreed. But the player issued a statement about Arsenal's lack of ambition and trophies, and the parting of the ways become increasingly inevitable. Sir Alex wasn't going to let him get away to City. It was almost as if the title was being played out in advance of the season — the winner of van Persie takes all.

Sir Alex was intent on making the signing that would ensure the shift in Manchester's balance of power back to Old Trafford, and remarkably he enlisted the aid of his old foe Wenger with a personal call to the Arsenal manager to thrash out the price after weeks of refusing to meet Arsenal's demands despite all the delicate negotiation with Wenger. "He could run a poker school in Govan", Ferguson later joked.

Despite doom laden predictions of an ageing striker who suffered from frequent injury problems, the arrival of van Persie was always going to prove key to success. The Dutchman was handed the number 20 shirt in pursuit of that 20th title.

As the Premier League title was decided at Old Trafford for the fourth time in the history of the competition - more than at any other ground, as United beat Villa with a Robin van Persie hat-trick inside 33 minutes, it was even more compelling to believe that one man had delivered the 20th championship. Roberto Mancini also knew the failure in the title race was the failure to sign the Dutchman. Mancini was bitterly disappointed that his four strikers were nowhere near as effective as they had been - one of them, Mario Balotelli, caused the usual mayhem until he was sold, while Dzeko, Agüero and Tevez took turns either out of the team or out of form.

Meanwhile Sir Alex had three strikers in reasonable form in Rooney, Hernandez and Welbeck and one who, van Persie, who seemed unable to miss the target from August until March by which time the title was all but settled.

It was by far the big difference between the two. Recriminations at City, their failure to deliver the stellar signings Mancini demanded, the hierarchy replaced with promises of the right big name acquisitions to again challenge United. City can offer greater riches, it will again be an interesting choice for the players most of which will be the same ones chased by the big Manchester outfits. As for van Persie, his head was not turned by the City once in a life time offer. City offered far more money but United had the greater lure from a player who eventually revealed that he put his heart before his head, well, his heart before his wallet, to go to the red side of Manchester. Not that a £200,000-a-week wage from Old Trafford was a shabby incentive!

Mancini knew the title was won and lost on 17 August, the day Sir Alex captured van Persie from the North London club. It was hard for Mancini to take. He was offering van Persie the opportunity to join a club with ambitions to retain domestic dominance and go for the Champions league. The fact that the prolific goalscorer felt that his best bet of silverware was at Old Trafford was a slap in the face for Mancini, and as it turned out a mortal blow to City's title defence.

Van Persie argued that it wasn't a question of money. However, did money really come into it, after all when you are earning so many millions a year, one or two hundred thousand here or there hardly makes a difference. It was a footballing choice.

The shutting of the summer transfer window on August 31 had seen United secure key forwards Robin van Persie and Shinji Kagawa, while City ended up with Scott Sinclair to bolster their attack and a midfield player way down Mancini's list, Javi Garcia. Half a team arrived on deadline day, but they were all squad players at best with the likes of Maicon and Scott Sinclair joining Garcia. Once the title returned to Old Trafford, how it was won and lost was pretty clear to all, and Mancini echoed the feeling that it was all in the club's transfer successes and failures in the summer window, which is considered far more significant than trying to push through an emergency deal in January when it is by and large far too late. Mancini remarked, "We wanted van Persie because we knew he could be an important player. He has changed their situation, he is the difference between us."

Gary Neville, the one time Old Trafford dressing room shop steward, turned TV pundit, made it known that Sir Alex often stressed that he never wanted to be beaten on goal difference; that was his old manager's biggest dread. When that nightmare scenario became, Neville knew that Sir Alex had sworn to himself it wouldn't happen again and his ruthless pursuit of van Persie ensured that it didn't.

Once he had got his man Sir Alex set out in pursuit of a goalscoring records and points totals, safe in the knowledge that with van Persie's almost guaranteed goal return he would not succumb to City again on the dreaded goal difference.

"The only thing I said to them at the start of the season was make sure we do not lose on goal difference again," Sir Alex confided when celebrating his and the club's 13th Premier League, United's 20th title in all. He told the club's in-house TV channel MUTV. "That was the first time we had ever lost on goal difference. That to me was the challenge – that goal difference must be better than what they've got across the road."

United accumulated 78 league goals, compared to City's 59, by the time they clinched the title with an emphatic 3–0 win over struggling Aston Villa at Old Trafford with four games to go, van Persie delivering a hat trick inside the first 33 minutes.

To underline the Dutchman's significance to the title race, almost a third (24) of the goals had come from United's new striker even by that stage. Normally van Persie's goal haul and input into the title would have been easily good enough to secure all the personal accolades in terms of Footballer of the Year trophies, but Gareth Bale was on fire and he took them instead.

When the title was secured with four games to go, United conceded 35, five more than City. The blues were secure at the back but United' were far better in attack. So Sir Alex got it spot on again, the glut of goals compensated for any lapses in the rearguard. Sir Alex added, "After what happened last season there's a lot of teams in the country that would have melted... but not us bunch, they did what Manchester United expect of them and raised the bar. It's a marvellous performance, 84 points, four games left, it's fantastic."

Sir Alex had sown the seeds of the psychological effects of City's title triumph from the very first moment he could. The Boss was determined that his United players knew as well as their manager the gritty determination that was required to emerge from the moment City took the title. The players feeling the hurt was just what Sir Alex wanted. He made sure they knew it too. It is easily the greatest motivating factor, in Sir Alex's bludgeoning book on 'mind games'.

United's 20th title began as the United coach made its way down the A19, in the hours after the pain failing to diminish from Agüero's soul destroying goal. "We were travelling home from Sunderland on the coach and the manager went round all the young players and said to them, 'Never forget this, because this will win you titles'," Danny Welbeck recalled. "He said: 'This will make some of you into men and be the best you can be'. When the manager says things like that to you, you really want to take note of it."

The players could see at first hand how much Sir Alex was angry and frustrated at the title-race collapse. Those players knew the repercussions if they failed to put it right immediately. Feeding revenge in his young players to harness the pain was the manager's motivational style,

The message from Ferguson and his players as they embarked on their pre-season tour of South Africa and China was that the top priority was regaining the title, arguably ahead of the Champions League, something reinforced by Gary Neville who suggested on Sky TV that the domestic title was ahead of glory in Europe as Sir Alex sensed that City were in danger of gaining a foot hold on the domestic game if they retained the title.

Van Persie's early-season goals, Nemanja Vidic's return to fitness following a cruciate ligament injury, which was complicated by an early-season setback, the resurgent form of Rio Ferdinand and Michael Carrick's emergence as the driving force in midfield were all key ingredients. It wasn't a one man show, despite the fact that it felt that way, as the United faithful took to their new goalscoring machine with absolute delight. Van Persie instantly become a focal point of the United fans chanting. However much Carrick was establishing himself as a central figure with his quiet efficiency and consistently to mark out perhaps his best ever season for United it is always a goalscorer who hogs the headlines and wins over the fans.

Van Persie's late goals at St Mary's and Anfield in September claimed crucial victories and endeared him to the support. Those goals also helped to prevent United trailing City. But the self doubts were already creeping into United's biggest rivals as Mancini increasingly became exasperated with City's failure to sign the striker. After beating Chelsea 3-2 in a controversial game in which the European Champions had two men sent off and Hernandez scored from what appeared to be an offside position, United could look ahead to the first derby of the season with a 3 point lead at the top of the table.

A Manchester derby is always going to be a defining point in a season irrespective of whether it is at the start or the end, irrespective of the manager's views that it is still only three points at stake; who are they kidding? Yet at the final whistle Mancini was totally frustrated as City were defeated by a near perfect tactical masterplan organised by Ferguson and his coaching staff.

Soaking up early waves of City pressure, United broke away twice with Wayne Rooney applying the finishing touches on both occasions. Thereafter City looked a shadow of the team that had thrashed United so convincingly over the two league games the previous season.

When Ashley Young notched a well-deserved third goal, it seemed little less than the away team deserved but the goal was incorrectly adjudged offside. Within seconds the game was tilted on its head as City broke away and pulled a goal back. When Zabaleta equalised with just ten minutes left many expected the blues to snatch all three points. Yet United were if anything more determined than the home team in the closing stages. With seconds left Welbeck wrestled back possession near City's box and was fouled by Tevez. As Robin van Persie struck the resultant free kick, Samir Nasri stuck out a leg that deflected the ball sufficiently to beat Joe Hart. United's celebrations were wild and the anger felt by the home crowd led to Rio Ferdinand being struck by a coin. Things got so bad City's keeper had to act as peacemaker as some fans ran on the pitch. Yet this was a giant forward step for United and a result that, if anything, flattered the home side.

Nevertheless, United's defensive frailties had been exposed on several occasions. By the time Newcastle United arrived at Old Trafford for the Boxing Day fixture, they had trailed in 10 of the 18 league games played. That afternoon produced a helter-skelter classic. Newcastle took the lead three times but still ended on the losing side by the odd goal in seven, a 90th minute Javier Hernandez strike capping an incredible afternoon's entertainment. Elsewhere, City lost 1-0 at Sunderland to hand United an 8 point advantage.

It was a lead that continued to grow as United pounded out win after win as the defence tightened up considerably. United took 16 of the next 18 points available before they faced Everton at Old Trafford in early February. Meanwhile City drew 0-0 at relegation strugglers QPR and succumbed 3-1 at Southampton. A win against David Moyes team would extend the lead to 12 points. Surely that would be game over as far as the title was concerned.

Fergie fielded a full-strength team, despite a trip to Real Madrid three days later, to illustrate the manager's desire to put City in their place even at the expense of the Champions League. Everton had put City on their way to the title by fighting back from 4-2 down to draw 4-4 at Old Trafford the previous April, so the United boss was determined to make sure it wouldn't happen again and knew his old pal David Moyes was plotting a top four place so their motivation couldn't be higher. First half goals from Giggs and van Persie secured all three points for United and while it wasn't a particularly sparkling performance there was a ruthless determination exhibited that could only have been instilled by the manager.

United were unstoppable now. Despite the set back of defeat to Real Madrid following the controversial dismissal of Nani, United maintained a stranglehold on their league lead, reeling off another four wins without conceding a goal, extending it to 15 points as City lost at Everton. After a cup exit at the hands of Chelsea on Easter Monday, the return derby a week later saw an entirely different Manchester City turn up at Old Trafford. The Blues dominated the game and were unfortunate not to win by more than the eventual 2-1 score-line settled late on by a fabulous Sergio Agüero dribble and finish.

However if there were any doubts about United's title credentials they were calmed by United picking four points in two potentially tricky away games. The 2-0 triumph at Stoke on April 14th saw van Persie score his first league goal in two months while the Dutchman's late strike at Upton Park rescued a point in an end-to-end encounter with West Ham that finished 2-2.

Despite a win against Wigan, City now had to win every game to stay in the race and despite taking the lead and performing impressively at White Hart Lane for 75 minutes their title was surrendered as Spurs, so often City's nemesis in the past, scored three goals in eight mad minutes to maintain their push for Champions League football. That left with United with relatively simple task of beating relegation candidates Aston Villa to win the title.

The title clincher was in total contrast to the taut nerves of the final day of the previous season, as Villa played the unwilling stooges to a Championship party with four games to go. It had been a forgone conclusion for some considerable time, and City's mathematical chances ended when van Persie opened the scoring after just 90 seconds in the title clinching win over Villa before netting a superb over-the-shoulder volley 11 minutes later, that was rightly hailed as one of the season's wonder goals, although he did exactly the same, identical technique in Arsenal colours a season earlier. He fired home a third just after the half-hour mark to move on to 24 goals for the Premier League season, with Luis Suarez (23) close behind, but the Liverpool striker was about to be suspended for the rest of the season after biting Branislav Ivanovic in the 2-2 draw with Chelsea.

For the first goal Brad Guzan stayed on his line as a deep cross from Rafael was knocked across the face of the goal by Giggs to allow van Persie a simple finish. The move was started by a marvellous raking crossfield pass from Wayne Rooney, playing deep in midfield. The United fans had been salivating from the start of the season at the prospect of van Persie and Rooney linking in attack, but as it turned out the partnership seemed far more effective with Rooney in a deep position supplying the ammunition.

While the sheer perfection of van Persie's second strike caught the eye, it was created by one of the passes of the season from Rooney as his long range ball was met by the Dutchman, who had spun away from the defence with a clever diagonal run before letting the ball drop over his shoulder for a trademark volley from the edge of the box. After 33 minutes, following a Villa corner, Giggs showed an age-defying turn of pace down the left, before picking out van Persie to complete his hat-trick.

Yet it was van Persie's spectacular second, a contender for goal of the season, that manager Sir Alex Ferguson described as, "[Goal] of the century for me. It was a marvellous hit, head down, over the ball, perfect timing – a magnificent strike."

Michael Carrick observed, "It has to be right up there, the movement for starters, then Wayne to pick him out with a great pass. The finish was textbook. There are not many people who can do that. Robin has had a terrific season. It is his first one here and if he carries on like this he will have a good career, that's for certain." In the second half van Persie was back defending when it mattered, executing a goal-line clearance from a Weimann header. Inevitably, he was named Man of the Match having scored the quickest Premier League hat-trick in nine years to make it five goals in three matches.

Ferguson's greatest praise was reserved for the Dutchman who has made all the difference and whom City had been able to only watch with envy. "He's been unbelievable. He has to take a lot of the credit, his goals tell you that. His performance level will tell you that (but) I'm sure Robin will be saying what a great bunch of players he's got with him."

Arsenal manager Arsene Wenger did not accept that van Persie had been decisive in his new club establishing a 16-point lead over City and a 21-point advantage over his own team. Well, he would do, wouldn't he? "United have won 20 championships and they won a few without Robin van Persie," Wenger observed. "No, the difference is that City have dropped off. Robin has made an impact of course, I don't deny that, but United lost only on goal difference last year. And if QPR did not know they were safe, they [United] would have won it last year."

However, the stats seem to prove otherwise. It had been predicted that his golden goals would give United the title, and they did. Van Persie's immediate on field reaction with a Sky TV microphone thrust before him, "It didn't really matter who scored as long as we won this game and we did win this game, from the first minute everyone played well and everyone wanted it. It was a great to score so early and it was a fantastic game of football. I'm very happy but it's weird. I had to wait for so long for my first title and it's a great feeling."

Speaking of his special second goal, van Persie modestly added: "It was a great ball from Wayne, so the only thing I had to do was guide it right and hit it properly and it went in great but more important was the result." The victory over Villa gave United an unassailable 16-point lead over City. Rooney emphasised how much the heartbreak against City spurred them on, "It's what we've worked all year for and we've fully deserved it. We won this game in the first half and it is a fantastic night for us. When you lose the title, it's hard to take and the way we did it wasn't a nice feeling last time so we've all dug in deep and all worked together and done fantastic to put ourselves in the position to finish the job off. You know how football is, so you never take anything for granted so we worked hard and thankfully now it's done. The manager has great desire and a winning mentality. We all buy into that and want to do well for the club."

Ryan Giggs had already extended his contract to play next season when he will turn 40. He was still a part of United's plans and justified his continued by such performances and how Giggs provided the assist for van Persie's second-minute opener. "He's a unique freak," Fergie said of the Marathon Man who featured in all of the 13 Premier League title wins and scored in every Premier League season. "He'll play for another two years, trust me." Ryan Giggs was offered his first professional contract with Manchester United on his 17th birthday on 29 Nov 1990. He is the only player to have played and scored in every Premier League season

Giggs won his 13th league championship and Sir Alex felt he would play on until 41. Giggs was in his 22nd season with the club and will become the third outfield player to play in the Premier League in their 40s, following Teddy Sheringham at West Ham and Gordon Strachan at Coventry. The number 11 made his 28th appearance for United this season against Villa and played the full 90 minutes. Carrick said for Giggs to still be playing at the highest level was "sensational". "I keep talking about him but what else is there left to say?" said Carrick, who partnered the 39-year-old in central midfield in the title clinching game. "It is sensational that he is still able to do that after all this time. It is not just physical, it is mental, having the drive and desire to do it every day. Ryan is out there training every day. The standard he has set is unbelievable. He is a legend. It is a throwaway comment too often. But he is the legend really. It is a pleasure to play with him and work with him every day."

When Giggs smashed the ball into the top corner of the Benfica goal on 14 September 2011, he became the oldest scorer in the Champions League at 37 years, 289 days. Uefa president Michel Platini praised Giggs's loyalty to United. "That is beautiful. I like the people that fight for their colours and don't change clubs every two months to make business. He's a guy who would never change clubs." Giggs has now won 23 major titles, including four FA Cups, four League Cups and two Champions League crowns. He has never received a red card during his club career, although he was once sent off for Wales, against Norway in September 2001. The veteran Welshman had now won as many as titles as Arsenal have in their entire history. Giggs completed the full 90 minutes on Monday night, his 28th appearance of the season. Yet even he would accept he must cede top billing to van Persie.

United won the title with five games left in 2001, but winning it with four games remaining to put City in their place made it one of the sweetest of all United's 20 titles, and of Sir Alex's 13. Rio Ferdinand posted a series of pictures on his account, including locker room poses, champagne drinking and a late-night party as he revealed on Twitter how champions really celebrate after winning a title. An image, tweeted at around 1.30am on Tuesday morning, following the Monday night win over Aston Villa that clinched the 20th title, showed the team dressed in casual clothes, in a bar smiling for the camera. The caption simply read: Here we are!

An earlier photo from the Old Trafford dressing room at around 11pm on Monday night showed Rio reaching for the ceiling panels, holding a bottle of wine. It said: 'We took the roof off tonight!' There were also images of the defender posing topless with Michael Carrick and Wayne Rooney, and Rafael. Rio's tweet, posted the next morning, said: "#NowPlaying Champion by Buju Banton on #Spotify fits the mood nicely this morning!" He was joined on Twitter by striker Wayne Rooney who said: "What a feeling to win the league. Champions 20" Their former team mate Michael Owen tweeted: "Congratulations Manchester United. I don't think anybody can say they didn't deserve it. The best team by far this season."

For the neutral it hadn't been a vintage campaign, there would be no "squeaky bum time", as Sir Alex Ferguson might put it. To win with four games to go lacked the previous season's drama, but it was seat revenge for the way they had lost the title to City.

It had been a stuttering start for both Manchester clubs. United started their league season with a 1-0 defeat at Everton. Sir Alex used the disappointment of that night at Goodison Park to drive his players on. City suffered an early season major setback in a 1-1 draw with a Stoke; normally a tough nut to crack but no one knew then that they would face a season of decline and relegation fears, but Peter Crouch handled before putting Stoke went ahead. Javi Garcia levelled on his City debut but Edin Dzeko was denied a late winner when Ryan Shawcross cleared off the line as the signs were already there that fortune would not favour them this time.

United's early-season form was inexplicable, their performance against Liverpool at Anfield in September was indicative of a very nervy start. Even against 10 men United struggled but somehow they found a way to win 2-1. It gave them a little breathing space when questions were being asked. Soon enough for United, the signs were quickly evident that they meant business in pursuit of getting their title back. A fiery showdown at Stamford Bridge saw United triumph 3-2 against nine-man Chelsea on October 28. A David Luiz own goal and a van Persie strike put United ahead but Juan Mata and Ramires brought the Blues right back in it, before Branislav Ivanovic and Fernando Torres were sent off. Javier Hernandez's neat finish made it 3-2 in a critical result. The concerns of vulnerability were dispelled.

United visited Chelsea twice in a week in October. They won the first game but lost the second, in the Capital One Cup, 5-4 in extra time. That was a blessing in disguise as the League Cup is a distraction United never need.

The van Persie show took off as his old club visited Old Trafford on November 3. The Dutchman received a hostile reception from Arsenal fans but was on target within three minutes. Wayne Rooney missed a penalty but Patrice Evra scored a second before Santi Cazorla scored.

Aston Villa faced a testing season at the wrong end of the table when but on November 10 they stormed into a two-goal lead courtesy of Andreas Weimann's double at Villa Park. However, United demonstrated they had not lost the knack of coming from behind with Hernandez scoring twice, either side of Ron Vlaar's own goal, his winner coming just three minutes from time.

United's early season was characterised by bad defending and concerns about their goalkeepers, with a 4-3 win at Reading on December 1, Anders Lindegaard was so poor that Ferguson decided to stick with David de Gea for the rest of the season. Good decision. Wayne Rooney's brace put United two goals up at the Etihad Stadium on December 9 in the first Manchester derby of the season. Yaya Toure and Pablo Zabaleta clawed City back into the game at 2-2 before van Persie's free-kick brought a dramatic injury-time winner that sent United six points clear at the top. The two Manchester clubs were hard to separate when United visited City in the run-up to Christmas and even closer together with the score locked at 2-2 late in the game. But van Persie's winner ensured United never looked back.

The Newcastle clash at Old Trafford on Boxing Day brought the usual glut of goals between these two clubs, as United won a seven-goal thriller 4-3. Incredibly, the Magpies led three times but Hernandez slid in to guide home Michael Carrick's cross in the last minute. It extended United's lead to seven points as City were losing 1-0 at Sunderland.

A slip up, a glimmer of hope. United draw at snowy Tottenham on January 20 handed City a way back, only for the defending champions to fail at bottom club QPR next time out. A big wasted opportunity for City. The injury to City captain Vincent Kompany in an FA Cup tie at Stoke on January 26, ruled out for two months and left Mancini's team exposed. By the time he returned City were 15 points adrift of United, the race virtually over.

City crashed to a shock defeat to Southampton at St. Mary's on February 9. Jason Puncheon and Steven Davis netted for Southampton while Gareth Barry put the ball in his own net. Dzeko replied but crashed 3-1, the title defence in tatters. Rooney scored a late goal at Fulham to secure a 1-0 victory in February, a difficult game which illustrated a dogged determination by United to grind out results when needed.

Van Persie went through an unexpected goal drought but it finally ended with a deflected shot in off Titus Bramble, that handed United three points in a 1-0 win at Sunderland on March 30. United remained 15 points ahead.

City's derby win at Old Trafford gave them one last chance, but United's next game, away to Stoke, saw Carrick scoring in the fourth minute and that was that. In his programme notes for the Manchester derby defeat by City at Old Trafford, Fergie reflected on the season. "How do we analyse this season – is it one of regret or celebration? For me it is something of the curate's egg, part bad but with great redeeming features."

*

Yet as the dust settled on the championship, so the bombshell of Sir Alex Ferguson's retirement rocked English football. It later emerged he had taken the decision at Christmas and confirmed to the board and directors in March. Within 48 hours of this announcement Everton boss David Moyes was confirmed as the new manager. A minority of supporters may have yearned for Jose Mourinho to become the new boss but United, conservative as ever, sought evolution not revolution. As far back as December Sir Bobby Charlton had ruled the Portuguese out of the running saying "he wasn't a Manchester United manager". Meanwhile

Moyes was described as being, "cut from the same cloth" as the outgoing manager.

After 11 years at Goodison, David Moyes had built a team capable of competing with the best domestically, even if he didn't have any silverware to show for his labours. Yet he would walk into an Old Trafford dressing room in need of some rejuvenation. Patrice Evra, Rio Ferdinand and Nemanja Vidic were all the wrong side of 32. Although in Chris Smalling, Jonny Evans and Phil Jones United appeared to be well stocked with quality defenders and Leighton Baines was rumoured to be an early transfer target.

Paul Scholes had retired following a series of knee injuries and even Giggs – 40 in November – could not go on forever, indeed his selection in big games was still a cause of concern for many supporters. The rebuilding had already started with the signing of Wilfried Zaha from Crystal Palace, while Nick Powell headed the new generation. Nevertheless Michael Carrick, at 32, was United's only proper central midfielder with the likes of Tom Cleverley, Anderson and Ashley Young failing to nail down first team places for one reason or another. By some estimates, Sir Alex hadn't bought a genuine central midfielder since the signing of Carrick in 2006.

Further forward Wayne Rooney had made a second request for a transfer following his demotion to support act to new star man van Persie, many assumed that Moyes first order of business would be to find a replacement for a man he once managed when he was just a boy. Meanwhile Danny Welbeck had only notched one league goal all season and there were rumours that Javier Hernandez was being courted by United's Champions League rivals.

On reflection, much of the brio of Ferguson's early teams had disappeared with the later vintages. Whether this was a consequence of the manager adapting to new tactics or the limitations placed on his transfer budget by United's parsimonious owners, it wasn't clear. Yet most felt that, in leaving having secured the 20th title, Ferguson had done the right thing for himself and the club. He had turned United into ruthless winners of leagues but the last few seasons had seen the club fail when it came to many of the big clashes in Europe or domestically – their meek surrender at the Etihad the previous season being a case in point.

The majestic swagger, flamboyance and drama of previous championships may have been absent but United were superb at stringing results against the lesser lights. City and the London giants couldn't live with them, delivering a level of performance that won games regardless of the conditions against inferior opposition – this was the hallmark of true champions.

Clearly the lack of edge in Rooney's game played a major role in his second, informal, transfer request. Fergie had dropped him for the game against Real Madrid at Old Trafford and although there was a sense of injustice in the manner of their exit, the loss to Chelsea in the FA Cup (having been 2-0 up at half-time in the first game) was perhaps a bigger blow. In his programme notes for the City game, Sir Alex confessed that the Chelsea defeat was his biggest disappointment as he put defeat to Real Madrid down to circumstances beyond his control after Nani's far from fair red card. He added: "What could we have done differently? The answer is not a lot so I don't dwell on things that have simply not gone our way and that we could do nothing about."

As usual the critics were divided on how this team measured up to others like the 1999 Treble winners or 1994 Double winners. Sir Alex commented, "There's a lot of youth in the team, it's a team that can stay together for a long time and hopefully they do and Ryan Giggs and Rio Ferdinand, the old codgers, still can carry on. I'm really happy with the squad, really delighted, they are a good bunch of professionals, of human beings. There is no reason why we can't go on and improve for next year."

Sir Bobby Charlton had labelled Ferguson's side as one of the best in the club's history. "Although it looks as though we haven't been playing attractive football, we've been winning with ease in lots of cases, it was impossible for anyone to follow us, we were right on song. This is maybe one of the best squads of players that we have had. The players are from all sorts of different countries but, somehow or other, Alex seems to be able to gel them together for the important matches."

Naturally van Persie was highlighted as the big difference, but as usual Sir Alex was recognised for his achievements in leading another new team to yet another title. "If we're talking about magic in football, the only magicians I know are people like Sir Alex," said England manager Roy Hodgson. Three of United's starting line-up in the title-clinching over Villa - Phil Jones, Michael Carrick and Wayne Rooney - are England internationals. Danny Welbeck came off the substitutes' bench, which also included Tom Cleverley. "I'm realistic in that I don't expect coaches to put teams together for England and I wouldn't dream of suggesting Alex should favour English players over others," said Hodgson. "It's very nice to see a lot of very good English players are coming through thanks to their incredible academy system and they are going to be very important for me. That is of course a major bonus. It's a particular bonus when I go to watch matches because when I go to see United play, there's a good chance I'll see a number of English players, which unfortunately isn't always the case when I watch other matches."

Asked about Fergie's latest title success, Hodgson added, "There's not so much you can say other than we'd all like to know how he does it. We'd all like to know what the secret is. Year after year he keeps producing incredible performances from his teams and his players, and keeps being able to rebuild sides from the ashes of the previous team."

So how would David Moyes approach his new squad? Eurosport 'expert', Paul Parker, a Manchester United legend, commented in his column that the majority of the reaction "rightly concerned" praising the signing of van Persie, and Sir Alex's ability to get his teams "playing an incessant, consistent level against the small and medium sides while grinding out close results against the big players". Instead he concentrated on the players United succeeded in signing, and those City failed to sign. He commented, "I think if United want to get the best out of a player like Shinji Kagawa, they needed to sign someone like

Mario Goetze, who is joining Bayern Munich instead. Kagawa is a wonderful technical player, but to succeed he needs the dynamic creativity that he was accustomed to at Borussia Dortmund, the ability of team-mates to show flair and panache at high tempo."

Parker helped United to their first League title for 26 years and won the Double twice, recognised the scale of Moyes task in walking into England's pre-eminent club. "The squad is balanced and strong, but the first XI needs an extra spark, particularly in wide positions. Ashley Young lacks the appetite required for this level, while Nani is too inconsistent; Antonio Valencia is consistent and determined, so he will stay in my view, but he lacks that extra guile United need in the final third." Parker stressed the need for a couple of world class players as he questioned United's ability to beat the best in English football, pointing out that if there was a Premier League title play-off system like in rugby or US and Australian sports, United would not be champions as "they have the collective mentality, style of play and squad depth to deal with all the average teams and largely avoid defeat (if not beat) the top sides." Parker felt that United did not have the best players in the league, "some way short" of City's or Chelsea's in terms of creative ability, certainly insufficient to win the Champions League.

Parker pointed out that van Persie chose United over City because the very top players value United's history and stability at management level over the "extra £30k a week they could get at Eastlands". He argued van Persie would also rather work with Ferguson, the great man-manager, over Mancini "does not appear able to control the top stars, and has a tendency to let his own ex-player's ego interfere with team matters". Fergie had the edge, Parker believes, with a "cohesive dressing room with a clear disciplinary code" rather than "a hotchpotch of superstars with a tendency to follow their own leads." How David Moyes copes with the big personalities at the club will be his first significant test of course.

As if the title was not enough, there was chaos at Manchester City before the season even ended as the Blues lost the FA Cup

Final 1-0 to lowly Wigan Athletic who had only entered league football in 1978. City were thoroughly outplayed at Wembley and the 90th minute Ben Watson winner brought the curtain down on Roberto Mancini's Etihad reign. The celebrations were just as enthusiastic in the red half of Manchester.

So in contrast to 2012, United would lord it over City who, despite their extra financial muscle appear to have fallen backwards during the past twelve months with their star players apparently content to rest on their laurels. Paul Parker perceptively pointed out that Mancini's managerial style "can motivate but equally frustrate players" continuing, "there is a difference between being a lightning rod, Jose Mourinho style, and actually making it all about you, which is Mancini's tendency (you would never have seen Jose scrapping with problem players on the training ground). Ferguson knew how to motivate his players regardless of their personality and profile and whatever the circumstances, whether off the back of a defeat or in an attempt to maintain a winning run."

Parker also put the current squad into perspective: "United's forward peak was arguably 1999, when they had a proper pairing – Dwight Yorke and Andy Cole – and two excellent reserves in Teddy Sheringham and Ole Gunnar Solskjaer. You could also point to the Ronaldo-Rooney tandem that brought United great success before the Portuguese left for Madrid. At the moment they have van Persie, Wayne Rooney – who is more comfortable deeper behind the forwards – Danny Welbeck and Javier Hernandez. Welbeck has only scored once in the league this season and is probably destined to be a squad player, while Hernandez is easily at his most effective as an impact substitute. United are still possibly a man short up front."

While Parker clearly favours United due to his obvious roots, Sir Alex doesn't see it very much differently, although he would never, of course, use such emotive language. Speaking to *Inside United* before he announced his retirement, Sir Alex was clearly confident he had a strong squad that can become even stronger with two or three specific improvements to the team. He said:

"You have to look at the structure of the club at present, in terms of the number of first-team players we have at 23 or under. David De Gea, Rafael, Phil Jones, Chris Smalling, Alex Buttner, Nick Powell, Tom Cleverley and Danny Welbeck. Shinji Kagawa and Chicharito are 24. Jonny Evans is 25 and Wayne Rooney is hitting his peak at 27. Older players like Ryan Giggs, Paul Scholes and Rio Ferdinand may be coming towards the end of their careers, but these younger players are the foundation for the next five or six years, irrespective of the players breaking through, like Adnan Januzaj, the Belgian boy, who's really looking very good. Hopefully the players we bring into the club in the next year or so will be of the quality we need. We're competitive in the market - we're not Chelsea or Manchester City in terms of money but we're competitive. We've been doing a bit of work on that over the last three or four months, targeting who the players are that we feel could enhance us, make us better or help us maintain the level we're at." Surely David Moyes would have his own ideas now regarding potential transfer targets.

*

The retirement of Sir Alex Ferguson seems to have left a huge void, not just at Old Trafford but at the top of the English game. He had been at the club for so long, 26 years, that no one seemed to know who would fill his role as the pre-eminent figure in the game. With City and Chelsea both likely to change managers during the summer, the Premier League seemed in flux for the first time in over two decades, dating back to Kenny Dalglish's first resignation from Liverpool in February 1991. There were more questions than answers ahead of what could be the most exciting period in English football for a generation.

Arsene Wenger was now the longest serving manager, perhaps with Arsenal's improved financial position, he could assume Sir Alex's pre-eminence in the English game? Or would Spurs make a decent fist of things under Andre Villas-Boas? Would Mourinho take English football by storm for a second time at Chelsea? Could Manchester City get their mojo back having secured Yaya Toure's future at the club but with a manager new to the English game? Could Brendan Rodgers' improving Liverpool see them back in contention? Would David Moyes continue Sir Alex Ferguson's incredible achievements with a seamless transition to another decade of glory? The top six all had reason for optimism and trepidation.

As the curtain fell on Sir Alex Ferguson's reign perhaps the biggest tribute to him was that no one really knew what the future held. The only certainty was that the game in England would never quite be the same again.

THE PLAYERS' PLAYERS POLL

"Bryan Robson was out of this world... a box to box midfield player with enormous energy, he was like Red Rum, never stopped running and would do so for the full 90 plus minutes, breaking up play one minute and scoring a goal the next...that's why I felt privileged to be a Manchester United player, to be in that sort of company."

RAY WILKINS

PERHAPS IT HAS NEVER BEEN attempted before but among all the usual lists of all time greats selected by individuals from time to time, this is the first time there has been a poll of The Players' Players for Manchester United. During research for '20|13', United Legends were consulted for their views on the 20 record breaking title years and the players who starred in them. It was a unique opportunity to conduct a poll of United legends to select their all time favourite United players and to evaluate who comes out on top as the Ultimate Players' Player. From elder statesman such as Sir Bobby Charlton to the modern day players, such as Dwight Yorke, everyone had the chance to vote for just one or a multiple of their favourites.

Sir Bobby talks about, in an earlier chapter, why he went for Edwin van der Sar ahead of Peter Schmeichel, opted for forwards Denis Law, George Best, Eric Cantona and Ryan Giggs and a midfield of Roy Keane, Nobby Stiles and Bryan Robson, with Steve Bruce, Gary Pallister and naturally Duncan Edwards at the back.

THE PLAYERS' POLL

Wilf McGuinness, who had the unenviable task of following Sir Matt Busby as manager at United, was also a player in the 50s, and his main concern was not to "insult' anyone he left out. In the end he selected Robson, Keane, Ince, Cantona, Bruce, Pallister, Stam, Irwin, the Neville brothers, Edwards, Beckham, Giggs, Scholes, Charlton, Law, Best.

Steve Coppell reached for the history books and declared that his starting point would be the great United team that first won the European Cup, hence his initial selection of Paddy Crerand, Bobby Charlton, Nobby Stiles and George Best. But, Steve added, "In the modern era, I would go for Ronaldo and Rooney. The club are synonymous with exciting, attacking players, so it would be very tough to find defenders with flair, certainly not compared to the forwards, so its a big problem choosing defenders, having said that, there is David Sadler and Bill Foulkes from that European Cup era. Then there is "Peter Perfect" Martin Buchan and there were none better than Steve Bruce and Gary Pallister as a combination. Steve Bruce might not be exceptional as an individual, perhaps he did not have a great deal of pace, but he was a great defender, a very effective defender within the framework of the team especially alongside Pallister. United have also had Jaap Stam and even the current crop of Vidic and Ferdinand would feature." Clearly, once Steve got going he found plenty of top class defenders, but a profusion of midfield and attackers.

"It's in the attack where it gets exciting, and my first choice there would be Ronaldo, Cantona, Rooney and George Best, which means Ryan Giggs in midfield, the roving role he has adapted to more recently. Bobby Charlton is an absolute legend and you couldn't possibly leave out Paul Scholes and how could you leave out Roy Keane?"

He went on, "You would have to have a rotation system because Denis Law would be in the squad, not a player I saw a lot of because he seemed to be injured whenever Manchester United played Liverpool but he and Nobby Stiles would have to be in the squad and so too would "Robbo", a player who would be your yardstick for any Ferguson team."

"As for the goalkeeper? Well, it would be Schmeichel or van der Sar, having said that Alex Stepney was great in the dressing room as well as a great keeper. But Schmeichel was literally and physically a giant who had an effect on the entire team."

Yet the process of selecting the Players' Player wasn't as facile as it would seem to be. Some of those selected were not always the obvious names the fans might have assumed would come under consideration. Ray Wilkins was one of those who came up with some surprise selections. Wilkins, who insists "don't call me a Leg End", picks out Frank Stapleton, Jimmy Greenhoff, and Stuart Pearson for special mention knowing that they are the kind of forwards that few might pick at first, but who he believes rank among United all time greats.

Wilkins told '20|13', that he admires Stapleton, Greenhoff and Pearson, as well as the usual suspects picked out for the Players' Player honours. "Once when I had a few friends round for dinner I told them that I was expecting a 'proper' centre forward, who would be coming through the front door shortly. 'Who is that?' they all wanted to know, they must have been wondering if Ronaldo was turning up for dinner! I explained that he was one of the best. It was Frank Stapleton. He was a fantastic footballer, and one who would be very difficult to kick out of any Manchester United side. I played with him for two years at United and he had immense qualities. Jimmy Greenhoff was another, so gifted, it was almost embarrassing the silky skills he had. He would point to where he would want you to pass the ball. Stuart Pearson was another in that category.

"Naturally, the likes of Bryan Robson and Roy Keane were out of this world. Bryan Robson was a box to box midfield player with enormous energy, he was like Red Rum, he never stopped running and would do so for the full 90 plus minutes, breaking up play one minute and scoring a goal the next. Roy Keane was another like Robbo who you would say believed there was no 'I' in 'Team'. They played for their team, and that's why I felt privileged to be a Manchester United player, to be in that sort of company.

"When I was growing up as a trainee at Chelsea, from the age of ten, it was Best, Law and Charlton who I most admired, a group of guys I would always watch and admire. I would see Best wreaking havoc on cabbage patches football pitches and I wish I would have seen George Best on the modern pitches, how even more wonderful he would have been. Then again, for me there was he was the greatest of them all... George Best. People talk about Maradona and Messi being the best, but Best was the best for me. It was such a shame that he was Northern Irish and they never qualified for the World Cup or the European Championships, otherwise there would have been no question about who was the best. Best was massive, a genius!"

Gary Pallister is most certainly a Manchester United 'Leg End' as Cockney Ray Wilkins might put it. One of United's fulcrum alongside Steve Bruce as the titles started to roll in, the centre half has no doubt about the pecking order for his comtemporaries. "Bryan Robson is the No1, the player who had everything; he was an unbelievable captain, great in the dressing room, played his game at break neck speed, was physically dominating and had a great range of passing. He had such drive that he carried people along with him, they wanted to fight alongside him. Little wonder he was dubbed Captain Marvel because that is exactly what he was like. I never played with Robbo at his peak but I saw enough of him to know that he was the No1 around during my time in the game

"Eric Cantona was No. 2, sheer genius, the player who could turn a game with the genius factor, and there is no doubt that he was the catalyst to us winning titles. Cantona would be closely followed by Roy Keane and Ryan Giggs. Keane is the closest thing I've seen to Bryan Robson and Giggs in his pomp raiding down the left hand side had such great ability. He was awesome for a player who didn't carry a lot of weight with a small frame but who was tough and caused such problems for defences."

Outside of his own generation of superstars Pally is steeped in the Old Trafford traditions, as he commented, "I was talking with Sir Bobby Charlton recently and he was singing the praises of Duncan Edwards, telling me how he was the best he had ever seen, and that is some recommendation. Personally, I have seen very little of Duncan, apart from a few snippets in the old black and white games on TV, so it is so difficult for me to say who was United's best. But you cannot help but talk of the very best in George Best, just a little bit amazing, wouldn't you say? You just have to start with George Best as the best and you hear that from those who played with him. Whenever I talk to Brian Kidd, Paddy Crerand, and Denis Law, they tell me what an amazing talent he was.

"Of course, no matter how much you rate Edwin van der Sar, there is only one goalkeeping selection and that is Peter Schmeichel, who was United's best goalkeeper without a shadow. Edwin came close and Alex Stepney too in the '68 team but Peter changed the face of goalkeeping, he made it into a different art form. Ronaldo was of course an amazing player for United, and that's the great thing about United, and why it's called the Theatre of Dreams, it's because so many wonderfully gifted players pass through it, why it's so entertaining to be part of it as player or fan. Giggs, Cantona, Beckham, Scholes, Edwards, Charlton, Law, Best – there are just so many nominations for the best players ever at United. Somehow the club excites their fans world wide by producing or buying some unbelievable talents, mainly producing them themselves and that distinguishes United from other club."

Alan Brazil has no doubts about United's greatest title teams, "Those containing Roy Keane, Peter Schmeichel and David Beckham. Schmeichel was the best I've see and I have played with and against some of the best keepers of all time; such as Shilton, Clemence and Jennings, and Schmeichel is the tops for me. Don't get me wrong van der Sar is a great keeper but you cannot compare him to Schmeichel, just as you cannot compare this [current] team with the team that Schmeichel played in. Roy Keane had his demons, but he was the driving force. The players from the Best, Law and Charlton team, plus the likes of Keane,

Schmeichel and Bryan Robson, who would be my captain of an team in any era, make up the best United sides." For Brazil, David Beckham was, "a wonderful ambassador as well as player". Alan also mentions Gordon Strachan, Norman Whiteside, Mark Hughes and Gordon McQueen. Explaining why he nominated his fellow Scot and towering blond centre half, the TalkSport host explains, "like Jim Holden, Greenhoff and Martin Buchan, you need real characters in your team and this player was one of the best in that category. Often you find it is 85% ability but the other 15% is pure character and McQueen had more than anyone in terms of character."

Garth Crooks named Rooney, Hernández and Giggs, as the stars of the 2011 team and mentioned Cantona, Ronaldo and Beckham of the more recent generation but also expressed his admiration for his own generation; Norman Whiteside, Frank Stapleton, Arnold Muhren and Mark Hughes, but was reluctant to go through all his top line United acts, as he explained, "I have too many friends, and have no wish to upset them!"

Dwight Yorke was emphatic about his choice of all time greatest Manchester United player – Paul Scholes He did mention the likes of Beckham, Keane, and Giggs, but his only vote went to Scholes .

Paul Parker selected his contemporaries first; Bryan Robson, Denis Irwin, who he rates a far higher than Ashley Cole, and next the players who inspired him as a kid, Jimmy Greenhoff, Lou Macari, and Arthur Albiston.

The ever popular Lee Sharpe nominated George Best based on his reputation and what little he has gleaned from TV, but goes more for his contemporaries; Paul McGrath, Gordon Strachan and Jesper Olsen, and naturally, Bryan Robson, Roy Keane, Paul Ince, Steve Bruce, Gary Pallister, and Peter Schmeichel as if to the icons and great players Lee associated with at Old Trafford. Mark Hughes also makes it onto Lee's list together with Eric Cantona and the group of young players who broke through the ranks such as Scholes, Beckham, Butt and the two Nevilles, as well as "absolute legend" Ryan Giggs.

Centre half David May selects Bryan Robson, for his inspirational leadership and mentoring skills, Eric Cantona, for being a genius, and a big surprise, a vote for Kevin Moran, the player who was such a big influence in the defender's career, first at Blackburn, and then at Old Trafford.

Alex Stepney didn't hesitate in selecting George Best as his all time No. 1 but of the modern generation he went for Paul Scholes. Of the players who inspired him when he was growing up, it had to be Duncan Edwards. While there has been a profusion of quality and world class foreign players, Alex felt the British players deserved to have far more recognition.

Viv Anderson journeyed from Forest, where he won the European Cup twice, to Arsenal before becoming Alex Ferguson's first ever signing, but as he recalls for '20|13', "I was a 15 and 16 year old schoolboy training at Manchester United; we were on one pitch and the first team trained on the other with the likes of George Best, Denis Law, and Bobby Charlton. How fantastic was that for a young kid? Those are the three players who I would select as my all time favourite Manchester United players, but also 'Robbo' sticks out for me, as does Eric, and Sparky, there were also the Giggs, Scholes and Beckham group of players that I admired."

In Martin Buchan's 11 years at Old Trafford he was regarded as one of the club's greatest ever defenders, one who demonstrated excellent positional awareness which, coupled with his pace, made him one of the coolest and classiest central defenders of his era. He made 456 appearances, scoring four goals and played 34 times for Scotland, including two World Cups in 1974 and 1978. Now working for the Professional Footballers' Association in their Manchester offices, there are few better placed to assess the all- time best United players.

Martin tells '20|13', "It is very hard, if not impossible, to put together your ideal Manchester United XI. I could easily nominate three United teams, we've had so many outstanding players down the years If I have left anybody out, my apologies, it is not because I don't rate them, it's just that there are so many excellent players to choose from, so I have decided to go with a few of my personal favourites, in no particular order.

"As a defender myself, I would have loved to have played alongside Jaap Stam. I had the pleasure of meeting him when I worked for Puma, the football boot manufacturer. I thought he was immense. He had not just an imposing physical presence but skill and a footballing ability that you don't often see in centre halves. Bobby Charlton would be on my list, not only the best two-footed player I have ever seen, but also the best ambassador England has ever had, not just in football, but in any field. Then there is The Genius that was George Best.

"When I first joined United there was a curious mixture of superstars such as Bobby, George and Denis Law and players who wouldn't have made the Aberdeen reserve team. I had the privilege of playing with all three for a spell and, although I didn't play against Pele, I played against all the other outstanding Brazilians of that time. I've always felt it was such a shame that George never had the chance to perform to a wider audience in the World Cup Finals. He had unbelievable balance, but he was also so brave. I once saw him play for Northern Ireland against Scotland at Hampden Park, and he took on Scotland virtually on his own.

"I'm also a big fan of Ray Wilkins, who I feel was much maligned in the press by some who should have known better. He was given the undeserved nickname of 'the crab'. What's wrong with keeping the ball when your team-mates are tightly marked or you cannot be sure that the pass you'd like to make will reach its intended target? He wouldn't be called the 'crab' today if he played for Barcelona, and kept possession in the same way that he did back then. Steve Coppell was a wonderfully gifted player and it was a real tragedy that his career was cut short in his prime, when he was injured playing for England. He had ten years' experience under his belt and was physically at his peak when it all ended so abruptly. I'm eternally grateful that I played at Old Trafford until I was 34 and then had another couple of seasons at Oldham Athletic under Joe Royle. I really felt for Steve that he was denied another three or four years at the top.

"So far I have gone mostly for players I played with, but when you look further afield, how can you ignore someone like Eric Cantona, whose work ethic in staying behind to practice his skills after training inspired the Scholes and Beckhams et al to do the same and become United legends? Eric also brought his influence to bear on the pitch where his supreme confidence was the catalyst for the Red's title success. Never mend his free kicks, David Beckham is one of the best crossers of the ball I have ever seen. He didn't have the pace of a Steve Coppell or the trickery of a Gordon Hill to go past defenders but then again he didn't need to. Arnold Muhren was also a wonderful player, he could open a can of beans with that left foot, while Bryan Robson was an inspiring leader. Looking back at my selections, I'm not surprised to see that many of them played in midfield. I was always a frustrated midfielder myself, because to play well in that position you have to have so many qualities; stamina, awareness, good control, passing ability, defensive as well as attacking qualities. Oh well, maybe next time!"

Arthur Albiston is well qualified to pick out a legend or two, as he helps to run the Manchester United legends team. He opts for four players who would be his personal choices; Ryan Giggs, Paul Scholes, Denis Irwin and Roy Keane. Irwin wins his only vote. Sir Alex named Gary Neville as "the best English right back of his generation." Arsene Wenger agreed. United can boast great full backs down the Premiership years; Phil Neville, Paul Parker, Lee Sharpe, Gabriel Heinze and Patrice Evra. Denis Irwin is one of them. Perhaps he is the best of them. Signed from Oldham Athletic in 1990 for a fee of £625,000, Sir Alex still talks of the unassuming Irish international as one of his finest signings alongside the more obvious bargains such as Peter Schmeichel and Cantona. In 12 years at Old Trafford Irwin made 368 appearances scoring 22 goals. He won 7 Premier League titles, 3 FA Cups, 1 League Cup, 1 Champions League and a European Cup Winners' Cup. Irwin played predominantly as a left back in his time at Old Trafford however he was equally comfortable on the right flank. This was evidenced by his performances for the Republic of Ireland where he played as a right full back for the majority of his 56 caps. The Cork-man was a true gentleman and was very well liked by everyone involved in the game. Denis was Mr. Consistent and finally left United in 2002 dropping down a division to play with Wolverhampton Wanderers. Wolves were promoted that very season and the United fans finally got a chance to say goodbye to Denis and to show him their appreciation when he returned to his old stomping ground in the 2003–04 season.

Peter Beardsley played just one competitive game for Manchester United and four years for Liverpool, famously once scoring a hat-trick against United. A product of the famous Wallsend Boys' Club, Peter was snapped up by Carlisle United in 1979. They sold him to Vancouver Whitecaps two years later for £275,000 but he was loaned back and helped Carlisle into the old Second Division. On his return to Canada, Beardsley scored in a friendly against Manchester United – only 13 seconds after Ron Atkinson's side had kicked off! Big Ron signed him up for £250,000, but his only appearance came in the League Cup before he rejoined Vancouver before Newcastle finally signed him for £150,000 in 1983 – his 20 goals in 35 games helping them gain promotion to the top flight.

After helping Liverpool to two titles, Peter moved to Everton in 1991 and two seasons later rejoined Newcastle under Kevin Keegan where, alongside Andy Cole, he formed a phenomenal partnership which produced 73 goals in 57 matches. Kenny Dalglish replaced Keegan and sold Beardsley to Bolton in '97. He was loaned to Manchester City and Fulham, then joined the Cottagers on a short-term deal before ending his playing career at Hartlepool United. He now coaches at Newcastle's academy.

Peter was one of English football's most successful internationals, providing the perfect foil for goal poacher extraordinaire Gary Lineker, who came within a missed penalty of equalling Sir Bobby Charlton's all time international goalscoring record. Unsurprisingly it is to his fellow Geordie that Beardsley first looks when selecting his best ever all time United player. "As a kid growing up in Newcastle, Jack was at Leeds and Bobby at United and I can recall seeing Bobby playing at St. James's Park for United reserves against Newcastle reserves – United won 5-1 and I thought 'wow, what a player!'. I was just a kid then and it wasn't until I learned of his role at the club; the Munich air tragedy, the first English club to win the European Cup 10 years, that I appreciated his part in their history.

"Meeting the man only makes it better. I was at the youth cup final last year at Altrincham and Bill Foulkes was there, and couldn't get about as well as he used to, and Bobby was helping him to his seat, it's the little things like that that stand out and mean so much. Beckham was a player that I worked with when Kevin Keegan was England manager and working close up you could see the unbelievable attitude he had. You can say this and that about him, and most people do, but within the England camp his football attitude was first rate, the same with Scholesy, they were two fantastic guys to work with, not just brilliant on the field but the way they had an attitude toward their job, and loved what they were doing. They trained as if each game was their last – quite sensational and it gave me a warm glow. It was fantastic to get two of them like that together. Then there was Bryan Robson with whom I played with for England, and there was no doubt that he justified his name of Captain Marvel, he was like Alan Hansen was to Liverpool, and it was just such a shame he was injured in both World Cups in 86 and 90. Ray Wilkins was another special captain and a special person."

Although, of course, no longer a player, and one who played for Bolton rather than United, Gordon Taylor is the players' union leader and a big United fan. So, although Taylor's selection didn't count in the voting he is in a rather unique position of having seen the Busby Babes as a fan, as well as admiring the qualities of Sir Alex and his numerous successful modern day teams he has built at Old Trafford. For Taylor the Busby Babes are his favourites, maybe out of nostalgia, but mainly because that is how he sees it. Taylor told '20|13', "The Busby Babes were a fantastic team and the one I would select as my best United team of all time but in saying that there is no one who admires Sir Alex more than I do, and the teams he has created at Old Trafford. Sir Alex stands out as the most admired football man I know.

"The problem with making comparisons, is that it is impossible with such great teams as the Busby Babes and say the United team that won the Treble. If anyone can compare to Matt Busby, it is Sir Alex. They shared the same principles, ideals and determination to make Manchester United a world force, let alone one to dominate Europe.'

Taylor's best ever United players are (in order): Edwards, Charlton, Best, Law, Giggs, Cantona, Robson, Tommy Taylor, David Pegg, Beckham, Schmeichel, Pallister, Solskjaer, Van Nistelrooy, Scholes, Roger Byrne, Eddie Colman.

THE PLAYERS' PLAYER POLL WINNER

"I am especially honoured being chosen by the lads, that is very nice, very nice. I'm well happy with this poll! To finish above George Best and Bobby Charlton! When you think of all the Bryan was genuinely surprised. When you think of all the great players over the years at United, and to finish above George Best, Sir Bobby Charlton and Duncan Edwards is a great honour."

BRYAN ROBSON

"SO, BRYAN, who do you think came out on top in this poll?" I am sat with the unsuspecting winner of our players' poll and he is none the wiser...

"Cantona", responded the man they called "Captain Marvel" for club and country.

"No", I replied.

"Ok, Bobby Charlton."

"No..."

"Well, I suppose it could be Duncan Edwards, although the players these days wouldn't know much about him, Paddy Crerand, Bobby Charlton, and George Best would bang on about Duncan Edwards being their all time favourite player, so I suppose he could have got plenty of votes from the players from those days."

"No."

The penny drops.....

"You have given me enough clues, if it's me then it would be a great honour."

"Yes, indeed, it is you."

Bryan Robson was genuinely surprised, pleasantly surprised and happy, very happy. Quite rightly so. "I am especially honoured being chosen by the lads, that is very nice, very nice. I'm well happy with this poll! To finish above George Best and Bobby Charlton! When you think of all the great players over the years at United and to finish above George Best, Sir Bobby Charlton and Duncan Edwards is a great honour."

Who would the newly crowned all time greatest Manchester United player vote for?

"I can't vote for Duncan Edwards despite how much George Best, Bobby and Paddy Crerand told me about him, because, apart from a couple of video clips, I have not seen much at all. The one player I have really admired and who comes trough as the correct choice for me would be Giggsy - a great athlete, dedicated in training and although you will suffer injuries through such a long career, he has done everything to keep himself in tip-top condition, with the right diet and Pilates. He is still going strong having played at the top since he was 15 or 16 and to think of all his achievements, he is right up there with George Best and Sir Bobby. George was a little like Ryan, or should I say, Ryan is a little like George but Ryan has had such a long career compared to George. Bobby stands out for both United and England, for the amount of goals he scored for both and for winning the European

THE PLAYERS' POLL

Cup the way he did, right up there."

Captain Marvel looks back on his United career with deep affection, as you would expect. There is no doubt that the turning point in the balance of power between Liverpool and United was the Red Devil's first title in 26 years. But from there to turn around Liverpool's dominance and for United to race away with the title lead is something Bryan Robson never envisaged.

"If somebody has said to me at that time that Liverpool wouldn't win any more titles for that length of time and that United would so many that they would over take them, I would have said, 'put your mortgage on that never happening.' If I was a gambling man I would have lost a fortune."

Bryan Robson knows how vital winning the first title in 26 years was to the eventually turn around in the club's fortunes. "We had come close a couple of times in the 80s, but throughout the 70s and 80s Liverpool was dominant. Yet there were a few times we had real opportunities, especially one season when we won the first 10 League games but then we suffered a lot of injuries. To win the title became an albatross around our neck and it was fantastic that the lads finally broke those shackles in 1993. It had to happen as people couldn't keep going; 26 years, 27 years, 28 years. It was such a burden and it got worse every year it went on, but once it arrived it relaxed the players and they were able to go on to greater achievements, but even though we thought it would release us for more titles, no one would ever have thought that under Sir Alex he would have won so many."

'Robbo' scored that first successful league campaign's final goal in a 2-1 win over Wimbledon at Selhurst Park, a fitting end to his season, when six days earlier he and Bruce lifted the League trophy at Old Trafford in a stop–start season with back and hamstring problems. "The season we first won the title I played plenty of games but when the club signed Roy Keane, to play alongside Paul Ince, I knew I wasn't going to be playing in as many games as usual. I was club captain and when I played I captained the side but when I was on the bench Steve Bruce was skipper and we lifted the title together, and that was a big thrill for me. I was getting on though, I was 36 and thought the time has passed me by to win the title, and it is one of my highlights of my career that I got my hands on the title before I left United. To win that first title in 26 years and be part of such an important historic moment and to think it started the ball rolling toward winning title 19 was a big part to play in all that happening.

"The magic moments were lifting the FA Cup in 1983, which was my first trophy. I had won promotion with West Brom, but a trophy like the FA Cup was something quite different and special. The European Cup Winners' Cup in 1991 was also special and the fourth big thing in my career of course was to be part of World Cup Finals with my country."

Various injuries plagued so much of his remarkable career for club and country. He suffered three leg breaks in a year at West Brom where he played nearly 200 League games, scoring 39 goals before new United boss Ron Atkinson returned to his former club and paid a joint fee of around £2 million to bring both Robson and Remi Moses to Old Trafford in October 1981. The deal rated 'Robbo' at a then-record £1.5 million. Although Atkinson's decision was questioned, Robson was destined to become one of the game's midfield greats, replacing Ray Wilkins as club captain.

Robson scored well over a century of league goals in his career, was an inspirational captain for both club and country and uniquely led United to a hat-trick of FA Cup wins in 1983, 1985 and 1990. In the 1983 final against Brighton and Hove Albion he scored twice in the 4-0 replay victory. He was a League Cup finalist in 1991 and collected a prized European medal when he lifted the Cup Winners' Cup in the same season.

Bryan won 90 caps for England, wearing the Three Lions in three World Cups. His 26 international goals included a hat-trick against Turkey in 1984 and a strike after just 27 seconds against France in the 1982 World Cup, which was the (then) fastest goal in the tournament's history (Hakan Sukur went one better for Turkey against South Korea with an 11 second strike in 2002). In his final two seasons Robson started only 15 Premiership matches but usually made a telling contribution when called upon and could hardly have ended his illustrious career on a more satisfying note than seeing United complete the coveted League and Cup Double in 1994.

He was coach and right hand man to England new manager Terry Venables but was quickly snapped up on a lucrative contract by Middlesbrough when he announced his impending exit from Old Trafford. After seven seasons there as manager in June 2001, and following a relegation battle, Robson left in June 2001. He later returned with his first club, West Brom, with whom he completed a remarkable escape from Premiership relegation in 2004/05 – becoming the first boss to lead a team bottom at Christmas to safety in the Premiership's short history. A year later the Baggies dropped down to the Championship. They were favourites to win promotion back to the Premiership at the first attempt, but after taking only twelve points from their first eight games, Robson left the club by mutual consent on 18th September 2006. Bryan has also managed Sheffield United and Bradford City. More recently he has been coaching in Thailand, until he resigned in June 2011, inheriting the position from fellow countryman Peter Reid in 2009. Thailand fell to 120th in the FIFA word rankings during Robson's tenure, which was interrupted by the former England captain's battle with throat cancer, for which he underwent surgery in March before reassuming his position as coach of the national side.

Robson is among Michael Owen's all-time greatest Manchester United players. In his time Owen was rated one of the world's greatest goalscorers, his momentous moment coming with his wonder goal against Argentina in the World Cup Finals. Owen tells '19', "I was too young to remember, and having not seen some of the greats in action, however, just seeing some of the clips, I would go for George Best, Sir Bobby Charlton and Denis Law, those of the ones who stand out from that era. Of the players I've seen myself; Cantona, Keane, Robson, Giggs, Schmeichel and Scholes wouldn't be a bad six-a-side team, would it?"

Sunderland manager Steve Bruce, who spent almost ten

years at Old Trafford, picks out 'Robbo" as his complete player, and puts him on a par with Eric Cantona as his one of his two favourite all time United greats adding the Holy Trinity of Best, Law and Charlton to his list. Gordon Strachan selects Paul Scholes as his personal No1 United player of all time, but is not surprised that Bryan Robson was selected as the Manchester United Players Player of All time. Bryan Robson and Sir Bobby Charlton would be his second choices yet Captain Marvel is the No1 player he has played alongside.

'Robbo' is described by so many as the ideal leader, more than one used almost identical emotive language in expressing the powerful emotion that they felt as though they would win a game merely by being led out onto the field by Bryan Robson. Gordon Strachan is a vastly experienced manager with a quirkiness to rival Brian Clough at times. He is one of the games most forthright advocates for the way it should be played and makes a compelling TV pundit. He was also a team-mate of Robbo's during the eighties and is well placed to assess the merits of United best ever players.

"When you talk about United and flair teams, my favourite midfield, being a midfield player myself, of course, was watching Beckham, Scholes, Keane and Giggs. When it comes to selecting my all time favourite United player, now that is a hard call, mainly because there have been so many over the years. You would go for Bobby Charlton because of the sentiment over the Munich air crash and coming back to win the European Cup, but also because he was so a wonderful player and a nice bloke as well, as nice a bloke as I have ever met. He was ever so graceful in the way he played, and the way he acts off the field. I suppose Roy Keane was the complete opposite of that, but still, in his own way, just as formidable a player and influence on the team. I loved Best, well, who wouldn't? I could sit and watch George Best all day. But of course, I haven't seen as much of Bobby Charlton as I would have done of say Paul Scholes, whom I have watched closely for the past 15 years.

"Bryan Robson is the favourite player that I have played

THE PLAYERS' POLL

alongside, and also to have as a mate. In addition Bryan was the very best of the players who never really won a major trophy, although at the end of his career he and Steve Bruce together lifted the League trophy. Best was phenomenal, Keane was phenomenal and they would all get a vote from me, but there are so many great players to pick from that you could select a couple of Manchester United all Time Great teams without too much difficulty. There is plenty of material for a Top Twenty of All Time Greats; Cantona, Scholes, Charlton, and Robson would be in my top selection for sure and Paul comes out on top because of the sheer number of goals, trophies and a European Cup.

"But I can see why, when you ask players to vote for their best or favourite player, they would go for Bryan Robson. When you ask a player like myself, I would say Bryan Robson was certainly the best I ever played alongside, that's for sure. It is no fault of Bryan's that he wasn't in a side winning European Cups or League titles, but if he is the top United player of all time, then I wouldn't quibble with that selection, not at all."

THE PLAYERS' BALLOT

Bryan Robson	15	George Best	14
Bobby Charlton	13	Paul Scholes	11
Eric Cantona	11	Roy Keane	10
Ryan Giggs	9	Denis Law	9
David Beckham	8	Gary Pallister	5
Mark Hughes	4	Peter Schmeichel	4
Duncan Edwards	4	Steve Bruce	3
Denis Irwin	3	Cristiano Ronaldo	2
Jaap Stam	3	Arnold Muhren	2
Ray Wilkins	2	Gordon Strachan	2
Frank Stapleton	2	Nobby Stiles	2
Norman Whiteside	2	Gary Neville	2
Jimmy Greenhoff	2	Phil Neville	2

ONE VOTE APIECE FOR:

Wayne Rooney, Edwin van der Sar, Paul Ince, Paddy Crerand, David Sadler, Bill Foulkes, Steve Coppell, Nemanja Vidic, Rio Ferdinand, Stuart Pearson, Gordon McQueen, Lou Macari, Arthur Albiston, Kevin Moran, Johnny Carey and Stan Pearson.